The Art of
Self Care

ISBN 9781922598639 (print)

Published by Upself in 2022
upself.com.au

Book production by Booktopia Publishing, a division of Booktopia Group Ltd
Unit E1, 3-29 Birnie Avenue
Lidcombe, NSW 2141, Australia
booktopia.com.au

Printed and bound in Australia by SOS Print + Media Group

The paper in this book is FSC® certified.
FSC® promotes environmentally responsible,
socially beneficial and economically viable
management of the world's forests.

The Art of Self Care

Tracey Jewel

CONTENTS

Section 7: Energetic Self-Care

Section 8: Financial Self-care

Section 9: Practical Self-Care

Section 10: Professional Self-Care

INTRODUCTION

Tracey Jewel

True fact: Most people don't give themselves the intentional self-care they need or deserve, yet they put their all into the things they do for others – children, partners in marriage, friends and family. So, it's highly likely you're neglecting the one person who needs the attention most – yourself.

Intentional self-care isn't all that mystical, though it does cover plenty of ground. To take proper care of your needs, you must learn how to take care of your physical, social, emotional and spiritual well-being. If you're one of the many who feel like it is selfish to help yourself, you're not alone.

Like most of us, I have gone through life with ebbs and flows of looking after myself. When I prioritise my self-care, life flows, challenges are easily overcome and life seems overall happier and more fulfilling. Then life gets busy, or something happens, and I forget my self-care practices. In these times, challenges seem overwhelming, my head feels muddled, my physical energy is depleted and anxiety returns.

The great news is, with the help of intentions, we can get back to basics of foundational self-care. We can draw a line in the sand, say today is another day and build ourselves back up to even greater than before, but only if we choose and make the intention to do so. We can put self-care back on the to-do list and make it a priority anytime we want, we just have to show up and commit. Don't we deserve that?

This book is just what you need to start checking all those boxes for yourself. It's not being selfish; it's self-preservation. Practising intentional self-care allows you to be fully present for the ones you love and those that depend upon you.

Self-care in all its many forms fills us up and makes us whole again. After all, it only makes sense that when we have our needs met, we have everything to give to the ones that count on us.

Some of the duties we must fulfil exhaust us, both mentally and physically. In order to stand up and take what life throws our way, we must work to be self-sufficient in intentional self-care to bring our best to the table in every situation. Whether work has become more challenging or you're struggling to care for sick relatives, young children or reach a goal you've always wanted to achieve, it all starts by putting your self-care needs first.

What you're about to learn will truly set you free. In these following pages, you'll find the keys to serving every area of intentional self-care. As you practise them and make them part of your life, you'll soon see struggles ebb away and focus return. That's because when you take care of yourself, you'll have the tools you need to naturally handle both the blessings and the challenges that you face.

In this book, you'll discover strategies for all areas of self-care, to help you bring balance to your life. From physical to mental, it covers all bases, so you can harmonise your entire existence and unleash your full potential.

And really, that's what self-care is all about. Once you start making time to truly nourish yourself and fulfil your needs, you'll discover how much fun it can be to make yourself a priority in life. Welcome to your next phase in life, the phase of intentional self-care!

SECTION 1:
EMOTIONAL SELF-CARE

INTRODUCTION

Tracey Jewel

Emotions are something we all have. Why then do we feel compelled to hide them away? We stuff them into a suitcase and leave them in the shadows, which isn't healthy. While it's certainly never wise to have an angry outburst, stifling that emotion doesn't bode well for emotional self-care.

Healthy coping skills are a necessity when dealing with uncomfortable emotions. Emotions such as anger, sadness and anxiety can tear us down when we don't confront them.

With emotional self-care, you'll learn activities and skills to both acknowledge and express those feelings daily. Writing about them can certainly help and gives you a memento to go back to when you're having a tough day dealing with the world.

Talking to someone you trust can help you with your emotions. So too can engaging in activities that let you release these frustrations. Exercise doesn't just boost physical wellbeing, it boosts the emotional side as well.

When you think about your emotional wellness, in what ways are you expressing your emotions? Are they healthy, or do you need a new way to work them out? What activities do you do to recharge your mind and reset your emotions?

In this chapter, you'll learn about the many ways you can take care of your emotional wellness with a positive and enlightening vibe.

BELIEFS: YOUR MIND IS BEHIND EVERYTHING … WHAT YOU BELIEVE IS EXACTLY WHAT YOU WILL EXPERIENCE

Deb Griffiths

Your mind is behind everything … What you believe is exactly what you will experience.

Are you ready to shift your status quo, challenge your current perspective and identify the limiting beliefs that steal your joy, creating unnecessary negativity, destructive thinking and suffering in your life? As an expert in re-programming empowering beliefs, in the next few pages I will teach you the process I used to transform my own life and the lives of many clients – simple, practical strategies and learnings that will guide you to master new powerful beliefs and behaviours that will rapidly transform your life experience to a greater sense of purpose, love, success and freedom.

For the last ten years, the story I have told myself is 'I cannot write'. I am great at speaking in person – to one, to many, showing up on video is fine too, but … 'I can't write!' (or so I believed).

Hmm, what an interesting belief. How on this planet did I come to be writing a chapter on the power of our beliefs? Did the universe set out to challenge me? Is it that I always had a goal to write a book? Or maybe, at a deep subconscious level, I know I have the creativity that will allow me to flow into storytelling just as well on paper as I do in person.

I have done the inner work to understand that any belief I have had in the past is merely created by a story I have repeated in my mind until I finally believed it was true. I have learnt that to receive a different outcome, the story I tell myself needs to change … and here we are.

She wanted to change so she changed her mind.

Growing up I remember experiencing a nagging, persistent feeling of 'less than or not good enough' – less liked than anyone I hung around with, not good enough to be in the group, less liked and not as popular as my brother, the outcast of my various friend groups, the least attractive one, the chubby one – and so the self-proclaimed stories about myself went on in my mind. As much as I tried to override this, everywhere I looked I successfully found the evidence to validate my belief of 'not good enough', and as I fed it, so it continued to grow.

I so clearly remember the day I became aware of the strength of my 'not good enough' belief and how it had held me back from experiencing so much joy, freedom and success in my life. It was like someone turned on a light in my head. I realised that every thought I had and every action I took (or didn't take) was literally driven from a place of 'not good enough'. I was constantly in search of external approval, checking in to make sure I was enough. The need for this outside validation was huge in my world. So much so, that when I didn't get it or I 'failed', I felt like I was being thrown under a bus. I knew this was not right, and there had to be an easier, more confident and fulfilling way to experience life.

Naturally, this newfound awareness fuelled my desire for change. I got support from coaches and healers around the globe, read books and researched. I studied healing, neurolinguistic programming, psychology and coaching. I did all this before going inward on a deep surrender process to connect and make friends with my inner childhood beliefs, releasing them once and for all. Phew, what a ride that was, filled with a mountain of learnings and wisdom that I now passionately share with my clients.

Through this process on my journey called life, I have come to learn that whether you believe you can or believe you can't, you are always right. The power of that belief carries an energy strong enough to determine any outcome. It all starts with you!

Change your beliefs, and your thoughts will change. Change your thoughts, and your actions will change. Change your actions, and you open your life to limitless possibilities!

Where do our beliefs come from?

Psychology tells us that our beliefs are formed in two ways: by our experiences and by accepting what others tell us to be true. In fact, most of our **core beliefs** are formed when we are **children**. Our parents and environment play a big part in moulding our **beliefs** from a young age.

Can we change them? Yes, absolutely, with a genuine intention and aligned action you can change your beliefs. But before we get to that, keep reading.

It's time to make magic with your mind.

Changing the belief

A small trick I love doing with myself and my clients is asking what something means to them and then having a look at the dictionary meaning. This is an excellent opportunity to see the meaning we have given to something and how far from the truth (or close) it may be. Let's use this technique here.

The dictionary meaning of the word belief is: 'An acceptance that something exists or is true, especially one without proof.' Isn't it interesting that we don't need the proof or the evidence to show up before we actually believe something? Think about how often you relate a situation, circumstance or life event to something in your or your parents past then connect the dots and create a link, a circle of relevance, further cementing your belief.

What if you took different action first or even created a new and useful belief first, then found the evidence to confirm your new belief?

Essentially our beliefs define our actions, and we cycle through life staying contained within those beliefs. In the two diagrams below, I have shown how, by simply switching the action to the first part of the cycle, you will find the corresponding evidence you need to create a new and more empowered belief. It's through this process that you can and will experience different results and greater success within your life. See the cycle below:

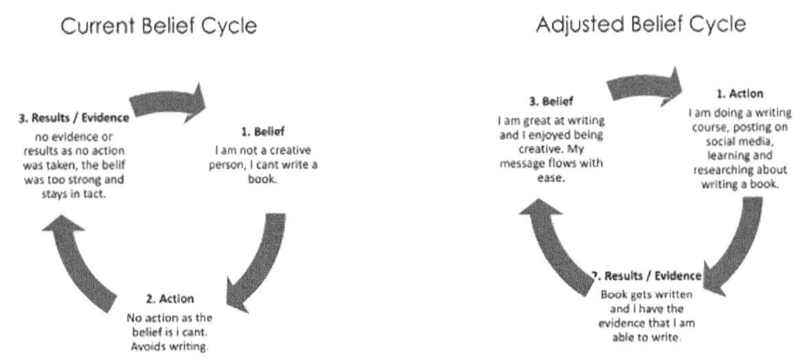

Emotion solidifies the beliefs

Beliefs are formed from family, friends, status, education, media and our environment. When a belief is present, emotions are naturally present.

Emotions are triggered by identifying with beliefs, applying beliefs, internal thoughts, external events and our interpretation of our now moment. When an emotion is triggered, it further confirms and even solidifies our belief, keeping it in reality and holding the belief strong. So, another key point to remember when looking to change a belief, is to identify and change the attached emotion associated with that particular belief.

Let's take the saying 'I'll believe it when I see it'. If you are not tuned in or your awareness is not focused on seeing that particular thing, because of course you don't believe it or don't want to believe it, you definitely won't see it, which means, guess what … you won't believe it.

So where am I going with this? If you want to see different results in your life, then it's time to get curious about the beliefs you are holding, become aware of when they are holding you back and take the steps you can to shift them … and fast!

Beliefs are choices.

I had a beautiful client – let's call her Claire – who had a firm belief that she was bad. Everything Claire did was to counteract her feeling of being bad. She put pressure on herself to have the dinner made before hubby got home, she was conscious of what she said in social circles in case she felt or looked bad, she went out with friends even if she was tired so she wouldn't be perceived as bad. Everything about who she was, was driven and impacted by this belief. It was wearing her down. She felt exhausted from putting herself and her own needs last, struggling to please every person except herself every day. Her tank was completely empty. She did not know how long she could keep going with this and wanted to give up.

During our coaching sessions, we would do deep dives using strategic, critical questioning techniques, and we discovered that this 'bad' belief was having a powerful and negative impact on Claire's daily life.

Thankfully, when Claire understood it was no longer hers to own, she became motivated and committed to change. She prioritised the aligned actions to create a new, more empowered belief and, just like someone had waved a magic wand, life started to show up differently for her. Claire became crystal clear around the choices she could make for herself, highlighting the difference between her old behaviours and the woman she could now be, aligned with her new belief systems.

To continue confirming her new belief, Claire attached new emotions and affirmations to it, making it easier for her to remember and connect to empowered experiences until the belief became her new norm. Claire is now experiencing complete freedom from her old thoughts and behaviours, which has had a successful flow-on effect into her relationship, her parenting skills and even within her workplace.

She believed it was possible, so it happened.

Before closing off, I will leave you with one last piece. I love using analogies to create relatable learning platforms. So, for this story, imagine your life is like a TV screen. Think of your favourite genre movie and select it from Netflix (aka your mind/thoughts). Now, what would you expect to show up on the screen (your life)? I love a good comedy so that's definitely what I would choose and what I would expect to see in my life. Would you be shocked if a different genre started playing? I certainly would.

If you are wondering why life is showing up in a certain way, check what thoughts or beliefs you have programmed into your mind. If the two do not align, change your action and beliefs, and I promise you, your life experiences will change too.

Are you ready to do the work, changing your life one belief at time? Below are some actionable steps for everyone who wants to change, to heal and to thrive. With a new awareness, a new belief and some committed action, anything is possible!

Actionable steps:

- Silence and connection – Sit quietly and write a list of your current and not so useful beliefs. Stay out of judgement as this will hinder your ability to identify and heal these beliefs. Once you have a list, identify where these beliefs came from. Take a deep breath. Ask if they still serve you, and create the space to come up with a new more empowering belief. Use this statement as an affirmation in your daily life. For example, 'I am not good enough' can be reaffirmed with the statement 'I am enough. I release all limiting beliefs that have come from my family or society and love all parts of who I am.'
- Play – Choose something to really believe in, and focus on it, put all your intention on it. It can be the next new car you desire; it can be your partner helping to tidy the house; it can be as simple as a new love for butterflies. Now go out and about your day giving focused attention to this belief, and see if you can find the evidence. I bet you will!
- Action – Follow this simple step-by-step process to sustainably change a belief:

1. Become aware of the different parts that make up a belief.
2. Release the emotions held in that belief.

3. Shift your perspective so you can see the identity as false.
4. Break the bonds that make that belief so powerful.

Bio

Deb Griffiths is a qualified mindset mentor and healer who is on a mission to transform and elevate the lives of more than one million women. Her passion is helping women just like you to discover and step into your power, giving you the confidence to take your life and career to the next level.

Deb landed in this space for reasons close to her own heart. After experiencing real emotional challenges in her own life, Deb made a bold and necessary move to challenge her belief systems, thoughts and behaviours, resulting in a better sense of self and a more fulfilling life experience. She learned you don't have to walk this journey alone and realised that with courage and self-belief you can create a different life. Deb knew her calling was to share her passion worldwide, supporting and inspiring her clients to take charge of their worlds and live the life they dream of.

Passionate about beliefs, Deb works with her clients to crush their old belief systems, doubts and fears, giving them the clarity to recreate more empowering beliefs and behaviours, which in turn catapults them into a more joyful, magical and exciting life.

Deb is a lifelong learner and a certified coach. Her qualifications include a ICF (International Coach Federation) Advanced Momentum Life Coaching certification, Neuro Transformational Coaching (including Transformational Timeline Therapy), Evolved Coach certification and a diploma in psychology. She is also NLP certified and practices Usui reiki, kinesiology and Theta Healing. Throughout this journey she has learned that with the right mindset, you can achieve anything. She is now truly living her purpose, helping women around the world with their own life-changing personal and professional transformations.

If not out walking her fur baby, hanging with family, drinking coffee or exercising, you will find Deb intentionally focused and having fun while embodying her powerful vision of inspiring personal transformation and creating conscious leaders worldwide.

Please jump onto Deb's website where you can book a complimentary clarity session or join her complimentary five-day Empower Me program, where you will get some practical tips on prioritising yourself, the first step to transformation.

If you wish to work with Deb, you can also receive 10% of her six-week Breakthrough program by mentioning this book.

Connect with Deb:
Facebook: @debagriffiths.coach
Instagram: @debgriffiths.coach
LinkedIn: @debgriffiths
Website: www.debgriffiths.com

THE UNHAPPINESS LIE

Shayne Brian

I hear the train a comin', it's rolling round the bend. And I ain't seen the sunshine since I don't know when. – 'Folsom Prison Blues', Johnny Cash

I stared at my hands in disbelief as handcuffs were placed around my wrists. It happened very differently to how I had imagined it. My faith in the universe had told me that, at most, I would probably face community service for my error in judgment several years earlier in using tax office money to prop up a start-up business in the music industry. I was the scapegoat for a failed record label, and the start-up was my effort to help the artists who had been so badly represented.

The shock of hearing I was to spend nine months in a correctional facility barely registered. The faces of my beautiful partner and two grown-up children would stay with me, especially during the first month as the gravity of the situation hit me. I was going to jail. Nearly a year in prison surrounded by murderers, violent offenders, drug traffickers and addicts was more than I could even think about.

I was handed a plastic cup and clothes two sizes too big and placed into a three-by-three metre holding cell that was home for the next eight days while awaiting transfer to a maximum-security correctional centre. Three walls and a window facing yet another wall gave me a lot of thinking time while riding an emotional rollercoaster comprising fear, sadness, anger, hate, disbelief and distress. I was worried for my life in prison; however, the concern faded in comparison to the fear for my family and what they would have to go through. Most importantly, how could I survive without Tanya, my best friend and partner.

This was just another step on a road I had been travelling most of my life: never satisfied; always looking for the next thing. The truth was, I was unhappy, and that unhappiness had given me a one-way ticket to the big house. I didn't see that in my life plan, yet here it was. I had been sold a lie, a lie that I had mistaken for a truth. I had to find myself and what more perfect place to do so than in the middle of a bunch of thieves, murderers and addicts.

> *Can whatever has gone wrong be fixed? If so, what is the point in being unhappy?*
> – Yogi Shantideva

Unhappiness is a multi-million-dollar business. We wake up unhappy. We're unhappy in our life, our marriage, our work. In fact, everything around us makes us unhappy. The lack of happiness boils up inside us. The people we speak to, the demands placed on us, the lies we are told – they all bubble to the surface of a cauldron that is constantly being stirred, every minute of the day, until we finally can't take it anymore.

The media reminds us that the key to a happy life is in the bottom of a bottle in our medicine cabinet, or in the next gadget, or the next relationship. We become so unsatisfied, so disappointed, so depressed. We numb our minds with alcohol, drugs, TV soaps. Nothing removes the pain we are going through in our unhappy life.

Most of us are programmed to believe we cannot be completely happy unless we have the next big thing: the car, the house, the perfect life. Even if we do obtain it, the happiness is momentary, and we quickly dive back down into our unhappiness.

In the mid-eighties, I remember reading a story (in a very dodgy tabloid) about a housewife who was jailed for beating her husband to death with a chicken leg. Now once you can get past the rather comic and bizarre scene, you see a woman who is unhappy, unappreciated and just plain exhausted. He sits at the table to eat and she brings out chicken for the third time that week, to which he angrily exclaims, 'Not this shit again!' Suddenly she snaps, grabs the roast, and the rest is a very juicy and entertaining news report.

In this 'chicken beating' case, we have two different types of unhappiness that come together to create a violent situation. One party has the impatience and unhappiness that leads to anger and violence, while the other party has the unhappiness and low self-worth that leads to frustration and hurt. Both sides have let the problems fester without seeking help of some sort. Like any ego-based emotion, once the genie is out of the bottle, the damage is done.

Now you might be reading this chapter thinking 'That's not me'.

'Sure, I'm not always enjoying my life, my marriage, my job.'

'Granted, I don't have the best relationship with my kids, but who does, right?'

'Yeah, I know I could try harder to get on with my family.'

'I know I'm depressed, but the next vodka will fix it, or at least numb the pain.'

That was me. I was unhappy. I was a multi-million-dollar property owner. I experienced the expensive lifestyle, the McMansion on the water, the fast cars. And on the outside I was telling everyone I was happy.

The truth is, I was wearing a mask. I was waking up at 4.00 am worried about how I was going to close the next deal. I was fighting off the short-term loan sharks, while I was desperately trying to settle the next property development so I could get the monkeys off my back. My marriage was failing, and my kids barely knew me.

And then it all came crashing down. I couldn't even mentally deal with the stress. For two years I bore the pain of losing my job, my property, my community standing. And so I settled for a job where I became the scapegoat for a failing record label. I had gone from reasonably sad to grossly unhappy in the space of a couple of years.

The body is amazing. If you choose to listen, it can tell you when there is something you are not dealing with. This time, the stress was manifesting in the form of hearing loss. When something as drastic as hearing impairment happens, most people will begin to realise and do something to change their circumstances, right?

Wrong. In fact, our human reaction is to try and deal with the problems ourselves. Friends, family, doctors, psychologists – they all heard the same thing. There is nothing wrong. I am perfectly fine.

How I was mistaken. How could I fix what was broken inside me when I didn't even really know what it was? Could I fix the problems I created? Nothing I did seemed to work.

> *If it cannot be remedied, what is the point of being unhappy? You are just rubbing salt into the wound and exposing yourself to the greater harm of anger.*
> – Yogi Shantideva

Now it wasn't all misery. I had plenty of amazing times before my visit to the prison. In fact, if my life hadn't gone down the path it did, I probably would never have met my wife Tanya, who has become my rock. And I would never have had the experiences I had and that I now draw on to help others with my new and successful podcast. Sure, it is an extreme way to meet a partner and launch a new business, but I was never one for doing things half-heartedly.

I have heard it said that there is a moment (or moments) in our life when everything suddenly makes sense and you understand that all the limiting beliefs you have held in your life, all the unhappy moments and the periods of stress and anxiety, can disappear in an instant.

When I entered through the gates of the prison, something clicked inside me. It was my watershed moment – the point in my life where I realised I had a choice. I could choose to be unhappy, or I could choose to be happy. It was the year that I lost my freedom, but it was also the year I claimed back my life and decided to be happy.

I remember so vividly the moment the guard who opened my cell door turned to me, looked me in the eye and said: 'Welcome to the start of your prison journey. Make yourself at home because it's a revolving door – you will be back.'

It was that comment and subsequent events that happened to me while in prison, that flipped a switch inside me. I spent nine months working on me – my mindset and my happiness. And the moment my time inside finished, I knew my life would never be the same again. I walked out of prison not knowing what I was going to do with the rest of my life, just knowing I didn't have to share a cell with someone who would scream out in the middle of the night. Nor did I have to share a meal with a guy who had committed so many atrocities that he was doing the end of his twenty-year stretch. And I definitely didn't have to share a kitchen with guy chopping up veggies while he was strung out on whatever he could lay his hands on inside.

I was actually happy, but that happiness only came to me when I realised I couldn't fix what had happened. I was only doing a nine-month stint for Australian Tax Office fraud, but, before you ask, yes, this was the real deal – just like you see in the movies and not the rom-com kind either. It was the place where dreams were crushed and you were told daily you would never amount to anything. Where the last words people heard on release was 'Y'all come back now!'

And they did. It was the cycle, the endless roundabout that society operates on – fear and unhappiness. Midway through, I started to notice that guys inside were driven by one of five things: anger, jealousy, desire, pride or ignorance. These are the five egos that most people who are unhappy live their life by. Until we remove the mask and see the truth behind the lies, we will remain in the cycle and become victims rather than empowered people who choose to be happy.

> Whatever is true, whatever is noble, whatever is right, whatever is pure, whatever is lovely, whatever is admirable – if anything is excellent or praiseworthy – think about such things. – Philippians 4:8

How can we be truly happy in the midst of terrible times like my period of incarceration? How can we set our mind on what is true, noble, right, pure and lovely, especially when there is so much around us that can make us unhappy? The road to happiness is peace … not accepting our limiting beliefs that hold us in a perpetual state of unhappiness, but acceptance and peace in knowing that we can change our lives.

We can change it. You can change it. All it really takes is the action of recognising the unhappiness and putting some practices into place that will begin to shift the mindset and unblock the limiting programmed beliefs.

For me that shift in peace and happiness came from mantras. You can use either traditional words of Sanskrit, which have an energetic signature that will empower you, or your own positive affirmation that will help you step into your own place of happiness.

During my nine months inside, I began a daily practice of mantra chanting. Fortunately, I was allowed to keep my mala beads, and every day I would walk around the complex silently reciting a mantra that Tanya had recommended … one time for every bead … 108 times each morning. The energy of the constant affirmation not only helped me maintain a positivity inside, I believe it helped me fly through the nine months.

Your happiness should be an important part of your self-care plan in your life. How can you shift that mindset towards happiness? This book is full of amazing tools you can use in bringing about happiness in your life. Mantras and positive affirmations are powerful tools you can use that will shift your attitude and your mindset.

Bio

Shayne Brian is head storyteller at Bad Boys Media.

Shayne co-hosts the popular Bad Boys Podcast with over 200,000 listeners and helps train others in using the power of podcasts.

As the host of the popular Bad Boys Podcast and The Beat Generation, which is broadcast over 150 stations worldwide, Shayne has interviewed high-profile artists and authors such as Jimmy Barnes, Toto, Simon Baker, Jon Anderson (Yes), Shane Howard (Goanna) and Scott Stapp (Creed).

In 2016, Shayne was placed in prison for Australian Tax Office related crimes. He now works closely with an organisation called Sapana to help with the education and rehabilitation of prisoners across the world using the incredible power of storytelling and podcasts.

Shayne currently runs Bad Boys Media which helps produce and distribute podcasts like Tracey Jewel's Upself, as well as helping people to uncover their unique story and turn it into podcasts and videos.

Work with Shayne:

Let Shayne start you on the journey of uncovering the story buried deep inside you, with a free thirty-minute discovery session.

Connect with Shayne:
Facebook: https://www.facebook.com/OfficialBadBoysPodcast
Instagram: https://www.instagram.com/officialbadboyspodcast/
LinkedIn: https://www.linkedin.com/in/shaynebrian/
Book a free call with Shayne: **http://bit.ly/ShayneBrian**

BOUNDARIES

Kyra Beasley

Self-care is giving the world the best of you, instead of what's left of you. – Katie Reed

Boundaries: a very valuable factor in life that many of us shy away from. I have had my fair share of lack in that department, which led me down a long road of resentment, bitterness and a wee bit of depression. From childhood up until my early twenties, I recall wanting to be liked and accepted. I did not want to be thought of as disruptive, mean, bitchy or selfish. So, I learnt how to diminish my own needs and make everyone else comfortable as a protection mechanism from rejection. Of course, this came at the expense of internal peace, but I felt safe belittling my personal terms and conditions. Little did I know 'safety' was an illusion in this scenario.

Downplaying my needs made others feel okay doing that as well. Still, it was my responsibility to make them aware of those terms and conditions. Therefore, I take sole accountability for failing to uphold my end of the bargain. How are people supposed to know what your boundaries are if you don't enforce them? That is just like an agent expecting a client to sign off on a blank contract. There is no safety or guarantee.

My very first relatable encounter with boundaries took place in adolescence. During this stage, I was experiencing massive acne breakouts and was completely ignorant of self-love/self-esteem. A loved one would constantly point them out, suggesting products to use. As if acne prone skin isn't caused by more than just having combination skin or a 'dirty' face. My triggers had grown much more sensitive after weeks of my acne being pointed out. Nonetheless, I kept quiet to keep from coming off 'disrespectful' … until I'd had enough.

'With all due respect, I get up every morning to wash my face as I look directly into the mirror. I see the acne and the scars it left behind. I don't need you reminding me every other day,' I responded, as small tears welled up.

I'm assuming they did not know how much their remarks affected me due to their reaction to my response. A lot of trapped energy could have been released and free flowing had I let them know the first time I was triggered.

This scenario brings me to my next point: children and teenagers are allowed to have boundaries. Their needs are just as valid and should not be shamed or called 'disrespectful', because what you're teaching is that their boundaries are invalid. If they're anything like me, they'll learn to shut down and suppress their emotions rather than standing up for their rights. This becomes a habit after a while, a dangerous one, unless, they're self-aware enough to catch it before becoming an adult, which is rare.

I had another encounter with boundaries at twenty-two years old, which probably was one of my most transformative experiences. I was hired as an account executive and later as a corporate trainer for a direct marketing company. While working, I built meaningful relationships. Nonetheless, the constant inconsideration and lack of integrity outweighed it all. There were several instances where my boundaries were disregarded and crossed. For the sake of this chapter, I will summarise. Before I get into this summary of experiences, I do not need to be viewed as a victim. Look through the lens of an optimistic, impressionable woman searching high and low for belonging and purpose. On a regular basis, I was called weak for being aware of the feelings of others and trying to respect their boundaries. I wasn't the savage marketing associate they wanted me to be. It was not in my nature. Yet, I kept trying to invoke that draining mentality I did not have. Soon, I began to lose sight of myself. I forgot who I was. Actually, I began to question whether or not I even truly knew who I was. Anyhow, just like little Kyra, I stayed quiet to respect the authority figures in the office ... again, which came at the expense of my internal peace. I had given up just about everything to be in this position – sacrificed my wellbeing with aspirations of climbing the corporate ladder and becoming a marketing mogul like Karen Civil. I mean, who was I fooling?! I was publicly humiliated, and I was discussed negatively behind closed doors more often than not. I had reached my breaking point. I remember pulling into the parking lot of the office and crying, because I knew I was out of alignment. The treatment was not worth the incentives they were presenting on the table. I made the decision to leave that environment as it no longer served me ... without giving two weeks' notice (oops.) I will admit, it was not the best move to make. I was severely burnt-out and on the edge of breaking down. My time was up. Sometimes setting boundaries is as simple as dropping what's holding you down and letting go of what does not pour back into you. Especially, if it is not in alignment with your divinity.

This experience taught me more about myself and purpose than any book I could ever read. It forced me to look within myself, where I was lacking boundaries and awareness. That experience, along with many other events that happened outside of my control, mandated me to go on the long journey of self-exploration and healing that led me here.

In this next section of the chapter, I will explain the value of placing boundaries and how to practise them daily. A boundary is something that indicates bounds or limits and can be found pretty much everywhere. Rivers, oceans and lakes have them. Otherwise mass natural disasters would happen more frequently than not. Boxing matches have them. When the boxer taps the opponent, it's for the safety of the boxer. State laws and regulations can be seen as boundaries as well. If you come from a rough upbringing and know anything about gang culture, you also know there are street codes represented as boundaries. You see, boundaries don't look the same for everybody. Therefore, your boundaries do not have to sound the same either. Set healthy boundaries according to your own needs, wants and desires. From personal experiences, boundaries are personal non-negotiables, standards and deal breakers that one is not willing to compromise for the sake of overall wellbeing – whether that be emotionally, spiritually, mentally, financially or physically – no matter who the person is or what the situation may be.

You know what happens to the ocean when the body of water has crossed its boundary? Tsunamis and hurricanes. When state laws and regulations are broken one can be fined or serve jail time. One faces personal and rather deadly consequences when the street code is purposely ignored. Just about everything in existence has boundaries. Where are yours?

Boundaries take self-awareness and self-love. This too is a vital part of self-care. People who struggle with setting boundaries typically (are):

- co-dependent
- lack self-awareness/confidence
- people-pleasers
- empaths
- very meek/too humble
- have the 'little ole me' syndrome
- were not listened to as children
- were indirectly or directly told their feelings were invalid

- have a fear of not belonging
- fear rejection and abandonment (anxiety preoccupied attachment style)
- desire to be disliked by no one

I often hear my clients say they sometimes despise having a big heart or being overly nice. I

always tell them 'Having a big heart and being kind is almost never the issue. Lack of boundaries is the issue.' It's almost like a muscle. It must be exercised over and over again before you gain confidence and assurance. It's a skill. Boundaries are essential for healthy relationships and lifestyle. Establishing poor boundaries leads to a lack of trust, fatigue, anger, hurt and bitterness. When someone or something acts out in ways that are inconsiderate, we show self-care by addressing the issue head on and making the boundary very clear and deep enough to see. This is not about revenge, being disrespectful or proving a point. It's about teaching others how to respect and love you. Generally, people who love and care about you will not have a problem adjusting to your needs. Some who do find a problem with this usually are co-dependent, lack their own set of boundaries or are not in tune emotionally. We are not in control of the inconsiderate actions of others. What we are in control of is how we respond and how we decide to put ourselves first by drawing the line.

Please understand that true self-empowerment and development is being able to articulate your needs and prioritising your non-negotiables. Every time you set a healthy boundary, you give yourself permission to stand in your authority gracefully. You cannot be afraid of losing people.

People who are meant to be in your life should fall together like a puzzle. There is no use in

trying to force pieces to fit that simply do not belong. I know you don't want to be looked at as difficult or a bitch. However, it's either that or take on constant projection, shame, guilt,

manipulation and being at the bottom of everyone's priority list. Including your own.

Setting a boundary is as simple as saying 'No'. You don't have to explain your answer if you don't want to. Also note, you do not have to sacrifice your wellbeing to prove that you are a good person. Being a good person has very little to do with what you can do for others. It has everything to do with your character, values and integrity. If we were to constantly give ourselves away, our time and effort wouldn't be seen as valuable. Plus, we leave no room for rest and replenishment. They say nothing in nature blooms all year round. So you shouldn't expect yourself to be on call all year round. You are deserving of rest and personal time that doesn't involve taking on the weight of other people. Don't take responsibility for the feelings of others. Lisa Nichols said 'The world is not going to stop when you say the word no.' People may very well get angry, disappointed, or upset. Again, it's not yours to take on. That said, know your standards and non-negotiables.

How to set boundaries in place? The one way I prefer to set boundaries is by using the 'sandwich method' for conflict resolution:

1. Build Up
2. Critique
3. Break Down
4. Build Up

Example 1: 'Thank you for showing concern about my health and weight. I really do appreciate it. However, I am not in the space to talk about my health comfortably with others during this time. I feel judged and even belittled when my health is brought up. I know you care about me so that is not your intention. As stated before, I just don't feel comfortable discussing my health with you. Thank you for your advice though. I'll keep it in mind.' (Begin to change the topic)

Example 2: 'I know this is a conversation that needs to be had. However, I'm putting an end to it, because it's beginning to be too intense for me. Perhaps, we can revisit when we are both calm and thinking clearly. Considering the tension that I feel right now … it is not the right time. I'd rather put this conversation on pause until we can both articulate how we feel respectfully.'

Key takeaways and things to keep in mind while enforcing boundaries:

- Boundaries are not mean or selfish.
- You teach people how to love and respect you.
- Setting healthy boundaries is vital for your wellbeing.
- Boundaries are your best friend when it comes to your growth and evolution.
- Everyone and everything has boundaries. So don't feel bad when it's time to enforce yours.
- Guilt comes from a place of co-dependency and/or people-pleasing.
- Your happiness and wellbeing are your responsibility. So are your boundaries.
- Boundaries are a part of self-care and self-love.
- Boundaries cannot and should not be compromised, belittled or gaslighted.
- People who love, care and respect you have no problem considering your boundaries while interacting with you.

How to respect others boundaries:

- Be mindful of your body language, tone of voice and facial expression.
- Avoid asking personal information that others have not permitted.
- If you are to ask, start by saying 'Let me know if I'm overstepping your boundaries' or
- 'I hope I'm not intruding, but ...'
- Treat people how you expect to be treated.
- Be considerate.
- Show empathy.

Bio

Kyra Beasley is a profound self-development and mindset coach who uses alternative energy healing modalities and divination tools to transform the minds of many men and women. The Houston native graduated from Clark Atlanta University with the intentions of climbing the corporate ladder; however, Kyra's route to society's idea of success changed drastically after experiencing an abrupt 'dark night of the soul'. This led her to a path of true self-exploration and development. After neglecting much of her own wellbeing to secure her position, Kyra soon realised that no one can truly grow, evolve or expand without a mind-body connection. She left corporate America with a new vision – a purpose. That purpose was for people to embrace their shadow while implementing inner child healing. According to the National AG Safety Database, ninety per cent of illnesses and disease derive from the everyday stressful lifestyles that are constantly being promoted. Kyra's intention is to step in before it gets to that point. With over ninety testimonials and reviews, she is currently expanding her products and services to give more service globally. Kyra plans to take the word 'mogul' to the next level within the spiritual community.

Qualifications:

- Certified Health Coach, June 2020
- Certified Life Coach, June 2020
- Certified Reiki Level II Practitioner, May 2020
- Certified Hypnotherapy Practitioner, (expected completion date TBA)

Work with Kyra:

Get a free one-to-one self-development assessment by booking a call with me today!

Connect with Kyra:
Facebook: Self Development & Mindset Coach
Instagram: @thehealingmogul
Website: https://www.kyrathemogul.com/
Email: kyrathemogul@gmail.com

SELF-CARE: RAISING YOUR VIBRATION

Katy Furnival

Be the energy you want to attract!

When the opportunity arose to co-author this book, I knew I had to do it. The last two years, starting from 2020, have demonstrated it is imperative to raise our vibration! This is not only vital in keeping our mind and body healthy, but it is also great for combatting fear and negativity.

I grew up on the island of Jersey in the UK. It was a tax haven back then, meaning cheap booze and cigarettes and a pub on every corner. Drinking and socialising was a normal way of life, and for me this progressed into partying on a regular basis. Before I knew it, I was leading a very unhealthy lifestyle. After a few years of backpacking, followed by living in Amsterdam (aka escaping reality). I was brought back down to earth with a nasty jolt. In 2002 my stepdad was diagnosed with cancer. He passed away just four months later. He had been an alcoholic and had always struggled with his weight, and I guess it all eventually got the better of him. His passing led me back to Jersey where I discovered reiki. It helped with my grief, and I decided to do a reiki course. It was there I met like-minded souls who opened my eyes to the world of healing and energy. I ended up moving to Australia with my (then) partner, getting married and having two kids.

In 2008 I discovered kinesiology and completed my advanced diploma. Kinesiology encompassed all the things I loved – energy, healing, health and spirituality (and so much more!) Slowly, I began peeling back the layers of my own childhood hurts and had many realisations, one of them being that I really wasn't happy in my marriage; I hadn't been listening to my intuition for quite some time.

I left my husband of thirteen years and started learning how to love myself and have healthy boundaries. In 2019 I went through one of the most challenging times of my life, and I really had to learn how to raise my vibration so I didn't collapse in a heap of victimhood and depression! First, my house got termites. Next, we got burgled four times in the space of two months! Then Centrelink cut off all my payments due to an error, which took twelve weeks to rectify. Everything around me was literally crumbling and being taken away from me. The final straw was my daughter becoming unwell. I eventually listened to my intuition, which kept telling me 'mould', even though I couldn't see or smell anything. To cut a long story short, we had water damage in the roof of her bedroom, and the spores had started to affect first her and eventually all of us. We had to literally evacuate our house, leaving practically all contents and belongings for fear of bringing the mould with us. It was absolutely devastating.

We moved to a new house in a new suburb, new school and basically built our life from scratch! It was so challenging but also probably the biggest period of growth I ever experienced in my life! People would ask me how I was managing to keep it together. Don't get me wrong, there were lots of tears and meltdowns, but I tried not to stay there. Funny how the universe works because I was actually in the middle of doing a gratitude challenge when it all started going pear-shaped! The timing could not have been more perfect. It made me realise there were still so many things to be grateful for, especially all the kindness and generosity I received from friends and even strangers. It was mind-blowing! I really forced myself to look at all the silver linings.

Years ago, if I heard the word 'self-care' I would instantly think of massages and pampering, and so on, but I now know that although those lovely things ARE self-care, there are many other ways we can energetically and emotionally take care of ourselves and lift ourselves up.

So how do we do this? Well, if you think about it, everything is made up of matter and matter is made up of protons, neutrons and electrons – which are made up of energy. This energy holds a frequency, and we all vibrate at different frequencies. When we energetically vibrate at a HIGH frequency, we feel light, joyful, at peace and on top of the world. We are productive, motivated and optimistic. We are at EASE and can deal with things in a positive way. The higher your frequency the more your life flows naturally and you seem to manifest things and situations with complete ease and synchronicity. Life feels EASY. However, if we are energetically vibrating at a LOW frequency, we feel heavy, sad, depressed, angry, frustrated and very LOW. We are unmotivated, and we do not handle things so well. Our energy and body are in a DIS-EASED state and we are more prone to illness and disease. Our energy feels HEAVY and life seems more challenging.

The universal law of attraction states that like attracts like, so whatever frequency we are vibrating at, we will attract the matching frequency. Have you ever noticed when you are feeling particularly low or one thing goes wrong, it feels like everything starts to go wrong and things start going downhill? If, however, we manage to shift our frequency and don't dwell on what went wrong and instead focus on something positive, we can change the course of our day. Our energy is affected by our environment, that is, other people's energy, foods we eat (food holds a vibration), things we hear, what we watch on TV, what we read, what we see, what goes onto our skin, the water we drink

– literally everything around us! How often has a person walked into a room and you have felt instantly drawn to them and lifted? And how many times have you felt 'drained' after being with a certain person? We feel the frequency of others. The great news is, we can change our vibration! We are magical, powerful beings!

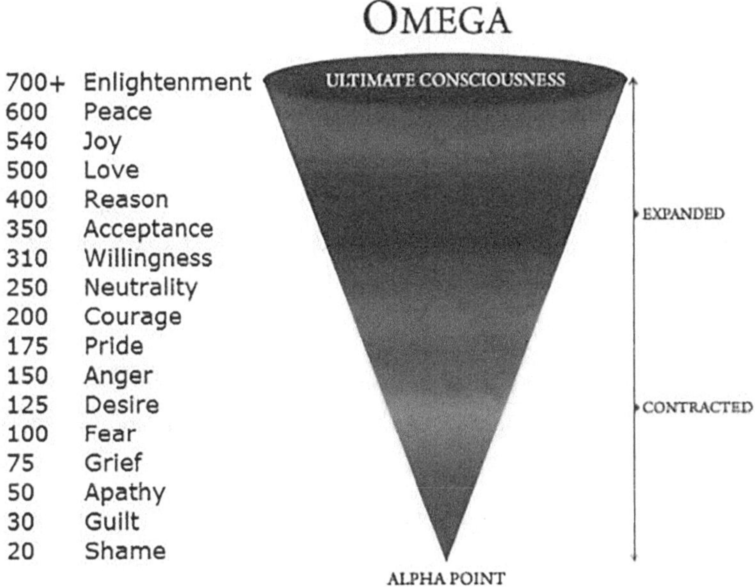

The human emotional vibration analysis frequency ranges chart shown above (reproduced with permission from the Love or Above Toolkit), illustrates the hertz frequency rate of a range of emotions from highest to lowest. As the vibration rate gets lower our breadth of consciousness and ability to deal with things positively is reduced, limiting our perception of the narrow band of reaction.

If you look at the picture of our emotional frequency ranges (above), you can see that shame and guilt are the lowest frequencies. The opposite of guilt is self-worth! The highest frequencies are peace and joy (just before enlightenment). If we can keep ourselves in a state of peace and joy and we love ourselves, we will be vibrating at a super high frequency! Sounds pretty simple, right? Until we get triggered! And let's be honest, we are always going to get triggered because it is how our subconscious brain protects us and keeps us 'safe'. But if you have some tools in your toolbox, you can always bring yourself back to a state of ease. Just by having this book, you have already made the conscious decision to take care of yourself. So well done!

Tools for your Toolbox:

1) Meditation/Breathwork –Try to do at least ten minutes of meditation first thing in the morning and then if you feel like it, add another five minutes each week until you get to your happy place. Make sure you are sitting comfortably. Start with ten very slow, deep breaths in and out through the mouth, breathing right down into the belly. Then do ten more but slightly faster and a final ten all the way down to the belly, but this time faster and really feeling your chest rise and fall. At the end of the breaths, hold for as long as you can, letting it all out and then feeling the energy pulse around your body. Now let your breath return to normal and stay focused on your breath. This is so beneficial because as well as sending oxygen to all your vital organs and cells, you are slowing your heart rate down, decreasing your blood pressure and activating your para-sympathetic nervous system. This instantly puts you into a state of peace, rest and restoration. It is important to seek out a professional breathwork practitioner to learn how to do breathwork properly.

2) Grounding – Visualise your root chakra (located at the base of your spine) glowing red and shooting down, deep into the earth and growing roots. You can also ground yourself by putting your feet on the earth or wearing earthy colours. Another way I love to ground myself is to put all my attention and energy down to the back of my womb space, imagining that all my power is there, and then breathing the energy up to the back of my heart space and then up to the back of my third eye (the space between my eyes). Then I picture all these energy centres lined up, keeping me empowered and centred.

3) Protection – As I mentioned before, other people's energy can affect you, and even drain you, so it is important to protect your energy, especially when going into public places. There are many different ways to do this, but intention is everything. I just visualise either a golden eggshell of protection all around me, trusting that I am completely safe and protected, or a dark blue cloak of protection and imagine zipping it up at the front and then pulling the hood up over my head.

4) Shake it off! – Have you noticed how dogs and other animals shake after being in an accident? They are literally shaking off the trauma from their body. You can either jump up and down and shake out your arms and legs, or you can actually hit your whole body, gently, with a closed fist or open palm. Work up from your legs all the way up to the top of your head, including your buttocks, stomach, chest, armpits, shoulders, back, neck, face and the back of your head. This activates your meridians, which are channels of energy running through your whole body. It instantly changes your vibration. As an added bonus you could also say a word that you wish to embody, such as 'love' or 'confidence'.

5) Daily Affirmations – Say whatever you like, but start it with 'I am the embodiment of' and repeat it at least twenty times. I like to do this in the shower or when I am driving. When I get to my destination, I am literally buzzing! To enhance it, you could look in the mirror straight into your eyes and say something like, 'I am the embodiment of love, health and abundance'.

6) Feel it to heal it! – When you are feeling down or negative, rather than try to suppress or ignore it, make yourself acknowledge your feelings so you can set them free! If you don't, eventually they could manifest into something physical. A lot of people try to avoid their feelings by using alcohol, drugs, TV, comfort eating, and so on. Journaling is a great way to get your feelings out, or screaming, crying, talking to someone, punching a pillow or just sitting with your feelings and breathing into them. Wherever you feel the emotion in your body, breathe down to it. Give the emotion a shape, size, colour and texture, and send it breath, really feeling into it. What usually happens is the feeling/sensation in your body will move or change. Repeat the whole process, always feeling it and breathing into it. Eventually you will be left with a sense of peace and calm, AND you will have acknowledged your feelings, allowing them to move on and not fester.

7) Nature – Regularly getting out into nature's sunshine and being around living breathing plant life is so beneficial. Plants and trees vibrate at a high frequency, so just being around them induces a state of calm AND raises your vibration. If you are feeling angry or frustrated, try putting your hands on a tree because it has the capacity to transmute all your negative energy.

8) De-clutter – Clearing out things like clothes, paperwork, books, old letters, birthday and Christmas cards and food in the pantry or

fridge that may have gone out of date, is a great way to make more room to receive. A clean house gives you a sense of ease and also allows the energy to flow better. Even letting go of toxic people, especially if you feel like you are not resonating anymore or you don't feel good around them. This can give you more time and energy to connect with those you DO resonate with.

9) Surround yourself with positivity – Be careful of what you listen to and what you watch on TV. If you are watching/listening to depressing news or fear-based stories, watching horror movies, reading scary books or articles, just be aware of how they make you feel. Try to listen to uplifting podcasts and watch heartwarming movies and things that make you laugh. Be with people who make you feel good. They say that the top five people who you hang around are the ones you become like, and that your vibe attracts your tribe! People can rub off on you and either bring you down or lift you up, so just be aware of how everyone makes you feel and choose wisely. When you do have to spend time with someone who you know brings your energy down (it can't be helped sometimes), make sure you protect your energy, like I mentioned earlier in tip number two.

10) Gratitude – Writing down what you are grateful for and why, and really FEELING it, can be life changing. That was my go-to when I lost my house and contents. No matter what was happening to me, I tried to find something I was grateful for. I have managed to turn many heart-aching moments around by using this strategy. When you make it a regular practice, it soon becomes habit, and you can't help but see the positive in everything.

Basically, you want to do anything that brings you joy and fills your heart with love! Doing anything that YOU are passionate about is going to raise your vibration. This might be as simple as going to the beach, hanging out with friends, hugging a pet, reading a good book, smelling some flowers, going rock climbing, or even sky diving! Do ANYTHING that lights you up. And when you feel lit up, try and savour every moment and feel into the gratitude and joy.

You now have your very own toolbox, and you can keep adding to it. If you create a daily morning routine using the tools from above or some of your own, stick to it, it will honestly change your life! Just set your clock half an hour earlier and do it!

Remember, YOU have the power to raise your vibration, which in turn will make you feel amazing!

Bio

Katy Furnival is first and foremost a solo-parent to her two gorgeous children. Originally from UK (Jersey), she has been living in Perth, Australia, for nearly twenty years. She first got into energy healing modalities when her stepfather passed away in 2002 and she discovered reiki. She has been a kinesiologist for over a decade, is a group sound meditation facilitator and has recently created her 'Elevating Your Life' online workshop. She holds regular sacred circles and has just started running retreats.

In 2020 Katy decided to put all her skills together and create her

'Inspirational Guidance' package. It incorporates her intuitive guidance with practical tools, kinesiology and EFT. It is designed to help women uncover the blocks and limiting beliefs holding them back in life and to create inner peace by loving and accepting themselves, creating strong, healthy boundaries and stepping into their power. This package allows women to shine their light bright and raise their consciousness.

Katy has a beautiful way with clients and holds a safe space for them, making them feel instantly at ease. She is really passionate about working with the subconscious and accessing and re-programming self-sabotaging beliefs. Katy loves to empower women who have grown up with addicts or narcissists and have lost their self-esteem and confidence. Her aim is to help them elevate their lives and raise their vibe by moving from victim to victor and learning how to love and believe in themselves, shining their light bright!

Work with Katy:

Go to my website to book a free thirty-minute clarity call to see how I can help you.

Special Offer: Send me your email address and I will send you some info on which essential oils to use for raising your vibration!

Check out my website for my upcoming retreats, circles and workshops.

Connect with Katy:

Facebook: www.facebook.com/katyfurnival & www.facebook.com/innerbalancekinesiology

Instagram: www.instagram.com/katyfurnival

Website: www.katyfurnival.com

SECTION 2:
PHYSICAL SELF-CARE

INTRODUCTION

Tracey Jewel

Our bodies have many parts that come together to keep us running. If you want yours to run efficiently, you'll have to take good care of it. The human body runs in conjunction with the mind. That strong connection means it is absolutely critical to look after the physical health of your body.

By taking care of your body, you'll feel better all round and have a deeper connection to your thoughts. With physical self-care, you need to think about what you're giving your body to provide nourishment and hydration. Sleep is another crucial factor involved with intentional physical self-care. Without enough sleep, your body doesn't have the chance to repair and renew and cannot maintain its peak performance.

Additionally, keeping active goes a long way towards this step in achieving self-care. Manage your health by digging into the physical aspect of things to ensure you're giving yourself what you need. A diet rich in nutritious foods coupled with plenty of exercise, rest and health management through your practitioner will serve your physical self-care well and allow you to strive to new heights.

Are you eating right? Getting enough sleep? Drinking plenty of water? Exercising? Taking charge of your health needs? In the following pages, we show how you can improve your physical self-care and bring everything into focus!

PERSONAL TRAINING

Hailey Schmidt

Find your confidence through fitness.

I want you to close your eyes and think about what the voice in your head tells you on a daily basis. Does that voice fill you with words of love and encouragement, or does it spew self-hate, constantly telling you you're not good enough? For most women, it's the latter. I call this voice your 'inner mean girl'.

She is the voice in your head who calls you fat when you look in the mirror, stupid when you're learning something new, ugly when you break out and disgusting when you eat unhealthy food.

She's the one in your head who tells you that you aren't good enough or skinny enough. *The one who knows all your flaws and all of your insecurities and uses them to get to you every day.* In this chapter we are going to talk about how to beat your inner mean girl so you can switch the voice in your head from your biggest critic to your biggest fan.

First, let me introduce myself. I'm Hailey Schmidt, I am a mother of one and an online fitness and business coach. I help women and mums find their confidence through mindset and fitness with programs that work. I have worked in the fitness industry for nine years and have a bachelor's degree in psychology. I am the ultimate hype woman, with energy that is contagious.

While I currently specialise in helping women find confidence,

I wasn't born with that ability. When I was growing up, my mum described me as 'painfully shy'. I would hide behind her or my siblings everywhere we went. Meeting others was painful, and new situations were daunting.

As I grew into my teenage years, I struggled with anxiety and panic attacks that would cause me to break down or pass out. I felt like I had no control over my body or my mind. This led to a lot of people-pleasing and constantly shrinking myself to fit in. Fast forward to now, and I don't even recognise that girl. People who know me today as the talkative, extroverted and confident coach that I am, don't even believe I could have ever been like that – but I was.

So what changed? What happened over those years that seemingly changed who I was? It is important to note that my personality and who I truly was didn't change, I was simply able to remove all of the fears and insecurities that held me back from BEING that person. I think you can probably relate to that. Feeling like you know you can be great and you have this amazing person inside you, but you just can't get her out. Taking that first step into the unknown and breaking out of your comfort zone to show people the real you can be terrifying. What if they don't like you, or they judge you, or you don't fit in society's mould of who you should be? I had those same fears.

The key to going from hiding who you are and people-pleasing your way through life to truly showing up as yourself is building confidence. Building confidence in not only how you look but in who you are. For me, this journey to confidence was through fitness. Let me explain why this journey is so effective in building confidence.

In a world where women are taught to sit back because we are weak, the feeling of being physically strong is inspiring. To break every standard that is socially acceptable and to lift weights and build muscle feels good. To finally have control over our health and our bodies and see our hard work pay off in a way that we love is empowering.

Through this process, not only does your body change but so does your mind. You start looking in the mirror and feeling powerful and proud of what you see, instead of avoiding mirrors because all you do is tear yourself apart. You start viewing clothing to see if you like it, not if you look good enough to wear it. You can get ready for a girls' night or a date in thirty minutes because you feel good in every outfit, instead of spending hours trying things on, never feeling good enough. You start to view your health and fitness journey as something to build you up, instead of a means of shrinking yourself to please others.

Slowly but surely, you beat your inner mean girl by proving her wrong. You beat her by overcoming challenges and reaching goals she told you that you weren't good enough to achieve. Everything changes.

So where do you start? Let me break down my three-part framework and the steps you need to get started on this journey.

Weightlifting

For a very long time, women's magazines and society have taught us that cardio is the key to reaching our goals, but that information is misleading. Cardio is simply calories in versus calories out. This means that you run and burn 200 calories on the treadmill, then you stop and step off and you stop burning calories. This isn't great for a couple reasons. First, if we then eat a piece of pizza, that is 300 calories and we 'ruined' all of our hard work. This leads to a bad relationship with food. Second, the calories burned by cardio aren't specific to fat alone; cardio helps you lose WEIGHT, which means you're burning muscle too.

Not only is muscle the key to sustained results and physical health as we age, it is also the only way to achieve the lean and toned look you want. To build muscle, your main focus needs to be weight training. This can feel very intimidating, especially if you are brand new to the process. So, start small. Find a plan, or hire a coach to create one for you, and start by committing to three to five days a week.

Learn proper nutrition

Diet culture has taught for too long that you need to cut calories and carbs to reach your goals. From personal experience, I can tell you that this is the quickest way to not only be miserable but also to gain all the weight back. This is because it isn't sustainable long term. When it comes to nutrition, we need to go in with the goal of healing and nourishing our bodies rather than just shrinking ourselves. I shared with you earlier that this journey has the ability to build us up as people mentally and physically, and part of that process is treating ourselves in a healthy manner rather than with restriction.

I recommend getting a professional to set your calories and macros for you, so that you can learn exactly how much food your body needs. You can reach your goals while eating real food and finding a balance that is sustainable for you. It is just a matter of gaining knowledge around nutrition.

Master your mindset

Realistically, this should probably be number one because it is the most important piece of this journey. It is also the most underrated piece. You can have the perfect plan, but if you don't have your mindset right, then you won't stick to it. There are two main mindset blocks that derail people on this journey: the 'all or nothing' mindset and a lack of belief in yourself.

The 'all or nothing' mindset is where we convince ourselves we need to be all in or all out. This stems from perfectionism and believing we have to nail our nutrition and workouts every day perfectly, or it is pointless, and we might as well not even try. The truth is that small changes can lead to big results over time. The key isn't perfection, it is consistency. If you are consistent with even small changes, over time this leads to results.

A lack of belief in yourself is self-explanatory; however, the hard part is acknowledging that this is what your struggle is. We blame our 'failure' on a lack of self-control or a lack of ability, when in reality you can accomplish anything you set your mind to. The problem isn't that you aren't capable, it is that you believe you aren't. The truth is you are wildly capable and you are so much stronger than you know.

On this journey, it is important to consistently work on each of these three parts of the framework to be successful. Success isn't just about abs or losing weight, it is about get healthy mentally and physically. It is about finally building the confidence and love of yourself that you have always wanted.

While this chapter hopefully helps you shift your mindset and has given you the steps you need to get started on your journey to finding confidence through fitness, I don't want to stop here. I would love to connect with you!

You can find me on Instagram, where you can grab a free copy of *Your Guide to Calories* and *Macros* to get you started on your journey! Let this chapter be the start of so much more in your life.

Bio

Hailey Schmidt is a mother of one, an online fitness coach and a business coach for fitness professionals. She is located in the US in Baltimore, Maryland.

Hailey specialises in helping women find confidence through fitness with plans that work, and in helping in-person trainers move and grow their business online successfully. Hailey teaches a three-part framework for her health and fitness clients: nutrition, workouts and mindset. She teaches balance and sustainability for long-term results that help women become healthy AND happy! She wholeheartedly believes that fitness can be the stepping stone to finding confidence and changing your life.

Free Guide:

https://boss-lady-hailey.mykajabi.com/calorieandmacroguide

Connect with Hailey:

Facebook: Women's Fitness Group: Learn Balanced Nutrition & Effective Workouts

Instagram: @bossladyhailey

Website: bossladyhailey.com

Email: bossladyhailey@gmail.com

YOGA MOTIONS FOR EMOTIONS

Madina Tanekeyeva

Love yourself, not despite your imperfections, but because of them.

– adaptation of a quote by Brené Brown

Imagine a yoga class.

You're all in and loving it. Suddenly, out of nowhere, a surge of emotions overcomes you.

And there you are, in the middle of a yoga studio on your mat wondering why this is

happening to you? Why the tears or this awkward laugh? What makes you feel so frightened or frustrated? It's just a yoga class!

Sounds familiar?

This was me about fifteen years back, coming out of a deep back-bend pose – sobbing and releasing. As I got on my knees and into a child's pose, a memory of me as a twelve-year-old popped into my mind. The image was so vivid, it was as if it happened yesterday. I am sitting at my desk and struggling with maths work. An adult is towering over tiny me. I look up and see how visibly annoyed she is at my stupidity because I am not grasping what she is trying to explain. As she raises her voice, repeating herself one more time, my mind blanks out. I am frustrated and lonely, and all I want is to burst into tears. But instead I try to keep it together by focusing my attention on the wood patterns of my desk. I stare at the intricate lace of lines and curves that shape the rich texture of the surface upon which my workbook and pens are laid out. I manage to push my emotions down ...

Ever since that encounter in 2006, I set on a path of understanding similar experiences I'd had, both as a teacher and practitioner of yoga. How come these memories and emotions from the past find their way to the surface on the yoga mat of all places? Why after such a release do I often see my body opening and pain going away? What triggers this emotional release?

Fast forward fifteen years, this enquiry and investigation is now systematised and put together in a yoga modality that helps us to become aware of, acknowledge and release emotions.

Today I am committed to helping others make sense of this process. My biggest passion is

to support others in learning how to process their emotions as soon as they manifest, so that instead of letting things pile up and spiral out of control, we can clear them straight away using the tools of yoga, cognitive work and spiritual mentorship.

So what are emotions?

Just like thoughts, emotions are caused by various nervous and neurophysiological activities in our body. Triggered by external stimuli, chemical compounds (neurotransmitters) are released and passed around from neurons to neurons to nerves. Each unique cocktail of these compounds defines what we feel and experience.

Fun fact: there are over 100 billion neurons and over 100 neurotransmitters. According to Dr Alan Watkins, a neuroscientist and internationally recognised expert on leadership and human performance, there are over thirty-four thousand emotions, of which he has mapped about two thousand.

Throughout the day, this chemical activity goes mostly unnoticed. But from time to time, we recognise that some thoughts and emotions get in the way of our wellbeing.

We all know that in order to thrive physically we have to move, eat and sleep on a regular basis. Not just once a week, but rather every day. But with emotional wellbeing, we are lucky if we can address our issues once a month with a therapist or occasionally share something with our close friends.

Pause reading now and take a moment to reflect on how you'd feel if you stopped caring for your physical body on a daily basis. What if you did not shower or brush your teeth? How long do you think you could go on like this without noticing decay and deterioration?

Let me drop a truth bomb here. The same goes for emotional body health, too! And I wonder why we regard it as less important than the physical.

Just like with food, hydration, sleep and movement, I value my daily moments of sitting with my emotions and holding space for myself in order to make sense of what I feel. It often looks like meditation, healing writing, crying (sweet tears of a release that is!), breathing or using essential oils. It's my emotional hygiene routine – something we should be taught at a very young age alongside brushing our teeth!

This practice is like a Marie Kondo method for emotional decluttering. Big chunks of a mess

should be done with a therapist, but day-to-day bits are up to us to recognise, acknowledge and clear.

Emotional Release Yoga is a simple process of four steps:

1. Pause – Slow down, exhale deeply, dedicate time to sitting with yourself and just being.
2. Feel – Look inwardly and sense your body on physical, emotional and mental levels.

3. Allow – Whatever you discover (pleasant or less so) is okay and is welcomed to be and exist.
4. Release – Using emotional release yoga, let go of whatever triggers you – clear it.

This process is really easy to follow, and I invite you to try it right now.

Pause

Choose your favourite place to sit or lie down by yourself. It can be in a comfortable armchair, on your bed or on your meditation cushion. Leave your phone in another room on silent and commit to ten to fifteen minutes of quiet time without any distraction. Take a few deep breaths in and out, and allow for your busy mind to settle. Hang in there for as long as you need to until you start noticing your thoughts slowing down.

Feel

Looking back on your day, ask yourself how you feel about it as a whole?

Was there anything in particular that triggered you in any way?

A possible power struggle or an uncomfortable interaction?

Maybe you got overly excited, overshared or said something you now regret?

Are you feeling inspired and energised thinking of your day or, on the contrary, deflated and tired?

If you noticed something that stood out for you, let's give it some compassionate attention. Go back to that particular situation and reconstruct it in your head using the three 'w' questions:

Where was it? Try to be very specific and remember every possible detail. Was it indoors or outdoors? Do you remember any specific features like a tree or a piece of furniture?

Who was involved in it? Who are the actors in this play, how many of them were involved in this interaction?

What was said and done (or withheld or not done)? Can you remember which phrases or words affected you the most?

As you live the situation once again, pay closer attention to what you feel and where you feel it. Hear your body responding to this memory. You can feel a gentle tingling, muscles tightening, some burning or numbness. Some people also see colours, hear sounds or experience flash memories from the past.

Whatever you feel, observe yourself, sense without judging, labelling and analysing. Hold space for yourself and breathe deep. It's very similar to listening to a close friend who just wants you to listen and is not seeking any advice. Feel. Sense. Breathe.

Allow

Acknowledging whatever you are sensing, read the sentences below out loud to yourself:

It's okay to feel what you're feeling right now.

Your emotions are welcome.

It is safe to feel whatever you're feeling.

Embrace yourself fully.

Breathe.

Release

There are many techniques and tools that I use for releasing emotions:

- visualisations and chakra balancing
- inner loving voice practice
- self-healing with golden light
- healing writing
- yoga poses, meditation, and breathwork

- myofascial release and acupressure points
- spiritual mentoring

And quite frankly, sometimes it looks like beating the hell out of my bed mattress with a

swimming noodle or singing at the top of my lungs while driving. Yes, in those moments I do look like a crazy lady rather than a yoga teacher. But who cares if it helps me!

Oftentimes, however, just the first three steps of pause, feel, and allow are enough to find deep relaxation and surrender. I'm sure that at least once in your life you've experienced that deep and meaningful exhalation. Remember how your shoulders softened, followed by your heart space softening straight after? Bliss…

However, if it's not enough for you today, I invite you to practise Emotional Release Yoga with me online. I created this especially for my readers, and it gives you a great bite-sized taster of a guided Emotional Release Yoga workshop.

It consists of:

- introduction and summary of the workshop
- practice session
- journaling prompts for reflection and healing writing
- opportunity to connect with me via email in case you've got any questions or need clarification on ERY

At the end of this workshop you will:

- KNOW how to process and let go of anger, resentment, and frustration
- FEEL balanced and in touch with your emotions
- BE less triggered by day-to-day interactions

I invite you to pause now and answer this question:

How would your life change if you could spot and process lingering emotions before they cluttered your energetic space and spiralled out of control?

Is it just me fantasising here or are you hearing lots of good things ringing through your head?

Head to my website or set a reminder in your calendar to check it out later. Grab your phone and do it now.

Let's sail the ocean of emotions together!

Be happy, healthy, and content.

Namaste,

Madina

Bio

Madina Tanekeyeva BEc E-RYT RPYT Dip CBed was born in Kazakhstan, grew up in The Netherlands and now resides in Sydney, Australia.

She is a mum and wife, a senior yoga teacher, yoga teacher mentor, creator of Emotional Release Yoga and Online Yoga Community (live and on-demand classes).

Since her early twenties she has dedicated most of her free time and resources seeking and deepening Buddhist and Yogic knowledge.

This intertwined with a career working for big corporations and being stressed and dissatisfied with her life. Despite having a bachelor degree in economics, at twenty-eight she made a dramatic career change to become a yoga and meditation teacher.

She set out on a path of self-discovery and travelled the world to study with many remarkable teachers. Her meditation practice is shaped by Namkhai Norbu Rinpoche, a renowned Tibetan Buddhist master. While her yoga practice is influenced by Ashtanga teachers Nancy Gilgoff, Rolf and Marci, and Eileen Hall.

She co-founded Astanga Yoga School Amsterdam, changed four countries and established herself as a successful yoga teacher in Almaty, Amsterdam, and Sydney.

Connect with Madina:

Website: www.madinayoga.com/upheal

SECTION 3:
MENTAL SELF-CARE

INTRODUCTION

Tracey Jewel

What you think plays a huge role in your psychological well-being. When we think positive thoughts, we attract positive energy. But when we dwell on the negative, it brings more of the same.

Additionally, keeping our minds healthy and happy requires exercises to sharpen things up. There's a lot of work to do for your mental wellness. Think of it like a glass that you can fill up with whatever you want. You'll need to choose wisely though for you can go for nourishing or toxic fillings.

With mental self-care, you will work on strengthening your mental health. That means more to stimulate the mind as well as filling it with good thoughts. Do you engage in any activities that mentally stimulate you? If not, this section will show you just how to use your mind to its fullest. Learn something new, read, and fill your mind with all good things.

Don't forget to be kind to yourself. What are you doing to help stay mentally healthy? Are you learning anything new or doing any activities to build up your mind? If you've neglected this area of your self-care, you'll learn everything you need for channelling that positive energy to boost your mental health on the following pages.

SELF-ESTEEM IS NOT AN OPTION: YOU WERE BORN WITH A HIGH SELF-ESTEEM

Raewyn Weller

You are the Architect of your Life, the Captain of your Ship. You have always, are presently and will continue to Create your Life, Accept, learn from and let go of the past, Love and be kind to yourself, Believe in and live your dreams. You can be the person you want to be.

– Raewyn Weller

Do you ever feel that you are not good enough? Constantly worrying about how you look, or how you think others perceive you? Lacking confidence in yourself? If your answer to any of these questions is 'yes', then you could be suffering from low self-esteem.

Having a low self-esteem affects all of us from time to time, however, if your self-worth is so low that you're struggling with your day-to-day life, it will be affecting your mind, body and spirit detrimentally.

The most important relationship in your life is the one that you have with yourself. The only mind you have control of, or not, and have the power to change is your own.

What you think about you is what matters …. love, respect, and believe in yourself.

Your self-esteem is how you think about yourself, whether positively or negatively. A healthy self-esteem helps you break away from the fear of being humiliated by others. You can look in the mirror and tell the person you see that you love them. You feel happy and confident.

When you have a low self-esteem, you feel you are not good enough one way or another. Most of your self-image issues are memories trapped in your subconscious mind. You are recalling and reacting to what someone has said or done to you in the past and allowing that person to make you feel small, insignificant, and unimportant. These memories are fuelled by what you continually feed your mind and will be there until you change them.

Always remember that the words you say and the pictures you create in your mind create your life.

Does comparing yourself with others and/or putting yourself down ring a bell? It did for me, especially when I was a teenager. I have always said that I went to school to eat my lunch. I never felt confident or clever, I felt frumpy and never good enough, thin enough, loveable enough, and certainly not beautiful. Would you call that a low self-esteem? I certainly would. If only I knew back then that I felt just like more than half of the girls at school, things might have been a little different. Statistics show that seventy-five per cent of women and eighty-five per cent of teenagers have low self-esteem.

When I was in my thirties and forties, I had a high profile in the community and business world. Looking back now, what I achieved was amazing, however I never felt amazing, at times I allowed others to make me feel small and insignificant.

Thank goodness that has changed, I am now often referred to as a 'ray of sunshine' or the 'self-esteem queen'. I accept and love it. It makes me feel good within. Having a high, but realistic, self-esteem is essential for good mental and physical health.

If you act and think positively and your thoughts and actions are aligned with your values, your truth, it doesn't matter what others think. How others think is their business, their opinion is just that, an opinion.

You don't need the approval of others. People who try to make you feel small are usually trying to prove themselves. They have a false self-esteem. Any time you feel better or worse than someone else means that you think someone is better or worse than you. We are all equal. Judging others is a sign of insecurity; you are trying to make yourself look better.

Life is a mirror; you see in others what is in you. Life reflects what you put out there.

Your attitude and moods are your choice, and are very catchy, so choose to be happy.

Happy confident people attract like-minded people, others feel and like your energy. Changing your words and thoughts from negative to positive will change your life. It's okay to make mistakes, you are human.

If you are feeling you are not good enough, know that you are not alone. Most people do not feel that they are enough – good, thin, clever, strong, whatever enough. Today's busy life and social media don't help. I had a client who, due to her perception of things done and said to or about her in the past, hated herself. She felt it was her fault that her parents split up. She felt she wasn't lovable enough for her dad to stay. And she heard boys at school say she was fat, even though she wasn't. Depressed, she turned to social media, followed an anorexic girl on Instagram and ended up anorexic and bulimic – extremely dangerous.

The good news is you can reprogram your subconscious mind and turn it all around. No matter what your current beliefs and insecurities are, they are just programming from your past thoughts, feelings and memories that can be addressed. You can turn your thoughts and life around. Get help if you need it. My book *Your Health is Your Greatest Wealth* will help you.

We often misinterpret what others say or do. Our imagination runs wild. We create pictures in our mind and start imagining things that are not true. Don't believe everything that goes on in your mind. Most of your thoughts are irrelevant or not true and are often the same as what went through your mind yesterday and the day before. Question your thoughts. Ask yourself: Where did this come from? Me or someone else? Is it true? Nine times out of ten it won't be true.

You are the captain of your ship; you have the control panel for your thoughts! To identify what or who is taking you off course, you need to look at how you are living.

- Who are you spending most of your time with?
- What is your attitude like?
- Do you exercise regularly, ground yourself, eat well and think good thoughts?
- Is there something from the past that you need to let go of?

The more you give something attention, whether good or bad, the more you attract it and it will grow. We create mountains out of molehills. No matter whether you perceive your issues as yours or someone else's fault, you have power over your mind, you can turn it around. Take responsibility for your life, start nurturing and loving yourself – mind, body and spirit. When you change your thoughts, you change your life.

What makes you feel good? Music? dancing? reading? being with friends? playing sport? games? Seek it. Do it. Laugh. Have fun. Life is for living.

I start my day with positive affirmations, exercises and music. I even sing and dance some mornings. I love rock'n'roll, bike riding, bushwalking and beach walks in fresh air and nature. Fill your life with fun things that raise your energy and ground you.

Be happy. Don't say I will be happy when I get x, y or z. It won't work, and you will always be searching. Be grateful for what you have, focus on the good and learn from and change the not so good. Start believing in yourself, and know that you are just like millions of other people; you are enough.

Your mind likes what is familiar, so you need to make being positive and happy familiar. Think about how you form a habit. That's right, repetition. Do you have to think about how to drive your car? No, because you have formed a habit. You know how to drive because you practised until you could do it. Replace habits that don't serve you with good habits.

Start each day with positive affirmations about yourself. Repeat them often, even if you think or feel it is false. It is okay to tell yourself little white lies if it is for the good. Believe me it works. However, if you say, 'I am a fantastic person' and then follow it in your mind or aloud with 'what a load of crap', you have just cancelled your affirmation and are back to square one.

Create a self-esteem bank. Make regular deposits of positive affirmations, praise and self-love. Just like your bank account, you must make deposits to be able to withdraw. Do and read things that make you smile and laugh, it releases endorphins, happy hormones, that make you feel good. Hang out with friends who make you laugh. Build positive relationships; avoid negative relationships, they drain your energy.

One of the most beneficial things you can do is to stop letting in and believing criticism. Read each question below and write down what comes to mind first. Trust your intuition. Be honest with yourself.

1. How do I feel about myself?
2. How does the image I hold of myself impact my life?
3. Do I rely on approval from others and make decisions based on what I assume they will think?
4. Do I need to become more assertive and learn to say No?
5. Do I need to improve my physical and / or mental health?

You can improve your confidence by identifying and challenging your negative beliefs.

Know that everything you need is within you. You do not need to search outside of you.

Identify, write down and work on the positives, your strengths. Set yourself realistic goals. Feel, say, write and imagine your goals and they will become much stronger, growing your confidence and self-esteem. Celebrate all achievements, big and small.

The following exercise will help you identify what you need to work on.

Rate yourself honestly from 0–10 (10 high) on each of the following statements:

1. I love and accept myself.
2. I am enough.
3. I have phenomenal coping skills and in control of my power.
4. I easily say 'no' when asked to do something I don't like doing.
5. I stand up for myself without feeling guilty.
6. I enjoy others, I have positive relationships with people in my life.
7. I have unique talents and skills.
8. I do not take other's actions or words personally.
9. I deserve good things in life

10. I forgive myself and let go of past mistakes.
11. I spend more time solving my problems instead of worrying about them.
12. Nothing and no one can disturb my peace of mind.

It's okay to score low. Create affirmations from the statements you need to improve, or create new ones that you resonate with. Repeat them with feeling daily. Positive affirmations will reprogram your subconscious core beliefs. Retest yourself regularly, and notice how your life changes.

Connect with your inner self often: Close your eyes, breathe in slowly with a smile on your face, hold it, feel the love and peace filling your whole being, then breathe out unwanted energy. Repeat several times.

Surround yourself with supportive, positive people who will fill your self-esteem bank. Be aware of your inner critic. You are harder on yourself than anyone else. You are your biggest critic, so praise yourself. Give self-approval rather than relying on the approval of others. Words and thoughts are energy, they can lift you or cut you down. Be aware of the words you use and those you accept from others.

Put yourself first, you are unique, there is no one else just like you, love yourself and you will shine and have energy to share with others. You are only a choice away from changing your life. If you say it is easy or hard it will be.

Step outside of your comfort zone with confidence.

If it is to be, it is up to me.

Bio

Raewyn Weller is the author of *Your Health is Your Greatest Wealth*, a self-health book, *Abracadabra*, a children's healing book, *Jan's Dash*, a biography of her sister, and co-author in *The Wealth Garden* and *Mum's the Word.*

Living in the Bay of Plenty, New Zealand, Raewyn is a public speaker, certified belief and energy clearing practitioner, life success consultant, holistic energy healer and Rapid Transformational Therapy practitioner. Raewyn is also a holistic energy healer; she uses qui gong and quantum-touch healing and works with bioenergetic healing frequencies. She is a life-long learner and her claim to fame is being a 'graduate of the school of life'.

Having studied and practiced many different healing techniques, Raewyn uses the most appropriate methods for each individual, working with mind, body and spirit.

Starting her working life nursing, Raewyn went on to create businesses for self and community, was a local body politician for two terms, a business mentor and has had government appointments. She has worked in schools and homes for needy and homeless children in Zimbabwe and India. Her passion is empowering people, giving them tools and teaching them to help and heal themselves.

Raewyn is grateful to have learnt so much through life experiences, clients and working with and studying the work of many amazing people internationally. They have all inspired and empowered her.

Special Offer: Tell me how this chapter has helped you, and I will send you an eBook and put you in a draw for a free consultation. Email: raewyn@raewynweller.com

Connect with Raewyn:
Facebook group: Your Health is Your Greatest Wealth
LinkedIn: www.linkedin.com/in/raewyn4healthymindandbody
Website: www.raewynweller.com (You will find videos to help you.)
Email: raewyn@raewynweller.com

TRICK MINDSET

Katrina North

When we focus on ourselves we can create anything, even when it feels like it's all going sideways.

I have been a pre-school teacher for about twenty years. We learn about theorists and the psychology of the mind. Psychology was not something I chose to venture into as I'd had some counselling and this was not very effective for me. So, I was recommended to try energy healing (access consciousness). I found this approach more effective for me. Then a friend of mine killed himself at the age of thirty-two. I was devastated and went on a venture to understand. This led me into suicide prevention and becoming a facilitator of Applied Suicide Intervention Skills Training (ASIST) with Lifeline New Zealand. After a while I thought 'This isn't working for me; there must be another way for people that also looks at a holistic viewpoint.' I have now adopted a way I have seen has been successful with the people I have worked with, both youth and adults. I am not saying that my method is better or is going to save you (this is just a different approach I have adapted from my education). If you are willing and looking for change from that space, then anything is possible with tools for life.

Recently, I have seen many clients – youth and adult – with the same underlying issues – OCD, PTSD, voices, destructive behaviour. I was curious to see what was really happening here. So, I went on a quest to gain more knowledge. I spent many hours researching these topics as they all seemed to link in. I am not here to diagnose, but in my years working in education in many areas, all the signs and symptoms were showing through (or were stated by the client).

Being able to have more clarity on what was being presented to me gave far more insight on how to best help and create something different for the people I am working with. I was fascinated about this, as in my work I have never seen anything this overwhelming or all in one go. I had to spend many weekends and late nights reading. Believe me, I had many tears, write ups and self-blame. I felt tired and overwhelmed. The curiosity was just so great as to what was creating all of this, as the clients couldn't really pinpoint it themselves. Some said Covid-19 lockdown and uncertainty. Others were not even willing to look at this and were in a state of what is known as toxic positivity, when you try to put positive affirmations on top of a belief that doesn't believe what you are saying. This makes things worse, and nothing changes apart from the belief becoming more affirmed. Not the most desired outcome.

So, let's look for the moment at what OCD is. This is a mental condition where people become obsessed with something. An example is cleaning, washing hands and worrying about germs. But OCD can be anything done compulsively. Anxiety then creates scenarios and stressing about nothing. To the person the scenarios are real, but they haven't happened yet. The mind sees it as real. This is the body going into a trauma state imagining that things are going to happen based on past experience. The mind creates the certainty of the uncertain to prove that it is right.

Post-Traumatic Stress Disorder (PTSD) is when a traumatic experience has occurred and is locked into the body. This can also tend to lead to self-wrongness. Everyone at some stage has had that niggle voice (contradictory thoughts). This is when you think or say something and the voice in your head says the total opposite. Some can just brush it off, while others believe what the niggling voice is saying is true and real. Imagine if something has been said to you over and over again and it becomes a silent voice that plays over and over in the background. This becomes a belief.

When we buy the voices as true and real, we start to create our lives from their lies. Before you do anything, there is this sudden pang of anxiety because what you would like to choose is pushing that belief. This can be a debilitating time. We can be too afraid to ask for help. So, we stay silent and remain in that space until either we have finally had enough or we stay there forever.

Anxiety can also be a sign of where you are choosing against yourself, so what you are asking doesn't happen. Like all of your power goes into this, instead of creating for yourself. When I say choosing against yourself, I mean going against a locked in belief or trauma that has been triggered by an event, or moving towards a target that the belief system says 'Oh, no you don't'. Creative energy goes into the undesired.

Self-harm can be anything from cutting, bullying, isolating, alcohol, drugs suicidal thoughts and action. With all of these aspects, always take the person seriously. It's not so much about the action, it's the things behind this that lead to it: emotions, thoughts, beliefs (a family member did this to cope) and learnt behaviour. It's the pain that holds this in place. The pain becomes a comfortable place and can get addictive – 'what's the point I will always be miserable'.

The process of coming out of this space takes repetition of doing things differently. I am walking proof of this. Now I am here writing this. So, this is lived experience as well as education. What I am writing about is experience with my clients and their journeys, not just my own. I get nervous sometimes and think of some of my strategies and if they are going to work for this person. It's not the easy talking to a suicidal person. I do what I can.

Also, this can be created by being in a family where everything is a problem, blame and everyone is at fault – a victim mindset. This can create a belief in a young child that this is how life is and they take this on. Guess what? Your life becomes one drama and problem after another, with everything and anything. Then anxiety and panic attacks happen.

In my techniques and working with people I try to avoid words with connotations. What are these? It's words that hold a lot of resistance or anything that a person can hold onto – labelling or categorising. If someone states they are something, then that's different. I am not a doctor, I am a holistic therapist. It is not in my scope of practice to diagnose.

Shame, guilt, regret are big ones that hold us back and keep us in our comfort zone. So, we never step into the unknown. What if we just step into the unknown and listen to that whisper and explore? 'Yes', I hear you say, 'but that voice says I can't' (contradictory thoughts). Well, what if you say 'hey, voice you have had your time. I am no longer choosing to listen to you. You no longer serve me.' Wow, just like that you took your power back. This is what we should demand of ourselves, the step we are required to take.

What's holding you back from moving forward? Let me tell you, it's always you. When you give thoughts, feelings and emotions power over your life, they will always win, as you have allowed them all of your power. It takes less energy to change your life than to fight to stay in your comfort zone.

How do I step out of this comfort zone?

Tools to help with this:

- Claiming your power back. Nothing is more powerful than you.

- Claiming and acknowledging the greatness of you every day
- Gratitude
- Forgiveness for ourselves
- Allowance for where we learnt things. Acknowledge that if we learnt this from family, they were only doing the best with the tools they had.
- Allowance for yourself for not knowing these tools before now.
- What am I really stressed about? If I choose to focus on something else, what can I choose now?
- What else is possible here? Now?

I would like you all to remember that you can change anything. It's the beliefs that stick us. Like, when you have had drama, trauma and upset, your creative energy locks into this space. This then becomes your creative space. We have to let go of the creative energy locked into drama, trauma and upset. Then we can allow ourselves to create the life we desire. Believe me this has taken a few years to learn. Then I just got it! The 'ah ha' moment changed it. Wow, life is so different. I no longer waste energy on trauma, drama and upset, which was my normal. I also let go of taking everything so personally. Like anything that was said to me I took personally. All that came from that was me beating myself up and eating away at myself.

When you ask a question, this shifts the mindset, this enables the mindset to change and you can see from a different viewpoint. This is where the ah ha moments come into place.

Acknowledge when you are changing old beliefs or stepping out of your comfort zone, and ask for the change to happen with ease, joy and glory.

Setting yourself up with a daily routine can really help.

I wake up early most mornings. Some mornings I don't get up right away. I stay in bed and do daily intentions. I set my day. Then I get up, go to the gym or yoga, come home, have a shower, have some clients and do some work for myself. I stay focused on my next move.

When things have got heavy, ask what you have you done for yourself or turned to. When you learn new ways and refocus your mind, a different life starts to emerge. It only takes that one step from you. Are you willing to take that step? Even if it's sixty minutes for you to experience a new door that can open, and all you have to do is be the key in the lock? Say to yourself 'I truly would like to have change in my life. I am the key.' What doors can you unlock now?

So where to from here? What could happen if you learnt some more tools or just chose to go 'Right, this all sounds great? Is it really this easy? Well, you learnt to tie your shoelaces, drive a car, how to use email. So, changing your mindset is just like these, you practise and then change will happen.

Bio

Katrina North has many years of experience in the field of energy work and has been a teacher for over twenty years. She is able to read people in a dynamic way and hear what they are saying.

Katrina has a methodology and tailors sessions for the needs of her clients and what works best for them. She has studied and became a suicide prevention facilitator. She has worked with many clients, both youth and adults, in this area, with the specific viewpoint that each person has very different requirements. She is always upskilling, whether it be through a class online or reading about specific topics. Katrina is dedicated to her clients and puts in 100 per cent into her work and clients, which shines through in her personality and character. Katrina has experienced her own life journey with suicidal thoughts. This is what brought her to finding another avenue to dealing with this from a holistic view, looking at all aspects and strategies – sometimes spending weeks working on a tailored program to suit the person. Katrina is passionate in her work and has an ability to connect with anyone she works with. Katrina lives in Auckland, New Zealand. She is working on a project in mental health designed for schools and corporate clients, utilising the Lego serious play method.

Let's have fun and play while we look at our 'mind health' and wellbeing.

Connect with Katrina:
Facebook: https://m.facebook.com/KatrinaNorthAccessConsciousness/?ref=bookmarks
Website: https://www.katrinanorthjoyofliving.com/

THE POWER OF MINDFULNESS: LESS STRESS, MORE SUCCESS

Virin Gomber

Breathe. Let go. And remind yourself that this very moment is the only one you know you have for sure. – Oprah Winfrey

My doctor gave me an inquisitive and semi-compassionate look and asked: 'Are you

stressed?'

Surprised at the sudden question, I paused for a moment, did a quick inner reflection and replied using some carefully crafted words.

'There are some life challenges at the moment,' I said. 'But I don't think I'm stressed. Why do you ask?'

'Your blood reports are alright, so I think the only other reason for your digestive issues

could be stress,' he shot back.

That evening, my mind took me back to the time when I had immigrated to New Zealand

from India in 2002 in search of a better lifestyle.

Navigating new moves

Moving countries wasn't easy. A completely different culture, with a different set of elements – language, lifestyle, foods and expectations – came as a huge shock to my system at all levels. At the same time, I was looking for a job to help me pay my bills, while also studying full time to qualify as an interior designer (though I had a quantum physics degree … But that's a different story!)

Navigating the smorgasbord of challenges was a big learning curve. My professional journey took me through a rollercoaster of different jobs in various areas, including interior design, journalism and public relations. A few years into it, I started to feel restless. I wasn't completely sure about the reason for this troubling emotion, but I was keen to address it quickly. At times I felt it was to do with some capped emotions from living in a new country. But, I also felt it was to do with lack of professional success.

Another 'But'

The mentality of that 'chase' and desire for the next best shiny object brought me to a point

of intense burnout. Despite being in a corporate and well-paying role, I felt deep within that it wasn't what I wanted my life to be like. That wasn't the only thing that seemed to be going wrong. I had been seeing someone for a couple of years, and that relationship was crumbling. These 'life dramas' were the pre-cursor to my increasing stress levels and overwhelm. And one morning when I woke up, I detested the thought of going to work.

'Well, I'm going to quit my job,' I decided.

That was a dire warning signal and a huge red flag. I had lost the desire to 'repair my broken life'. The pain and dejection impacted my physical health, as I started getting lazy, and losing weight and energy. That was the reason I went to see my doctor to 'fix' my digestive and other health issues. And he guessed, rightly, that 'stress' was the cause of all my health issues.

Our anxiety does not come from thinking about the future, but from wanting to control it.
– Kahlil Gibran

Apart from the damage to my health, I witnessed negativity creeping into all my personal

relationships. I also suffered financial losses. Above all, I began losing the connection with myself. I was stressed, depressed and clueless … That was my lowest phase in life!

Hope survives

But, for some weird reason, deep inside me I had a little corner with a glimmer of hope and belief that I was destined to create something bigger than I could even imagine. I think because I had been regularly meditating since my teen years, it helped me stay sane and stable at a deeper baseline level.

What you're supposed to do when you don't like a thing is change it. If you can't change it, change the way you think about it. Don't complain.
– Maya Angelou

The search for the solutions to all my problems led me to discovering mindfulness. Initially, I thought it was another form of meditation and a fad that was gripping the world, just like some diet fads. But, as I dived deeper into it, all the pieces of the puzzle fell in place for me.

I realised that mindfulness is a way of living that can lead us to the 360-degree level of success, happiness and balance that everyone is looking for. It's about understanding our own neural system – the way our brain operates and the infinite power it has. It's about applying this understanding to build a more mindful and conscious way of living.

This was a huge turning point for me. As I embraced and applied mindfulness, it

transformed me at all levels, inner and outer. I established my Success Consulting business in order to share these lessons and strategies with others. I was able to eliminate all the stress and overwhelm from the past. I reclaimed love in all my relationships and boosted my health, fitness and energy levels. Through this journey, I also became an Amazon best-selling co-author of a self-love book – *The Missing Piece in Self Love.*

As I reflect back on the past, I feel a sense of gratitude and appreciation for mindfulness,

which has provided me with the tools to overcome overwhelm, stress and anxiety, and the

opportunity to empower others to achieve the same.

Modern day stress

While our modern lifestyle has made our lives easier at many levels, there's also a lot of

aspects that have increased the levels of stress and that continue to perpetuate anxiety.

I agree we've got a world of information and thousands of apps at our fingertips that promise to make our lives easier, but is all this working in our favour? The most important reason for increasing stress levels in this day and age is the lack of awareness about stress and how to prevent it in the first place.

According to the World Health Organization (WHO), stress has been classified as the health epidemic of the 21st century. Two of the main sources of stress, as we know, are professional (work-related) and personal. Of course, as I write this, humanity is facing some major stress and anxiety from one of the biggest challenges ever faced – Covid-19!

The impact of stress

The stress hormones cortisol and adrenalin have a range of harmful effects on our physical health, including: irregular blood pressure, heart disease, digestive issues, fatigue, lack of sleep, diabetes and more. Then, there's a set of harmful psychological effects including: anxiety, depression, overwhelm, fears and doubts, anger and frustration, low self-esteem and low self-confidence. All these effects can lead to a range of chronic risks including: lack of focus, decreased memory, relationship conflicts, procrastination, productivity loss, work-life imbalance and even financial losses. So, where does mindfulness fit into all of this?

Mindfulness – myths

Like everything, there are myths around mindfulness that prevent people from opening their mind and heart to it.

1. One of the biggest misconceptions people have about mindfulness is that it means 'meditation' and sitting cross-legged every day.
2. Some people think that mindfulness is a religious practice, which is completely untrue.
3. There's also a misconception that apart from stress relief, mindfulness has no other 'real' benefits.
4. Some people also think that mindfulness makes you turn inward and become more isolated.
5. One school of thought says that mindfulness wears down your grit and courage to take bold actions, because of its focus on 'acceptance'.
6. And then there are people who think that mindfulness is difficult and it takes years of practice to see any results with it.

These are all myths and completely untrue assumptions, resulting from various misunderstandings around mindfulness.

Mindfulness – facts

Let me tell you that mindfulness is simple and easy to practise and, at the same time, immensely powerful. Scientific research also provides evidence that mindfulness is proven to give lasting results. There have been thousands of studies done over the years, and the ongoing research continues to provide strong evidence of its effectiveness.

Some of the key (and documented) benefits of mindfulness include:

1. reduces stress and anxiety
2. improves relaxation and peace of mind
3. promotes emotional wellbeing and physical health
4. increases focus and cognitive functioning
5. improves sleep

Research proves that mindfulness is actually a way of living that can provide significantly greater vitality, enthusiasm and drive to be successful. And above all, with mindfulness, you can get started right now even if you've never practised it before.

Even more evidence of its effectiveness is that mindfulness is being used by businesses globally, like Google, Nike and Apple.

> *The best way to capture moments is to pay attention. This is how we cultivate mindfulness. Mindfulness means being awake. It means knowing what you are doing.*
>
> – Jon Kabat-Zinn

How to live mindfully?

If you have experienced stress, anxiety or overwhelm, or are likely to experience it, the first step towards learning how to manage and eliminate it is recognising you are experiencing it.

Here's five simple and proven mindfulness steps to address these challenges:

1. Practise mindfulness meditation

Learn strategies to relax your body and mind, and control your breathing. You can do this through meditation and advanced breathing exercises, which will dissolve the energy of stress and prevent any more build-up.

2. Become mindful of your health

Getting regular physical exercise helps sharpen your mind, empowers you to push through pain and exhaustion, get stronger and have fun. Choose your workouts mindfully so you can get the most out of least effort.

3. Choose mindful nutrition

The first step is to be mindful of the kind of foods you're consuming. Since the gut has a direct connection with your brain, whatever foods you consume have an impact on your mental and emotional health. And then, understand that the 'how' of 'food' is much more important than the 'what'.

4. Recharge your batteries

Make time regularly for yourself to recharge. This includes getting regular mental breaks, having a good night's sleep and nurturing great social relationships. Press 'pause' whenever needed as well as having set times to do so through the day.

5. Declutter and simplify

The real clutter happens inside your mind as you consume all sorts of information through the day – news, social media stories, TV, Netflix, and so on. The quality of this information determines the quality of results in your business and life. Declutter your mind and simplify your life so that you can adapt to stressful situations and avoid unnecessary (and avoidable) causes and sources of overwhelm.

As you learn to recognise how stress manifests in your body, mind and life, and address them with mindfulness strategies, you will start to experience improved energy levels, more balance and enhanced productivity.

The only thing that is ultimately real about your journey is the step that you are taking at this moment. That's all there ever is. – Eckhart Tolle

The mindfulness mantra

According to one 2015 study, mantras help create a major shift in your brain activity — specifically in the part responsible for internal evaluation, rumination and mind-wandering. Further research from Harvard Professor Matthew A Killingsworth advises that 'A wandering mind is an unhappy mind' and that 'about forty-seven per cent of our waking hours are spent thinking about what's NOT going on.'

When researchers compared results between participants in a resting state who used a mantra against those that didn't, the ones utilising the mantra reached a more advanced state of psychological calm. So, one easy way to stop your mind from wandering is to develop a mindfulness mantra for yourself.

An example of a mindful mantra that I like to use: 'Happiness is a choice, not a condition. I choose to be happy.'

The key to success with practicing mindfulness is to start with an intention, and at the same time not to have any expectation of the outcomes. It works best when you experiment and explore with an open mind.

When you open your mind to just being present, the present presents itself to you with infinite possibilities and opportunities for self-growth. – Virin Gomber

Bio

Virin Gomber is a mindfulness success coach, speaker and author dedicated to helping people become top achievers.

He is a thought innovator with a strong passion for consistent and ongoing growth in all areas of life including – health, career, wealth, relationships, spirituality and learning. With an enthusiasm for personal growth and an endeavour for comprehending various forms of success modalities, Virin has researched and discovered some immensely powerful and transformational methods to enjoy a successful and well-balanced life.

His professional background is an exotic mix of varied careers and qualifications including – interior design, marketing, public relations, journalism, neurolinguistic programming and a master's degree in quantum physics.

Virin has gathered more than twenty-five years of mindfulness self-practice and experience, as well as coaching entrepreneurs and training corporates. In 2015, he also co-authored an Amazon international bestseller *The Missing Piece in Self Love.*

Born and raised in India, Virin is now based in the gloriously beautiful and peaceful New Zealand. In his free time, he likes to travel and connect with nature.

Virin's WHY: To empower people to create accomplished personal skills so they can achieve next-level success, happiness and balance.

Qualifications:

- Mindfulness teaching accreditation, Ovio Mindfulness
- Certified coach by Life in Balance Pty Ltd
- Mindfulness practitioner by Renew Your Mind
- Certification in the neuroscience of learning
- Certification in Leadership Foundations: Leadership Styles and Models
- Certified NLP Master Practitioner IANLP by Transformations International
- Master's degree in quantum physics, the University of Delhi

Awards:

Ambassador for Peace Award 2014, Universal Peace Federation

Work with Virin:

Virin offers a unique blend of mindfulness, smart strategic planning and neuro-science. The core of his work is with driven professionals, executives and entrepreneurs to help them achieve next-level success, happiness and balance.

He offers the 'Mindfulness Powerhouse' program that's transforming his clients lives by transforming their fear, stress and procrastination into maximising their peace, performance and productivity.

Connect with Virin:
Facebook: https://www.facebook.com/virin.gomber/
Instagram: https://www.instagram.com/virin.gomber/
LinkedIn: https://www.linkedin.com/in/viringomber/
Website: www.viringomber.com

HEALING TRAUMA WITH SOMATIC THERAPIES

Moniquea Spiteri

When we heal trauma at the root cause, not only does the mind and body heal, but we open ourselves up to emotional and spiritual transformation, breaking free from the states of pure survival to an overall feeling of relief, comfort and safety.

– Moniquea Spiteri

The Key to Resolving Trauma and Living a Thriving Life

I have come to the conclusion that human beings are born with an innate capacity to triumph over trauma. I believe not only that trauma is curable, but that the healing process can be a catalyst for profound awakening.

– Dr Peter Levine

I didn't originally set out to be a trauma therapist, and it's not something I aspired to until the tragedy of losing my father to suicide when I was twenty-nine. After his death, driven with a burning desire to know how and why his death had happened and how could it have been avoided, I began to dive deep into my own past traumas, and I subsequently set my life on a trajectory of self-mastery and deep healing.

I believe losing a loved one to suicide leaves a deep hole in one's heart and sometimes a void that feels like it can never be filled. For me, no amount of talk therapy was going to resolve the trauma of his death or the experience of my own abuse. As I felt strongly that unresolved trauma was at the root cause of his death, and that the mind and body are intrinsically connected, I began my search for practitioners who were trained to understand both.

I have always had a fascination with the human body coupled with a deep knowing that we all have the power to heal ourselves and to move forward in life with hope and vitality, and I discovered somatic psychotherapy a few months after my father's death and began doing my own deep trauma healing. For me, it felt like a part of my body was frozen in time – frozen in unexpressed grief and anger with an overall feeling of numbness. It was as if I was functioning but I wasn't feeling, and I knew that I needed to be healed at the core level for me to move forward with my life and to free myself from the pain. It was from that experience I began to gain my qualifications in somatic psychotherapy, somatic experiencing, somatic touch therapy and a host of other body-oriented healing methods.

Somatic Psychotherapy and its Distinctiveness from Talk Therapy

Somatic psychotherapy is a branch of somatic psychology. The word 'somatic' comes from the Greek word 'soma', which means 'the living body'. This umbrella term is often used in relation to medicine or psychological treatments. In the field of somatic psychology, somatics refers to an array of theories and techniques that take you a step ahead of your regular verbal therapy; this form of therapy presumes bodily experience as correlative, causative and caused by psychological experiences.

Although considered a member of the family of psychotherapeutic treatments, somatic psychotherapy is rather distinctive from other forms of treatment in that it introduces the concept of body mind – the idea that your bodily experience and emotions are inseparable. It takes into consideration the fact that the root of your emotions lies in the physical sensations created by your body; therefore, your bodily experiences can serve as a source of information and a resource for healing against trauma. By tapping into this resource that is often unused by conventional talk therapies, somatic psychotherapy helps you alleviate the symptoms of trauma at both a physical and psychological level.

Since somatic psychotherapy encompasses all aspects of 'the living body', it also includes verbal psychotherapy; however, it adds to its effectiveness by using various somatic techniques that directly engage with the bodily experience of the person affected by trauma. These somatic psychotherapy techniques can enable you to:

- understand and engage in non-verbal communication
- use the tools of creating meaningful narratives around posture and activating novel movements and breathing patterns and then correlating them psychologically

- develop increased awareness and bodily control over affect (emotions and emotional energy), physical pain and felt experiences
- deactivate and explore the psychological causes of patterns of acute and chronic tension
- carefully and respectfully resurface the emotions disavowed previously

The tool of touch, once explained and consented to, is used by the therapists to achieve the outcomes described earlier. Specific massages and bodywork practices such as ortho-bionomy, neuro affective touch and somatic practice may be used as a potent therapeutic pathway to affect psychological change.

Somatic psychotherapy belongs to the broad class of psychotherapeutic treatments, but it's a specialist field. It's built on the principle that not only can change be achieved in one realm of experience by consciously accessing another, but also that bodily experience, emotion and thought is intimately connected (forming a body mind). Similar to other modern psychotherapies, focus is on the individual's uniqueness, and the nature of the therapeutic relationship between the therapist and the client. Various philosophies and, more recently, studies in attachment theories, neurobiology, polyvagal theory and infant development guide the work of somatics. They all agree that:

- The body mind is directly and positively influenced and regulated/mediated by interpersonal interaction in terms of appropriate, safe and respectful relationships.
- The human body mind has an innate ability to heal and grow under the right therapeutic environment.
- Body and mind are inseparable entities that mutually influence the overall organism.

Also called body psychotherapy, somatic psychotherapy employs various approaches to psychological health It recognises the role of the body in creating our life and actively utilises the body in treatment as a resource and source of information for healing. Our life experience largely depends on our body's impulses, emotions and feelings, but because of our psychological and physiological conformity to the limitations of our environment, we often disregard, cut off or repress them.

Involving the body in psychotherapy provides an abundance of options for healing, experiencing and understanding that are often unavailable in conventional talk therapy. This is attributable to the body's capacity to maintain the muscular tension that supports and strengthens our characterological reactions to our environment, the body's ability to create the physical sensations that give rise to emotion, and the influence of the conscious over verbal expression and cognition. By making us more conscious of our behaviour, thoughts, emotions, impulses, feelings, and sensations, somatic psychotherapy enables us to address our concerns at the root cause of many disorders.

The Somatic Experiencing® model is another type of body-based therapy treatment for trauma and other stress conditions. It is a product and life's work of Dr Peter A Levine's multidisciplinary research on medical biophysics, indigenous healing practices, neuroscience, biology, ethology, psychology, and stress physiology, coupled with more than forty-five years of positive clinical application.

The Somatic Experiencing® technique eliminates traumatic shock, which helps to transform the scars of emotional and early-stage attachment trauma and PTSD. Somatic Experiencing® provides a system for assessing a person's position in the fight, fawn, freeze or flight responses and offers tools and support for resolving the 'stuck' physiological conditions. Its skills are effective and suitable for many professions, like first responders, addiction treatment, education, occupational and physical therapies, medicine, mental health, bodywork and others.

Trauma and its Affect Upon the Entirety of Your Being

Trauma is considered by many to be entirely psychological. This approach is being questioned by the recent advances in neuroscience, which suggest that a purely cognitive model of trauma is incomplete. Trauma affects every fibre of your being – physical and psychological. It can put your mind and body into a self-destructive and often a self-defensive mode, which dissolves your sense of identity, weakens your ability to keep track of space and time, undermines your interpersonal relations, and compromises your capacity for emotional regulation.

Since the reverberations of traumatic experiences can encompass the entirety of your being, the treatment approaches must also heal those affected by trauma from the perspective of a whole person instead of behaviours and thoughts alone. Cumulative stress, or intense stress from an apparent life-threatening situation, is what causes trauma. A person's resilience and equilibrium can seriously be impaired by both types of stress. Fear, conflict, pregnancy anxiety, loss, natural disasters, war, neglect, emotional abuse, physical or sexual assault, invasive medical procedures and accidents are some of the stressors that can lead to trauma. People often relate the word 'trauma' to major life events or incidents; however, the truth is that traumatic stress can be a lifelong experience that affects everyone. It can occur in the form of falls, accidents, invasive childhood procedures, or early developmental incidences and disruptions. At certain times in our lives, we have all experienced or encountered a traumatic event, regardless of whether it has led to post-traumatic stress or not.

Some people can live their lives free from the symptoms of such stress for a number of years after a traumatic event. However, our psyches and nervous system must overcome challenges and dysregulation for us to stay healthy. We can become depressed when this does not happen, or we become overwhelmed by life's challenges leading to anxiety.

The consequences suffered by people who are survivors of major accidents, natural disasters, abuse, war, and other traumas can be more severe. However, the effectiveness of an exclusive cognitive behavioural model has been challenged by recent neuroscientific discoveries, especially in reference to the effect of trauma. The point here is that trauma does not only affect our behaviours and cognition alone. Consequently, trauma should be treated from a holistic perspective. Essentially, every part of our being, not just our behaviours and thoughts, must be considered in any trauma therapy or trauma healing.

In closing, I am passionate about mental health, and I honour the courage it takes for someone to do the work on themselves to resolve their past and move forward with freedom and vitality. Underpinning my professional qualifications is twenty-five years of personal development and self-exploration, enabling me to take a holistic approach to mental health and wellbeing, incorporating a number of these modalities to help people to develop a strong bodily container and a greater felt sense of nervous system regulation and embodiment.

Many people have asked me how I take care of myself when working in the trauma field? My self-care involves a team of high calibre professionals to support me. I have the most amazing team including:

- body worker for a weekly ninety-minute massage
- osteopath
- naturopath
- kinesiologist
- holistic GP
- clinical supervisor
- body oriented psychologist for my personal therapy
- support network of close friends and colleagues

It is important as a professional in this field to take care of myself so I can better serve my clients. Vicarious trauma can affect many professionals in a range of sectors, which can lead to burnout and compassion fatigue. It is important to see the early warning signs or use preventative measures to take the utmost care of ourselves before this happens. Finding the right work–life balance was important when I went into private practice. Learning to listen to my own body and be present with my nervous system allowed me to understand that I can only work three days a week with clients.

With deep transformational work, nearly fifty per cent of trauma survivors experience post-traumatic growth after a traumatic event. Post-traumatic growth (PTG) is where someone has been affected by trauma and finds a way to take new meaning from their experiences in order to live their lives in a different way than prior to the trauma. Examples of areas for growth include personal strength, appreciation for life, new possibilities in life, spiritual change, and relationships with others. Examples of PTG can be vast, ranging from writing books, spiritual awakening, starting charities and many more. It has been through my own growth that I formed a social enterprise that will assist those living with mental health conditions regain wellness, retain employment and be supported in their personal recovery in a nurturing therapeutic community setting and launched a podcast called Transcending Trauma.

Key Takeaways:

- At certain times in our lives, we have all experienced or encountered a traumatic event, regardless of whether it has led to post-traumatic stress or not.
- The word 'somatic' comes from the Greek word 'soma' which means 'the living body'.

- In the field of somatic psychology, somatics refers to an array of theories and techniques that take you a step ahead of your regular verbal therapy.
- Although considered a member of the family of psychotherapeutic treatments, somatic psychotherapy is rather distinctive from other forms of treatment in that it introduces the concept of body mind – the idea that your bodily experience and emotions are inseparable.
- Involving the body in psychotherapy provides an abundance of options for healing, experiencing and understanding that are often unavailable in conventional talk therapy.

If you would like to learn more about the work I do or take up my free offer to do a thirty-minute discovery session, contact me via my website: Somatic Synergy www.somaticsynergy.com.au

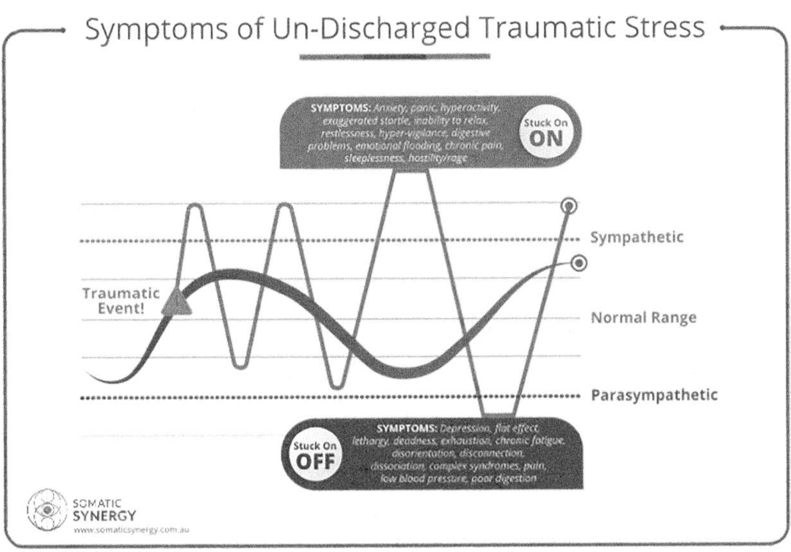

Bio

Moniquea Spiteri is a social entrepreneur, change maker, somatic psychotherapist, teaching assistant at Somatic Experiencing® Trauma Institute at Somatic Experiencing® International and host of the Transcending Trauma podcast.

Moniquea has worked in the field of mental health, personal development and trauma for over fifteen years and is a passionate and engaging speaker, coach and mentor. She was awarded as highly commended in the 2016 Victorian Premier's Volunteer Champions Awards for Change Maker and 2017 Soar Collective Business Woman of the Year and winner of the 2017 Emerging Not for Profit Business of the Year.

Having been involved with numerous holistic and innovative projects funded at a state and federal level within Australia, she was the chairperson of the national leadership group for the Partners in Recovery program in Victoria.

Moniquea is also the founder and president of Enveco Health – a social enterprise that will assist those living with mental health and trauma conditions to regain wellness, retain employment and be supported in their personal recovery. Moniquea has a natural strength for creating new ways of doing things and helping others ignite their own inner spark to achieve their goals. Having had direct family experience with the frailties of the existing mental health system, she is unwavering in her commitment to changing the mental health sector. Moniquea knows the value of collaboration and applies her vast array of knowledge in building community support, key coalitions and strategic interagency partnerships to drive her vision today.

Qualifications:

- Somatic Psychotherapist
- Somatic Experiencing® Practitioner (SEP)
- Somatic Touch Practitioner
- NeuroAffective Touch® Practitioner

Work with Moniquea:

Book in for a free thirty-minute discovery session via my website.

Connect with Moniquea:
Facebook: www.facebook.com/somaticsynergy
Instagram: www.instagram.com/somaticsynergy
LinkedIn: www.linkedin.com/in/moniquea-spiteri/
Website: www.somaticsynergy.com.au
Enveco Health Website: www.enveco.org.au
Transcending Trauma Podcast:
https://podcasts.apple.com/au/podcast/transcending-trauma-with-moniquea-Spiteri/id1535631499

TRANSFORMING STRESS: LIVING LIFE WITH NO REGRETS

Kim Wagner

The moment you change your perception is the moment you rewrite the chemistry of your body.

– Dr Bruce H Lipton

My mother died of cancer when I was six months pregnant with my son. I'd also lost my dad to cancer just twenty months earlier so it had been a very difficult time. Although I knew that the feelings and emotions I was experiencing were a normal part of losing a parent, every instinct was telling me that my unborn child would be affected. When my son was born, although physically healthy, he was suffering emotionally. I had no idea how to help him, which was a horrible feeling and tore me apart every single day.

I started to research and read everything I could find. There was new information emerging about the expression of genes that was groundbreaking. When I discovered we are not controlled by our genes, my life changed forever. Up until then, I thought we were at the mercy of the genes we were born with. The truth is that how we live, what we eat and how we experience life has a direct impact on our health and wellbeing. Most importantly, I realised that we need to take responsibility for our own health.

A few years later I watched a Dr Bruce Lipton interview. He was explaining how our thoughts, emotions and perception affect our cells and our gene expression – how we feel and perceive things directly changes our existence. He also mentioned that of the few ways to improve these thought patterns and replace limiting beliefs, PSYCH-K® was the quickest and easiest. I booked my first PSYCH-K® course, and it changed my life and also that of my son.

Our conscious or decision mind contributes to five per cent of our behaviour, whereas our subconscious or habit mind contributes ninety-five per cent. A prime example of the subconscious mind is when you are driving somewhere. Often you will arrive at your destination and not remember most of physical driving. This is because our conscious mind is thinking about something else and our subconscious mind takes over.

Everything that we are exposed to from around the third trimester to the age of seven years old is effectively recorded and stored in our subconscious mind. The subconscious mind cannot choose what it accepts, which means that in their very young years our children are really open and vulnerable to what they see, hear and experience.

Generational belief systems are also present, which means the subconscious programming is a mystery as you have no personal point of reference. It's really easy to see how a cycle will continue through generations when you understand this. For example, as my child is exposed to my habits and beliefs, my habits and beliefs will then become theirs, and so on. Trauma from generations ago can be present in your subconscious mind, and unless the beliefs are replaced, the cycle will continue.

Thankfully there is a quick and easy solution. PSYCH-K® is a simple, non-invasive and lasting process, which in my experience assists with healing intergenerational trauma, replacing limiting beliefs and transforming the perception of stress. A facilitator is able to work with clients by creating a 'whole-brain state', which allows changes to be made in the subconscious mind. The good news is that online sessions are just as effective as in-person ones, and PSYCH-K® allows us to work with clients in any location by way of surrogation.

We all react to stress differently. What bothers you may have very little effect on me. And often we react very strongly to some things more than others. Our reactions are often shaped by a traumatic event, our belief systems, life experiences and particular circumstances. Generational beliefs also play a big part in our physical and mental reaction. You've likely noticed that some things really trigger an intense response, yet there is no logical explanation and you have no memory of it.

During our lifetime we all have trauma: situations and conditions that cause a stress response – things such as losing a job, a broken relationship, health issues, a sick child or family member. The intensity of the physical and mental reaction to these circumstances is what will be different for all of us. For example, if our child is unwell or is struggling in an area of their life, as mothers we will have a very physical, primal response to that. We may get a knot in our stomach, find it hard to concentrate, get really overwhelmed, have a hard time sleeping or get headaches. This is the physical and mental response to a stressful situation. Every time we think about it, the response is right there. It's as though it never really goes away and is just waiting right below the surface.

When working with clients, we begin with focusing on the perception of stress around the trauma, situation or condition. In my experience, once we have worked through the process, they are happier, feel lighter and have a huge sense of relief. It's almost as though the stress took up physical space inside their body and now there is room to breathe. Whilst the situation or condition still exists, and the traumatic event did occur, the overwhelming stress response related to it is diminished, which allows us to be more effective, make better decisions and be more present.

For my situation, I was able to remove the stress around how my son was affected during pregnancy as well as how he was suffering. I was then able to work with him directly to reduce stress, replace belief systems and help him to heal. The beauty is that we are able to work with any age, even if clients are not old enough to communicate easily. The key is that we ask for permission and are working in their best interest only.

During our lifetime, we all encounter many stressful situations which can cause a physical reaction. Once we remove the negative physical and mental responses, we are able to live a calm and happy life. The negative beliefs and reactions are no longer on repeat twenty-four seven, and our entire system is able to relax.

There are many ways we can introduce change in our everyday life that will assist in our overall healing and will elevate our self-love and self-worth. These action steps are easy and will make a positive difference.

Awareness is the key. Often, we get so caught up in the moment or in our life that we don't take notice of the thoughts that emerge or what exactly we are reacting to. When we are in a heightened state, it can be so overwhelming we cannot pinpoint any one thing that has contributed to it.

- Self-love is the cornerstone to a happy and healthy life. If we do not love ourselves or believe we are worthy of love on a subconscious level, then we will make all of our life decisions based on that. It's time to start being kind to ourselves. Rather than negativity and judgement, show compassion and understanding. As you notice any negative thoughts about yourself that come up during your day, replace them with something positive. At first it may be a real struggle to show yourself love, but over time your belief system and habits will change.

- Begin the habit of keeping your thoughts in the present. Oftentimes we overthink and worry about things in the past and also about what might happen in the future. There is usually an element of guilt and self-blame involved, and we can have a negative physical or mental response. These thoughts are not serving us and will add to our stress, overwhelm and anxiety. Bringing your mind back to the present and focusing on the here and now will help to keep you centred and calm.
- Establish healthy boundaries in all areas of your life. It's important to know what you will and won't accept and to firmly place some appropriate boundaries. Most of us are so worried about hurting others or letting them down that we end up doing ourselves a disservice. From a very young age we are taught that we need to make others happy. Now it's time to discover what makes you happy. Whilst it is a bit tricky saying no the first couple of times, it won't take long for you to feel free of other people's expectations of you. Having boundaries in place is the ultimate form of self-love.
- Focus on one task at a time. Rather than trying to do multiple things at once, focusing on just one thing at a time is a game changer. When we are in a rushed state and doing too many things at once, our stress levels go up and our mind will be in chaos. That feeling of never having enough time and always being on the go is a fear-based reaction. By focusing on one task at a time your mind will be calm and you achieve more.
- Make yourself a priority – it has to be all about you. Our belief systems will have us think that looking after ourselves first is selfish. It's not, and in fact it's a big part of the healing journey. Taking the

time to nurture yourself and build on that self-love will not only help you to heal, but the ripple effect will help others. What do you enjoy doing? What fills your cup? It can be as little as walking on the grass with no shoes, exercise with a friend, a nice cup of coffee in your favourite café or a regular massage. The important thing is to incorporate things that make you happy into your everyday life.

- Simplify your life. Society has conditioned us to think that being busy is better and having 'all of the things' will make us happy. In fact, we tend to always refer to how busy we are like it's a badge of honour. That is a really damaging way to live. The key is to cut back on the things that we do and also the things that we have. Reduce your daily tasks to things that are absolutely necessary, and then spend time doing activities that fill your cup. For example, you could start a vegetable garden, read a book, learn a new language or find a new hobby. It's also important to reduce our physical clutter as it really does impact our lives in a negative way.
- Our inner dialogue is running twenty-four seven, and often it can be quite negative. A great way to change this dialogue is to replace it! Take some time to write a script about how you would rather things be. You can focus on any area of life. Write the script in the first person and in a positive manner. For example: I am worthy of success; I can learn new things easily; I deserve to be happy; I am in a loving relationship. Once you have your script, record it on your phone and then convert it to an MP3. There are plenty of free apps available to help. Using headphones, listen to it as often as you can on repeat. Over time you will notice really positive changes.

So, where to from here? In my experience, simple is always best. When it comes to belief patterns, becoming aware is the first step. Start listening to your body and become aware of negative and limiting beliefs. An easy way to pinpoint an area of lack is to see where things are not working well in your life. Often there will be limiting or negative beliefs present which are holding you back. It's also important to take notice when you have an adverse physical or mental response to a situation or condition.

Once you become aware, you can begin to heal. The most important thing is that you are kind to yourself and allow the time and space to make changes at your own pace. Now is not the time to be harsh or judgemental – self-love and nurturing is required. It's taken some of us many years to get to where we are right now so the journey will be different for all of us.

When you are ready to begin your healing journey, PSYCH-K® is the perfect place to start. By working together we can begin to heal trauma, reduce the stress from any conditions or situations and replace negative thought patterns that are holding you back from living the amazing life you deserve.

Bio

Kim Wagner is a PSYCH-K® facilitator, PER-K® catalyst, reiki master and educator. She is an expert in stress transformation and replacing negative subconscious beliefs.

Losing her mother to cancer when Kim was six months pregnant with her son, having also recently lost her father, began a healing journey that Kim could never have imagined. Kim likes to refer to it as her healing adventure with many twists and turns. Along the way she discovered so many things that affect our health, particularly the impact that our thoughts and perceptions have on our body and mind. Kim believes that discovering PSYCH-K® is one of the most impactful things that has ever happened to her. It has changed Kim's life and that of her family – especially her son.

Using her knowledge and extensive PSYCH-K training, Kim has become an expert in transforming the perception of stress and replacing any limiting or negative subconscious beliefs. Kim is very passionate about it as it literally changed her son's life right in front of her eyes. Her mission is to help as many people on the planet as possible to transform their lives.

Kim is currently living in Far North Queensland, Australia, with her family. She continues to focus on living a simple, happy life while working with clients around the world.

Connect with Kim:
Instagram: @kimwagner.simplynourish/
LinkedIn: https://www.linkedin.com/in/kim-wagner-0b73bb185/
Website: www.kimwagner.com
Email: info@kimwagner.com

SECTION 4:
SOCIAL SELF-CARE

INTRODUCTION

Tracey Jewel

Has it been weeks since you've met up with your best friend? When is the last time you nurtured those close connections? Life happens, of course, but making time for friends and loved ones that make us feel happy and whole is important no matter how busy life gets.

These special relationships require time and energy. You can't plant a garden and then turn your back on the plants you've seeded. They need water and care, just as friendships require you to invest time and effort into them.

Face-to-face time with friends is the best way to maintain these connections. Sometimes though, distance can be a factor keeping you apart. What are you doing to bridge that gap? Is your best friend the one always reaching out to you, or are you putting in the time to look in on them, even when you can't physically be there?

Everyone gets caught up in the chaos of life. With your self-care journey, you'll be working on uncluttering that energy. You'll also learn how to nurture the social self-care that tends to fall by the wayside when life gets hectic.

People need people, and we need the ones that are always on our side through the darkest of days. This chapter will help you put those relationships on track and find the time to maintain them so that you can give and receive the love and friendship needed for a healthy social life.

THAT'S NOT LIKE YOU: LESSONS IN SOCIAL SELF-CARE FROM A BURNOUT SURVIVOR

Sue Tsigaros

One of the most beautiful qualities of true friendship is to understand and to be understood.

– Lucius Annaeus Seneca

Social self-care happens in the context of relationships. The presence or absence of other human beings in our lives and the quality of our interactions with them, determine whether and how we satisfy our needs for social connection, love and belonging. The way we live the dances – of intimacy, individuality, togetherness and aloneness – the interplay between wanting to be seen and yet fearing being exposed, together with how we value and are valued by others, are the building blocks from which our sense of self-worth is created. Attending fully and lovingly to our social self-care needs is part of our soul's journey and is essential for our mental and emotional health.

When we do our social self-care well, we are uplifted and expansive. We feel fully seen and heard. There is reciprocity and enrichment.

When we do it badly, on autopilot or taking it for granted, the results can be dull, disappointing or even drastic.

That's not like you! My story.

People usually see me as a bright light – a positive, strategic leader, committed member, congenial host – and would most likely classify me as an extrovert. At times, however, I find that the social and public roles I occupy demand a significant contribution of emotional, physical and mental energy. My husband often remarks that I seem to be receiving less than I am giving out, and I hear him, but nothing changes. I have often said yes to social activity when I really needed my solitude. I actually enjoy working alone for periods of time and habitually underprioritise this. When I am in abundance and alignment, I feel endlessly fulfilled and love to be with people. I hardly notice the drain when it begins, its subtle.

Can you relate to this? Do you always feel obligated and committed to deliver, no matter what? Do you see it as a sign of integrity?

By late 2020, after so many meetings-turned-into-performances on Zoom, I was dangerously close to the edge of burnout. When I started to tell people, they would typically say 'That's not like you!' I had contemplated freeing up some time by stepping down from my two voluntary leadership roles, but I couldn't seem to do it, and I would keep myself going by doing my maintenance practices – just to get me through the next meeting.

This pattern was not sustainable, and one day I hit the wall – full burnout. Unable to work because of headaches, fatigue and body pain, I was overweight, not sleeping well and miserable. How shameful, being a supposed 'role model' and being in such a state! 'That's not like you,' they kept saying, and I kept agreeing. The truth was that my dedication to always being 'like me' was the reason why I was ending up like this now!

Over the preceding months, when away from the spotlight, as exhaustion was taking over, I had started feeling resentful about my commitments. I became judgemental, highly critical and short-tempered. I knew I was not bringing my best self to my interactions with others.

Fortunately, I have a deep and mutually supportive friendship with my niece, Marilyn, which allows each of us the space to share without being judged or advised. And in that deep listening, my emotional and energetic healing could begin. I soon regained access to my capacity to be fully present and not so reactive; however, my resting state was 'vulnerable', and I was still in a very low state energetically and physically. Even my go-to practices of yoga and dance were becoming so hard to do, let alone enjoy. This was certainly 'not like me'.

My recent burnout and healing process has delivered deep reflection and valuable learnings. In this chapter are some of the models and perspectives I have found useful, and I will elaborate further on my story as I offer personal explanations and reflections of each. If you are already relating to any part of my story, I hope these reflections will offer you some insight and assist you in your own process.

Reflection #1: Social Foundations

During my early school years, 'how you do social self-care' was modelled by my parents, who had moved to Australia from England on a two-year contract that ended up being permanent. My sister was born soon after we arrived, and it was just the four of us, in this new country with no other family or friends.

Mum and Dad needed to forge new connections, which they did very well. They were quite active socially, and their social self-care practices were to regularly engage with their preferred group of friends with:

- laughter and affection – openly exchanged
- entertaining – lots of food, drinking and dancing (Our house was the party house.)
- playing active games like sports, table tennis, darts and twister, and intellectual games like cards, puzzles and charades
- ladies having tea and cake, long conversations about health, relationships, beauty, gossip and missing the 'old country'
- watching TV, going to a movie or live theatre and discussing it afterwards
- drinking at Dad's bar, celebrating life and solving the philosophical and political problems of 'the human condition'
- taking a picnic or barbecue to a national park or bush with a bunch of friends, or going wine tasting (As kids we would play outside while the adults were inside and laughing a lot.)
- a lot of alcohol (It took me many years to realise that it's actually possible to function socially without it!)

Going to the park for a walk and marvelling at nature with Mum and Dad, which I always wanted more of, was an activity I deeply cherished and which generated much greater closeness than the 'social' activities.

I still loved the joy, intimacy and belonging of those times with Mum and Dad and their friends, but the other children I met through these social functions did not really become friends of mine. We had no cousins, aunts, uncles or grandparents, so my school friends would regularly abandon me for the more important 'relatives' who were coming. I was growing intellectually and in relationship with adults, but not really socially amongst my peers. I tended to be either observing (and would discuss later with Dad) or performing (as I enjoyed the attention, praise and recognition). My role as an outsider at school became even more pronounced when I won an entrance scholarship to a private school, where I was not welcomed by the in-crowd at all, as our family had no pedigree or social capital in their eyes. Coming into my teens, my self-esteem crashed to an all-time low. By the time I went to Uni, I was experiencing severe anxiety. My poor choice of boyfriends did not help, and I had very little in the way of peer or extended family support to help process the pain when I was serially dumped – for being too 'intense'. My parents were never able to understand my lack of self-esteem, so I learnt to pretend that I was fine and carry on.

My early experiences of needing and wanting social connections that were not readily available, have provided me with two important foundations: the gift of being a curious observer, as well as the gift of being a highly motivated connector.

Because of these gifts, most of my personal growth has come either directly or indirectly through connection with others – through being in a relationship. While the threat of rejection is always present and has at times created huge heartache, these human connections, along with all the conversations and experience, we have shared, have led me to places and opportunities I may never have otherwise experienced. This has made me richer in every way – personally, materially and spiritually. The special relationships I have nurtured over many years have provided a foundation for my wellbeing that continues to grow.

How was social self-care modelled in your family? Have you maintained these practices in your adult life? What roles do you occupy socially, and how well do they support your social needs?

Getting What we Need

Aristotle is quoted to have once said:

Man is by nature a social animal. An individual who is unsocial naturally and not accidentally ... who either cannot lead the common life or is so self-sufficient as not to need to … is either a beast or a god.

Abraham Maslow's theory of human needs gave us the well-known five-level model.

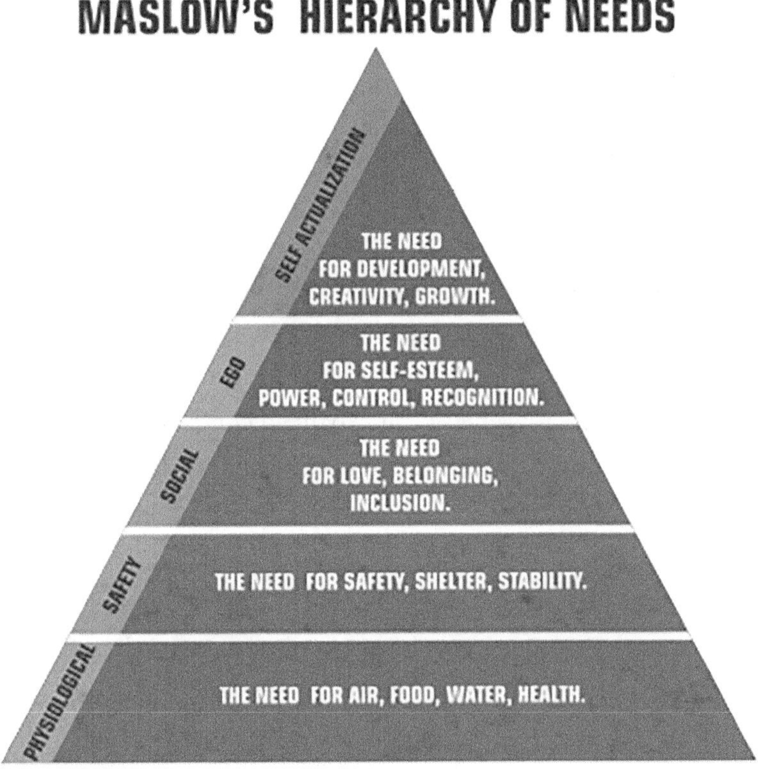

Our social needs are placed at position number three, evolving from the more primal needs of survival and safety. Our social needs are met and exchanged through the heart, whereas our survival and safety needs mainly attend to our physical body.

Included in our social needs is the need for belonging, which arises from the safety of being part of a tribe and is related to the primal needs for survival. Our ancestors used banishment as the ultimate punishment for wrongdoing. We still fear being outcast lest we perish in the wilderness.

A sudden change in physical circumstances can activate the safety and survival needs – such as a natural disaster or a pandemic increasing levels of anxiety that can undermine our sense of autonomy and being in control (safety needs). Our resilience, wisdom and capacity to reach out for support can also assist us in making sense of and overcoming the setbacks and upheavals in life.

Unconditional love is a building block to the esteem needs. When we have not developed a solid sense of our own value – through the receiving of love that we did not have to strive to earn – we may overcompensate, try too hard to be liked and take on too much in our efforts to overcome the haunting mantra of 'not good enough'.

From a place where we feel accepted and valued for who we are, we can access the higher-level needs of expanded consciousness, contribution and spirituality. Our self-development work in relationship is thus pivotal and can form the bridge between Aristotle's animal-self and God-self.

Coming back to my own story, the drive to connect – in order to avoid the unpleasant feelings of being shut out, isolated and alone – had created a pattern of people-pleasing, compromise and making an extra effort to belong, including often being the one who would travel the longest distance for a meeting or putting in the extra hours of preparation to give others the best experience.

Where do you see your social behaviours in your own story? What roles are you currently taking on, in order to have those social needs met? How well is this serving you?

Reflection #2: The Work Ethic

During the pandemic-generated 2020 lockdown era that led up to my burnout, I was serving as leader with two business communities – membership organisations, which needed to 'pivot' and adapt to the online environment to survive. My business model also needed to adapt. There were so many more interactions and decisions to make, along with a rising tide of general anxiety worldwide. The fast pace of so many conversations and connections, which I had previously enjoyed and been uplifted by, began to drain and deplete my energetic reserves. There was little reciprocity for many leaders like me, whose default was to be of service and be a role model for organisational values like contribution, respect, flexibility and going that extra mile. This was how we habitually fed our esteem needs. Eventually after almost a year in this new reality, the energetic burnout wave crashed through my world like a tsunami.

But really, this did not happen overnight, or even in the space of one year! The foundations of my work ethic were laid long ago.

My twenty years in corporate roles and further nineteen as a business owner have offered many opportunities for meeting people, collaborating, competing, networking, play and friendship. I love to live life to the fullest, including long hours when required. I've cared for and supported many others and hold space energetically for current clients twenty-four seven.

From my earliest days at work, thanks to my strong desire to belong, I was recognised as a team player. I was also very open to learning and was easy to motivate with praise and recognition. Consequently, I did well at sales. I also loved the satisfaction of making a difference and seeing people happy, as well as being a contributor to something significant.

This became the 'winning formula' that defined my work and

brought me some great opportunities, while after-hours I was still playing hard – like Mum and Dad did in the old days.

Outside work, I am a highly enthusiastic member of the classes, groups and organisations where I learn and develop as a person – dance classes, yoga, meditation, and so on. I am often invited to step into leadership roles or committee work – some formal and others informal. All have been extra-curricular activities. My childhood experiences of being the outsider left me with a strong drive for inclusion and acknowledgement. Consequently, I have spent a significant amount of my 'social life' in service to others or in a service role for a social group.

I have also learnt and practiced many modalities for physical, mental and emotional self-care, applying them and integrating them into my teachings.

My typical trajectory goes like this:

1. Eager participant who does well in class. Likes the teacher, the work and what it stands for.
2. Becomes enthusiastic and embraces the community – 'her tribe'.
3. Joins as a member. Her participation is appreciated and she becomes a fan and promoter.
4. Recognises where some things could be done more effectively and/or is recognised as a special contributor with leadership energy.
5. Is invited into the 'inner circle'. Says YES.
6. Occupies a role that starts to demand more and more time and energy.
7. Earns reputation for being reliable and accountable – putting others first.
8. Over time feels resistance and resentment but pushes through, using the physical, energetic and spiritual self-care practices she has learnt.

9. Eventually becomes ill and needs to take a break OR something happens to the organisation and she leaves.
10. Occasionally a real friendship blooms during this time and survives past the era of infatuation/engagement with the organisation.
11. These relationships are the ones that last more than a season. They are the lifetime connections, worth investing in.

What are your patterns when it comes to forming social connections? What roles do you easily fall into? What is your trajectory? In what areas are your safety, social and esteem needs driving you to overextend and deplete your own resources?

Having frequent and varied social contact with as many people as possible might seem like social self-care or torture, depending on your own makeup. Even the activities that in smaller doses can nourish us can turn into self-sabotage unless we bring awareness and discernment to the social commitments we make. But there is no simple answer to this puzzle. Although we share very similar basic needs as human beings, each of us has different needs at different times in our lives. Everyone has a unique story and set of key drivers. It's an evolving relationship with self in relationship with others, and it is exquisitely complex.

When I work with organisational leaders and business owners to help them access clarity, develop a strategic intent and advance without burning out, we always personalise rather than generalise. That's why I use an in-depth psychometric, the Hogan Motives, Values and Preferences Inventory, with every client I work with. This assessment reveals exactly what are our underlying needs in the key areas of status and recognition, enjoyment and fun, social and community, security and safety, financial, investigative and creative/aesthetic areas of life.

We also take a deep dive into the potential as well as underlying challenges in behaviours and habits that led the client to the roles they are functioning from, so that we can change and redirect the narrative, if they so choose. This way we are able to liberate their inner flame of true talent and allow it to work its magic in the world.

Which is better: quality or quantity?

In the context of social self-care, the quality and quantity of connections are equally important. How many people can we connect with in a meaningful way and what degree of intensity or intimacy is needed in order to feel nourished, are the questions that drove British anthropologist Robin Dunbar's social research over several decades.

These studies suggest that our capacity for engagement in friendship is limited to 150 people.

[This is] due to a cognitive limit to the number of people with whom one can maintain stable social relationships, in which an individual knows who each person is and how each person relates to every other person.

https://en.wikipedia.org/wiki/Dunbar%27s_number

These limitations are observed across several primate species as well as across cultures in human beings. Our range of relationships vary in their degree of trust and intimacy and can be represented as concentric circles, relative to the degree of intimacy or closeness we feel.

The number sequences* look like this:

1. Me = 1 – nobody else can know everything about me
2. Intimates = 5 – people we relate to deeply and openly, strongly nurturing
3. Best Friends = 15 – people we feel comfortable and have much in common with

4. Good friends = 50 – a positive enjoyable relationship, more casual and less intimate
5. Friends (Dunbar's number) = 150 – my 'tribe', we identify as like me, my kind of person, I feel belonging here
6. Acquaintances = 500 – I've met them and know a little bit about them
7. People I recognise = 1500 – may not have met them but know something about them

** A comprehensive and well referenced explanation of Dunbar's number can be found at https://en.wikipedia.org/wiki/Dunbar%27s_number*

Beyond the limit of 150, for example in a club with a large membership or in the broader reach of our social media accounts, we move beyond the sense of tribe to the level of acquaintances and meaningful relationships to a possible 1500 'people I recognise'.

Maintaining social self-care means 'grooming' our circles from time to time – the relationships that nourish, stimulate, expand us. Have we apportioned our time in a way that enriches these relationships? Do we need to declutter, re-prioritise or have some hard conversations about boundaries?

Some key questions to ask yourself around social self-care are:

- How do I feel when I come away from each meeting or gathering?
- Who are my the most intimate and unconditionally positive relationships?
- How do I know when I am well seen and heard?
- Am I making time for the relationships that are most nurturing?
- If I was having a party, who would I invite and why?
- How have I changed, and are the good friends I used to have still nourishing?

- What if I want to launch a new product or service – who do I need around me then?
- Are there people I treat as acquaintances who could really become friends?
- And are there best friends with whom I no longer have the same degree of ease, shared interests or understanding that I have with most of my friends now?

In the world of work, we spend a significant portion of our time with people who might be at layer six or seven (acquaintances and people you recognise). Over time and through interacting on collaborative projects or at social events, these have the potential to move closer, to the inner layers. A portion of your work colleagues might become friends, and a few may become good friends, or closer still.

I have found that good friends are more likely to appear when I am in an environment where I feel congruent, and my values are supported. When the environment is all at acquaintance level or I am feeling like an outsider, I need to seek out any individuals who seem to be like me and get to know them. They might become level three or four relationships (best friends or good friends) or even closer if we're lucky!

In the world of small business, developing genuine trusting relationships through networks can be a very effective way to grow yourself and your business. It also introduces a number of conflicting motives, because many people who are new to networking and trying to grow their start-up business want fast results. They may try to accelerate the progression from 'acquaintance' level to a level where I 'know, like and trust you' so that they can do business with you. This is an area where we must learn to exercise social self-care and discernment, so that we move at a pace which is comfortable and congruent for us.

Reflection #3 – Maintaining a healthy inner circle

I was blessed with my first true friendship (outside my immediate family) when I was fifteen. I was sitting in my usual seat on the bus that I caught every day, on the way to that private school where I was the outsider, and a beautiful girl boarded the bus. She was a being of light and joyful friendliness, and her radiance seemed to fill the whole bus. Our eyes met and we smiled and she sat next to me! Her name was Joanna, and she said I could call her Joey. She was generous with her sharing and genuinely interested in me. She almost missed her stop. Over the coming weeks, months and years, our conversations continued on the bus and we became firm friends. She was and always remains in my inner circle, at level two, along with my husband Tony and some family members. Our friendship has lasted more than fifty years. In our late teens we moved into our first shared house with two other girls, and we all went to Uni as well as starting our first jobs, which for some became very successful careers. There were many parties and a few rotations of housemates, but Joey and I stayed together. Thanks to Joey, who is the ultimate connector, the four of us can still reconvene, reminisce and feel deep connection, so many years later; however, the others are at other levels for me.

When I was first introduced to this circles idea, many years ago, I called Joey and told her that she was meant to be in my inner circle, but we hadn't been able to catch up for such a long time. I really wanted to have five people in there so I gave her the ultimatum: Are you in or out of my sacred inner circle? Of course, this produced some tears and then much laughter, and we processed things and made a renewed commitment to getting together more regularly!

A few years before my burnout experience of 2020, I gave up alcohol. As part of my self-care, I also needed to limit my contact with a number of 'best' friends, allowing them to move outward in my circles, because enjoying quality wine together was something we had based much of our social ritual around. This was a sad part of letting go of the old me. My level three friendship circle was getting pretty lean, as the drinking buddies became level four connections! A lot of my time was spent working and networking, and circles at level five and beyond were filling, but it was initially difficult to feel the support of those inner circle connections as my identity was changing.

Fortunately, my letting go has opened up new parts of the true me that are healthier, stronger and more independent, as well as bringing new treasured connections into my life who are now occupying some parts of my closer circles? My relationship with alcohol has changed, as 'it' is no longer one of my 'best' friends! I am now free to spend time – albeit less frequently – with those old drinking buddies, and the old rituals no longer apply to me. Conversely, I know of a few people with a family member suffering from addiction who have chosen the substance over them as an inner circle member.

If this has happened to you, please allow yourself to let go, and don't take it personally. You can find yourself some new soulmates to hang out with who are more aligned!

The process of getting to clarity about the 'right amount' of contact is where the learning and growth happens, often through luck and circumstance and sometimes by design or intention. It can be both painful and exhilarating to learn what truly nourishes our being in a social sense. Our choices and actions in our social lives, as with all habits we develop, can be self-enhancing or self-sabotaging.

Looking in the Mirror

Social self-care really boils down to spending the right amount of quality time with the right people and being properly seen, heard and valued – whilst also reciprocating this to the other.

Friends hold a mirror up to each other; through that mirror they can see each other in ways that would not otherwise be accessible to them, and it is this mirroring that helps them improve themselves as persons.
– Aristotle

In a sense we can only know ourselves in a healthy way through adequate mirroring, whereby our identity is reflected back to us through the eyes of another. Being well seen, accepted and affirmed as who we are supports self-reflection without judgement, building a stronger sense of identity and capacity for discernment, which is an essential component for social self-care.

My role as coach is to help clients develop this capacity for non-judgemental self-reflection, as well as gaining confidence and discernment about self-disclosure in a trusted relationship. Once we recognise and own the patterns of behaviour and belief that play out in so many areas of our life, we are free to choose – to do more of what's working and less of what isn't.

Fast forward to early 2021

My path from burnout to recovery was actually quite simple, and recovery happened fast. It required an honest, tearful and vulnerable conversation with my coach (one of my most valued relationships) and some simple maths with regard to timeline and priorities. This led to a decision – which required a declaration – that I was stepping down from my voluntary leadership role and that 26 February would be my final meeting in that leadership role. It was for health reasons. I did not need anyone else's permission or approval to do this.

I dedicated myself to my healing and cut back the amount of time spent with level six and seven contacts, while increasing the amount of time and willingness to be vulnerable with my best friends and soul sisters.

I now have a team of professionals (and revitalised practices), to keep me in optimal health (which I chose through trial and error) as well as a team to support me in my business (same), and I am enjoying my membership in each of my business and on-business communities. I am also listening to my husband and appreciating his suggestions, rather than reacting to perceived criticism. Getting to this took a few months, some courage, some hard decisions and a lot of humility.

Performance, Permission and Purpose

I had always understood – but now fully realise – that we all have a performative layer, sometimes referred to as ego or the 'winning formula', that we apply, largely unconsciously, in order to receive gratification and avoid pain.

Within this layer are the things that others like and reward us for, as well as the mistakes, embarrassments, judgements and other shadows that we keep running from and trying to out-perform. Its real purpose is to deliver what we are called to do from our deeper core; however, much gets lost in translation as we strive to adapt and please. People who are on our inner circle are more likely to have touched that inner part of us.

The performative layer is exhausting and ultimately unsustainable or somehow lacking. This feeling of lack keeps the performance going. We try harder.

But we can never be satisfied until we are purposefully present and at peace with this performative layer and all its shadows. The essence of my journey and the work I do with leaders can be seen in this simple model:

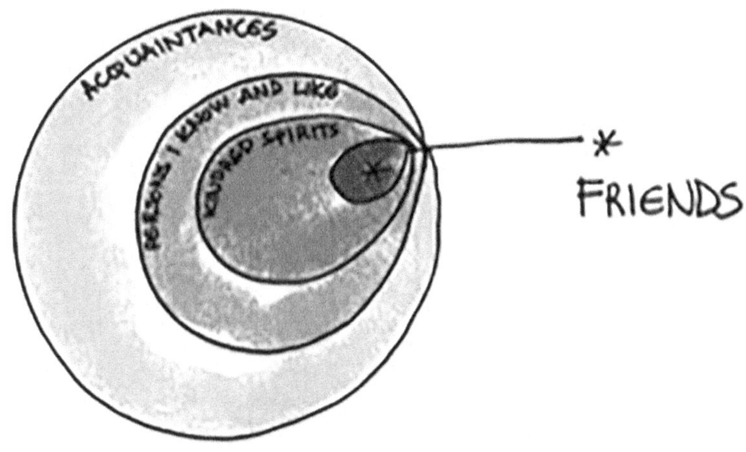

We must develop the capacity for self-reflection and self-disclosure through quality relationships so that we can identify the dynamics of the performative layer and step back from it and let it go.

Only when we have exhausted the game of performing, and we give ourselves full permission – to ask, receive and to be – can our uniqueness and passion find its way to fully living on purpose and in alignment with our true brilliance. Our quality relationships allow us the space to BE. Social self-care is about taking responsibility for the quality of – and access to – those essential relationships.

My recovery happened fast because I had prepared fertile soil for it over many years of personal development. I only needed to make one hard, ego-shattering decision to set my healing in motion. Whatever stage you're at on your own journey to living beyond the performative layer and into the expression of your true passion and purpose, I would love to support you in the next stage!

If you are resonating with this and would like a full Personality

Profile or an inspiring Breakthrough Session, please reach out for a Complimentary Conversation with me!

https://irisgroupcoaching.com/contact/

Bio

Sue Tsigaros is a leadership coach and mentor for women on a mission

Sue launched Iris Group in 2002 and is now recognised as a strategic thinking partner, a gifted and generous leadership coach, mentor, facilitator and an inspiring speaker. Iris was the Greek messenger goddess and Sue's work provides that rainbow-bridge between divine vision and grounded manifestation.

Sue contributes extensive experience, knowledge and skill built over an entrepreneurial, corporate sales and academic career spanning more than thirty years. Her practical and commercial business savvy is balanced by a lifetime of deep philosophical inquiry and spiritual work, and she skilfully blends a range of modalities – from evidence-based, solution-focused coaching approaches to transpersonal, spiritual, linguistic and action-based methods – in an atmosphere of authenticity, spontaneity, courage, hearty humour and deep connection.

Sue is passionate about the power and potential of feminine wisdom in leadership. She empowers her clients to own and draw from the whole of self – embracing body, mind, energy, intuition, spirit and heart – so that they can transform the organisations and communities they serve, while growing themselves to their full potential in a sustainable and satisfying way.

Qualifications and Memberships:

- M. Appl. Sci. (Psychology of Coaching), University of Sydney
- Member, AANZ Psychodrama Association since 2008
- Certified Women Power and Body Esteem™ coach since 2012
- Associate of the Australian Psychological Society (2007-2012)
- Accredited Hogan Practitioner since 2005
- Accredited provider of The Leadership Circle™
- Mastery coach, Money Breakthrough Method™
- Board member, Sydney Hills Business Chamber (2018-2020)
- She Business Community Mentor (2014-2016)

Work with Sue:

If you are a leader seeking a grounded and inspiring sounding-board to help clarify and accelerate your current process, let's chat! Simply follow the contact link.

Connect with Sue:

Contact: https://irisgroupcoaching.com/contact/

FIND YOUR FLOW: HOW TO FREE YOUR VOICE, CONNECT WITH YOUR PEOPLE AND DO MEANINGFUL WORK

Rebecca Kornmehl

There is always light. If only we're brave enough to see it. If only we're brave enough to be it.

— The Hill We Climb, youth poet laureate Amanda Gorman

When I'm underwater, no-one else exists. There is only me and an endless silken expanse. My ears fill with the loud whoosh of silence, and my limbs, strong and practiced in this fluid medium, stretch and pull rhythmically. Here I am a seal: free, fierce and pulsing with life. Here I am in flow.

When I bring this mindset to life on land, I coast over obstacles and the world brims with possibility. But the truth is that flowing on land has not always been easy for me. For most of my life I have been the quintessential people-pleaser. Time and again I swallowed my voice, compromised my values and complied with the most unreasonable demands. I did this all in the name of peacekeeping, yet I felt anything but peaceful inside.

For years, anxiety, exhaustion and a slew of mystery ailments plagued my life. Food bothered my stomach. Work befuddled my brain. Home … well, let's not even go there. The thing is that no matter how bad it got, I was not willing to stop. I had a successful management consulting career to tend to. I had children to care for. I had a husband to support. I did not have time to pause for a breath, let alone question the direction I was running in, until one morning I was forced to.

I was in my pyjamas, stowing baby clothes into a high cupboard, when my foot slipped on the ladder's top step. Gripped by gravity, I was yanked downwards – fast. It wasn't like being underwater, where I am light and buoyant. I was a dead weight, forcefully dragged down the ladder's metal rungs until, in a final insult, I cracked my shin hard and landed in a crumpled heap on the floor. It was only 6:30 am. I hadn't even done the morning school run.

Immobilised and clutching my pulsing shin, I lay on my back: a helpless infant who had lost her flow. Yet, pain can be a powerful catalyst. The shock of my fall stirred in me a longing. A longing for freedom from pain, and a longing for a second chance at life. I did not know what to do with this sudden hunger, but soon the world began to throw up answers.

I began to notice the warm and wise people in my community. I took a leap of faith, cleared my throat and dared to speak with them. It wasn't nearly as scary as I had imagined! One by one, beautiful friends and strangers opened their arms and doors for me. They soothed me with their company, compassion and clues to their own successful lives. 'I back myself', they told me, 'I know my limits', 'I follow my heart'.

Courtesy of my newfound support, my spirits picked up. Hope replaced despair, and I began to invite more people into my network.

I befriended a yoga teacher, who taught me exercises to soothe and strengthen my body. I engaged a therapist, who helped me plan a more joyful path forward. I enrolled in a year-long compassionate communication course, where a team of coaches revolutionised my relationship with myself and others. And still, I kept connecting.

One day, a school mum unexpectedly offered me a partnership in a purpose-driven start-up. A fireball of delight spun through my chest. I was so excited at the opportunity to contribute my skills to a meaningful project. Before I knew it, I was working on this initiative and a series of other engagements that culminated in the launch of my very own coaching business.

It seems that once I made the decision to make a change, the universe opened up for me. It showered me with incredible people, who offered empathy, honesty and a fresh perspective. But most of all, these people gave me the gift of unwavering belief. Their faith helped me rebuild my strength, free my voice and find my flow. Success is truly a collaborative experience.

Today, I live a free, vibrant and meaningful life. I'm privileged to run a thriving coaching business and nurture loving relationships with my children, partner and close friends. I spoil myself with a wide range of hobbies from yoga to poetry and cycling. And I dive into the ocean as often as possible to reconnect with myself, reignite my flame and recharge for a life that's worth bringing my best self to.

Get 'unstuck'

When you are in flow, you are deeply content with yourself and empowered to make a positive impact. You have no cause to doubt or criticise yourself. Sure, you may seek external input to inform your decisions, but you don't defer to others or seek their approval. When you are in flow, you genuinely believe in yourself, make peace with your current abilities, respect your natural rhythms, and have the courage to speak your truth and act in line with your values. You're not afraid of falling (or failing) because you trust in your ability to pick yourself up.

When you are in flow, you are strong, healthy and vibrantly energised to:

- make clear, strategic decisions
- take confident steps in your chosen direction
- invite more nourishing relationships
- embrace your natural leadership potential
- contribute your unique gifts to create a more wonderful world.

You're perfectly capable of operating at this level, so what are you waiting for?

If it feels like you've reached the limit of what you can achieve alone and would like a leg-up to get 'unstuck', here is a simple structure to help you find your flow.

Tune in to your body.

Embrace your values.

Shape your environment.

If you're familiar with the biopsychosocial model from psychology or the 'top-down, bottom-up, outside-in' approach from neuroscience, you might recognise the pattern in these steps. That is to say, your wellbeing depends on your ability to look out for your body, mind and environment. Let's take a closer look at this.

Tune in to your body

Every single day, your brain orchestrates a symphony of emotions and physical sensations to keep you alive and thriving. From fascination to fear, singing with joy to being sick to the stomach, your brain's messages guide you towards nourishing experiences and away from dangerous ones.

When you tune in to these subtle (and sometimes not so subtle) messages, you feel confident to make decisions that optimise your wellbeing. This is your natural state of flow. In contrast, when you silence these messages, you make choices that undermine your natural rhythms, values and wellbeing. The result? You become tethered to commitments that drain your strength, energy and lust for life.

If you have lost the ability to read your body's messages, here are three steps to start reconnecting with yourself:

Pay attention to your feelings and physical sensations.

- Are you afraid, angry, joyful?
- Do you have a knotted stomach, lump in your throat or fluttering heart?

Notice the thoughts or events that precipitated your feelings and sensations.

- What's going on in your head, and what's going on around you?

Approach your sensations with curiosity.

- What messages do you think your body is trying to convey to promote your wellbeing?
- What action is it prompting you to take?

Embrace your values

The messages your body sends you are an attempt to move you closer to your values. Simply put, values represent your priorities in life. They are the things that matter most to you, and when you embrace them, you're empowered to take decisions that honour who you are and what you want to achieve.

Clear values help you navigate complexity. When you encounter a conflict of interest, dip in motivation, threat or opportunity, knowing your values keeps you focused on what matters most so you can stay on track to achieving your goals or pivot with intention.

Here are three questions to help clarify your values. You can answer them with reference to your life in general (after all, some values are constants in your life), or you could ask them with reference to a particular situation or point in time.

What would make your life more wonderful (right now)?

What is missing from your life (right now)?

What do you need to feel in flow (right now)?

When you pause to answer these questions, you move closer to the most authentic version of yourself. And when you land on an answer that feels just right, you get to experience the most cathartic sense of relief, like the thrill of solving a particularly enigmatic puzzle. This relief allows frustrated energy to pass through you so you can flow with clarity and confidence towards your best results.

Shape your environment

As you become adept at listening to your body and making decisions that honour your values, you can start shaping your environment to support your flow. You can do this by consciously choosing whom you surround yourself with, the resources you buoy yourself with and the contributions you empower others with.

Humans are inherently relational beings. As such, your wellness relies heavily on your ability to choose the people you spend your time with. I encourage you to pay attention to the specific combination of qualities you value in others and seek these people out. Do you crave respect? Fun? Safety? Passion? A sense of belonging? You have the right to surround yourself with people who will help you thrive.

As you cultivate healthy relationships, you'll have the privilege of seeing yourself more clearly. Your strengths will be validated and your deficits gently illuminated. This provides a wonderful opportunity for personal growth as you can seek out physical, educational, financial or even human resources to nurture your strengths and supplement your deficits.

Finally, the pièce de résistance of finding your flow is to make your unique contribution to our world. In the words of poet Amanda Gorman: 'There is always light. If only we're brave enough to see it. If only we're brave enough to be it.' Yes, it's true: **you** are the leader you are seeking; **you** are the solution you are craving; **you** are the light that will heal yourself and the world around you.

It's time for you to flow with abandon and shine bright on this earth, so here is a handful of questions to help you do just that.

Who do you wish to support and be supported by?

1. Which resources can you gather to maximise your success?
2. How will you make our world more wonderful?

Your turn

If you would like to shine your light for the people and causes you care about, it's essential to find your flow. The more often you access this easeful and empowered state, the greater your gifts to our world and the greater its gifts back to you.

It is my privilege to support passionate entrepreneurs and leaders as they create positive change in our world. This is why I offer complimentary email support to The Results Coach community. This includes access to my latest thinking and highly practical advice to help you find your flow, as well as a direct line of communication with me. If you would like to find out more about this support or access it now, I invite you to join my community.

Bio

Hi, I'm **Rebecca Kornmehl.**

I believe that your voice matters and your unique contributions matter. When you share these with the world, you make it a better place for us all.

As a results coach, I draw on over twenty years of human-centric experience and education to help you achieve your most meaningful goals. My background includes work with global consulting firms like Deloitte and EY, diverse start-ups and purpose-driven leaders, along with education in neuroscience and compassionate communication.

Outside of work hours, you can find me scratching out poetry, splashing at my local beach or meandering through the curly Australian bush – my partner, two children or close friends in tow.

Work with Rebecca:

If you'd love to feel more focused, energised and empowered to do meaningful work, get in touch.

Connect with Rebecca:

Website: https://www.theresultscoach.com.au/

BOSS BABES: SOCIAL SELF-CARE

Daniella

Embrace your inner Boss Babe.

About Boss Babes Australia

Boss Babes Australia™ is a sacred community and creative studio born out of an insatiable love to help women in their mission to create their best life through soul-aligned work, following our hearts truest desires and celebrating the journey of business ownership.

We believe that there's nothing more beautiful and powerful than seeing women step into their own power, purpose and presence by fully embodying their message and boldly owning their voice, unapologetically!

Through all areas of our community and business, we hope you feel empowered and inspired to uplevel your mindset and elevate your personal and business growth game to become the empowered, embodied Boss Babe you were always meant to be!

My story

I'm Daniella, the founder of Boss Babes Australia™ and an empowerment and business mentor for big-hearted women who desire it all.

I'm also a multi-passionate, big-hearted mama and partner and an ocean-lover to the core, who loves to dance to the beat of my own drum (I know, typical Aquarius right here!), based in Melbourne, Victoria.

My personal and spiritual journey has had many twists and turns, and I know firsthand what it's like to confidently rebuild and embrace a new path in life. That's why I am deeply passionate about helping women to rise and conquer in life, business and motherhood.

My entrepreneurial story began back in 2017, when I first became a mama and created my business, Boss Babes Australia, a sacred community and creative studio for women.

I initially started Boss Babes Australia™, after feeling disconnected, lost, alone, stuck in a world and life where I felt like I didn't belong and where I didn't have any like-minded women around to go to for support and guidance. But I had a huge passion to empower women to step into their unique power, build a magnetic brand and elevate their social media presence from a place of alignment, strategy and flow.

The following year, I came out of an abusive, unfaithful marriage and became a single mama. And in that moment, everything changed.

I finally went through a complete breakdown and had my first spiritual awakening.

From there, I became committed and devoted to doing and being everything my heart desired, living my purpose, making my dreams my reality and living life on my own terms. I fully immersed myself in learning everything I possibly could about spirituality, inner work, the law of attraction, manifestation and everything in between.

All of which has led me to following my soul purpose to empower women to love and embrace the Boss Babe they are, to tap deeply into my sacred feminine power, to trust in the guidance of the universe and to merge my spiritual, business and creative worlds together.

Less than two years later, I had built confidence and belief in myself more than ever before, had met the true love of my life, had healed old trauma from my past, had scaled my business to create an abundant income, had walked away from the corporate world, had become a co-author in the Upself self-care series, had launched the Sacred Boss Babes podcast and had helped hundreds of women create a magnetic online presence and embody their purpose and Boss Babe power.

Along with my true desire to empower women to live their best life, I'm also a certified energy healer and trainer/assessor, with over a decade of corporate business management, social media and digital marketing experience up my sleeve. I love merging my spiritual, business and creative worlds together.

I'm here to help you to step fully into your Boss Babe power, share your unique gifts with the world and create the life and business you truly desire!

How to work with me

You can work with me through my heart-centred approach to social media and digital marketing services, empowerment and business mentoring, networking events and brand collaborations with an abundance of business support.

Bio

Daniella is a mother, partner, empowerment and business mentor, and the founder of Boss Babes Australia.

Her mission is to empower women to step into their unique power, build a magnetic brand and elevate their social media presence from a place of alignment, strategy and flow.

Daniella offers a heart-centred approach to social media and digital marketing services, empowerment and business mentoring, networking events, brand collaborations, an abundance of business support and an engaged community of women supporting women.

She is currently working on the Sacred Boss Babes podcast, personal development courses and events to help empower big-hearted women to live their best, most intentional life!

Qualifications:

- Women's Empowerment Coaching
- Reiki Master
- Crystal and Chakra Energy Healer
- Training and Assessment
- Human Resources Management
- Business Administration

Work with Daniella:

You can work with Daniella through her heart-centred approach to social media and digital marketing services, empowerment and business mentoring, networking events and brand collaborations with an abundance of business support.

Connect with Daniella:

Facebook: Facebook.com/bossbabes.au

Facebook: Facebook.com/groups/BossBabesAU

Instagram: Instagram.com/bossbabes.au

Instagram: Instagram.com/sacredbossbabes

Email: hello@bossbabesaustralia.com.au

Website: www.bossbabesaustralia.com.au

THE ART OF SELF-CARE IN CONSCIOUS PARENTING: CONSCIOUS PARENTING BEGINS WITH US

Chantel Rose

When you nurture the parent, you nourish the child.

– Chantel Rose

It begins with a decision, a change, a fresh perspective and a whole new way of being. It enables us to enter a deep-rooted world of discovery, about ourselves, our parents, and our ancestors. It binds us to our children on a physical, spiritual and emotional level, and in ways that we may have abandoned or neglected in our own inner child. It opens doors and memories to reveal the parts of us that we may have chosen to forget or to ignore. It takes us to the places of who we thought we were or who we needed to be, in order to make a positive impact in this world or in the lives of our children.

Parenting is not a new skill that we are required to learn; it's about unlearning, releasing old ways, and allowing ourselves to love more openly and freely; to accept and trust ourselves more fully and deeply; to embrace healing, forgiveness and togetherness.

Becoming a conscious parent is a journey into the unknown, with courage, intent and a burning desire. It's the willingness to follow our inner guidance, to speak gentle, loving, kind words in relevance to ourselves, others, and our children. It's creating a space from which all this magic can unfold as we gift our children with this life and show them that all that we are is enough. It is from this place that we can step into the unlimited potential of our existence as a parent and make an impact in the evolution of humanity which resides in the hearts of our children.

For this journey to unfold, we need to begin with ourselves: committed and immersed in the messiness of healing the parts of us that we have left feeling shattered, lost, and broken. It's about welcoming in self-love, devotion and care. But first it's important to understand how so many of us potentially became so disconnected from ourselves to begin with.

The Journey to Self-Discovery and Care

The modern world has often pulled us away from our natural and authentic way of living – from the depths of our intuition and innate wisdom. It has severed our connection with the earth, the trees, the animals and with the simplicity of what truly matters. We are no longer anchored in our presence, in a state of mindfulness or peace. Instead, we lose ourselves in the busyness of our everyday lives. We chase external goals or expectations and prioritise career, money and insatiable desires over our own wellbeing.

I too was sucked into the allure of 'modernity'. As a child, I was raised in a family of domestic violence, which very early on made me strive for something more meaningful in life. By the age of twenty, I had left my home and moved abroad in the hope of creating a more enriched way of living for myself and my future family. I joined the corporate world and worked endless hours, working my way up the ladder. And whilst I achieved great success, the reality was I was investing my energy, time and headspace into serving everyone else's needs, rarely my own.

During this journey, I soon realised that my career drive was simply a band-aid solution for what I longed for so much as a child: safety, connection, recognition and freedom. In the fast-paced modern world that idolises action, assertiveness and logic – where achievements in business, career, and money were the only determinants of success – there was no room for my instinctive feminine intelligence to thrive and make space for a family of my own. Without that connection, I felt lost and out of balance. It seemed that the one thing I was striving for was now so far out of reach.

In an effort to try my hand one more time at creating the joy and abundance I truly desired, I quit my corporate career and went on a journey of reclaiming balance. I learnt the importance of self-care, embracing my feminine energy and listening to my intuition. I undertook the work of healing the parts of me I had neglected during my corporate life. Most of all, I discovered that the majority of what I needed to heal and work through was from when I was a child. That process of discovery, awareness, and healing led me to a passionate connection with conscious parenting.

Although, this path led me deep into self-care, the true healing journey began when I became a mum myself. Only then was I fully aware of the importance of my own self-care. And with this, I realised how far back in my life I needed to go in order to make deep and meaningful change.

You see, conscious parenting is in realising that when you have a child, not only is a child born, but a parent is born as well. The importance given to love, care, and preparation for the coming of a child should be the same as the one given to becoming a parent. And that is something we often forget. As we nurture the adult through self-care, we naturally nourish the child.

Within every one of us is an inner child waiting to be heard, loved, and cared for. As I embraced loving, nurturing ways of taking care of myself, I was able to transform the way I thought of motherhood. I realised that sometimes, by taking time to nurture our soul, we come back grounded, rejuvenated and refreshed. And that's the place from which we want to connect with our children.

My work as a conscious parent continues.

The Work of the Conscious Parent

Becoming a conscious parent gives us an opportunity to access deeper, more meaningful parts of ourselves, which is where we hold so much wisdom and our ability to navigate through the demands of parenting.

You see, my vision is not to tell you how to parent, because the beauty of individuality lies within each of us and that of our children. Instead, I'd like to provide you with the tools to access, unlock, and magnify your inner brilliance.

When we look at the challenges of parenthood, patterns may emerge:

- parents feeling overwhelmed with emotions and not having the time or headspace to invest in themselves
- parents finding it hard to cope with the demands of parenthood and creating balance for themselves and their family
- parents struggling to navigate between past, present and future expectations.

Often these patterns feel like they are far beyond our control, difficult to manage or to understand where they stem from. Patterns are generally not those of our own, but those we have inherited from previous generations: our parents, grandparents, and ancestors. And whilst times have rapidly changed over the decades, often the experiences of those who have walked before us have been held within us and passed down from one generation to another. This perpetuates the patterns until we make the decision to break these generational cycles and find ways to move through them.

Most of the work of a conscious parent happens when we gain the awareness around what may be occurring, acknowledge our circumstances, and accept that we need to focus time, energy and effort on our own mental, physical, spiritual and emotional wellbeing. This is because when we operate from a space of love through our own heart's desire, we make the most profound impact in the lives of our children and create healing for future generations.

To master the power of conscious parenting through self-care we can channel our energy into three key areas that can contribute to breaking the patterns we mentioned in this section:

Healing Past Trauma

Conscious parenting requires that we travel back in time. First, we must go beyond our own childhood experiences to access any intergenerational trauma held within our DNA and passed down by our ancestors. Recent research has shown that there is a legacy of trauma passed down from one generation to the next. In one such study, three generations of fifteen Ukrainian families exhibited transgenerational impacts such as risky health behaviour, food hoarding, and overeating. These behaviours were linked to their ancestors who had lived through the mass starvation of millions of Soviet Ukrainians from 1932 to 1933. Even though the circumstances have changed since then, the effects of the trauma were felt three generations down. As such, our healing journey fundamentally begins at the DNA level.

Often, we identify patterns of behaviours, words and actions we recognise in ourselves as similar to those of our parents. Acknowledging that these experiences reside deep within us is the first step in being able to let them go. However, making a conscious effort to release them is key.

I began to realise that my past trauma would always become obvious when I felt triggered by a situation because the response mechanism was being expressed subconsciously (without much thought, energy or processing time). It was instant and 'out of character'. So, I began to sit with my trigger responses and go through the necessary internal work by doing the following:

Pause and process before reacting/responding.

A. Take a deep breath and acknowledge the thoughts, feelings or emotions that are coming to the surface. Be kind to yourself and allow these things to move through you.
B. Remain calm, ground yourself and either hold space or create space between yourself and the situation at hand.
C. Mantra: 'Higher self, take control.' We are handing over our need to be in control of the situation or the outcome, and we're unblocking the restriction of energy so that it has space to move. We are allowing peace and wisdom to flow through us.

Nurturing the Parent

How wonderful is it that you are reading this book! It's a clear testament to your commitment towards enhancing your relationship with yourself. And this area is solely devoted to that.

While healing may sometimes feel like 'hard work', in that it is fundamentally a process, nurturing ourselves can be a lot of fun. It's taking the time to prioritise ourselves and our wellbeing in a way that spills over to improve our entire existence and that of everyone in our circle.

As it stands, the day-to-day demands of family, work, relationships, and business often occupy the majority of our time and energy. As an entrepreneurial mum myself, I understand that it's not easy and we often feel drained by the weight and breadth of our responsibilities. However, just as we've prioritised all of the above, we need to prioritise our own self-care.

Here are a few simple steps to take into consideration when investing in ourselves:

Dedicate a day, time and place where you have communicated your plans and expectations with your family or friends so that everyone is aware of how you can be best supported to take that time for yourself.

A. Do something you love! No matter what that looks like, use this time to immerse yourself in something that lights you up and connects you with your inner world.
B. Kick off your shoes and spend time barefoot outdoors. Nature is exceptionally healing and grounding. Moreover, it connects us back to ourselves.
C. Speak gentle, kind, loving words to yourself. Acknowledge all that you've achieved and how deserving you are of this time.
D. Mantra: 'I am worthy of receiving. When I invest in myself, I achieve balance, energy and flow.' As humans, we often give so much to others, yet when we stop and reflect on the fact that we deserve to have our glasses filled, naturally we have more to offer the world.

When we indulge in these practices, balance naturally occurs. As a result, we feel energised, replenished, and able to give more of ourselves again.

Nourishing the Child

As a parent, we know we have a very important role to play in the safety, development and growth of our children. We are blessed with the gift of guiding and facilitating their unique journey in this world. When we hold space and operate from a place of love and understanding for our children, we allow them the freedom to navigate through situations without restricting their course of direction. We create opportunities for growth and expression which are in alignment with the child's character and perspective on life. We allow for their emotional needs to be met and show them through our own experiences that we are worthy of the love and care that is required for our ability to thrive. The way our children observe us being treated – either through our own actions or of those around us – creates the foundation from which they accept being treated throughout the course of their lives. Therefore, we have a responsibility to take care of ourselves and to try our best to live consciously and remain present, all the while showing, rather than telling, our children how life is best lived.

Here are four simple steps to help you make a positive impact in the eyes of your children:

Speak a language of love and positivity, for the words we choose and use with ourselves and our children are the seeds we plant within their minds. These begin to sprout over time as our children grow and express themselves.

A. Show compassion and kindness. Be patient and kind to yourself. Accept that not all of your days will flow with simplicity and ease. It is the challenges that make us more resilient to the changes and enables us to appreciate our blessings.
B. Hold space. Surrender and become comfortable with not having to be in control of the situation or the outcome. Allow yourself and

your children to feel all of your emotions as they move through you.

C. Mantra: 'I am the change that I wish to see.' When we lead from a space of love and intention, we become the change maker for future generations.

Healing past trauma, nurturing the parent and nourishing the child are three of the most transformative, empowering and rewarding self-care practices we can incorporate into our life's journey. By making these three areas a priority, not only has my life become more enriched, fulfilled and meaningful, it has given my family the ability to experience the same.

Call to Action:

Are you looking to embark on a powerful self-care journey? As the founder of Reignite Enterprises, I would like to personally invite you to access one of our Reignite Retreat experiences.

The Reignite Retreat is an online or in-person transformative self-care retreat that provides you with a place and a space where you can elevate your energy, wellbeing and happiness.

You will be guided and supported by world-class experts who will hold a space for you to renew your energy, nourish your wellbeing, rewire your mind and optimise your habits and behaviours so that you can leave with practical tools that can enhance your life moving forwards.

The Reignite Retreat takes you through a healing. Here, lifelong connections are made and the discovery of our deep connection with our Self is had.

To learn more about The Reignite Retreat, simply visit: www.reigniteretreat.com

Bio

Chantel Rose is an author, educator and a conscious entrepreneur.

Chantel is the wife of James Yates. Together they founded Reignite, a life enhancement company that creates unique programs, products and experiences that bring people together for causes that support the evolution of consciousness and the expansion of human potential.

Chantel specialises in supporting women and their families to gain greater clarity and awareness on their lifestyle choices, energy and wellbeing so that they can live optimally with greater happiness, joy and quantum flow.

She believes that when a woman's energy and wellbeing is in alignment, she has a greater ability to support her family, grow a successful career or do the things she loves.

After a highly demanding corporate career running major projects for the IT sector, Chantel was faced with her own health challenges, which led to severe mental, emotional and physical burnout.

After embarking on what would become a decade long quest towards her own self-healing, Chantel discovered a plethora of ancient modalities, self-care techniques and wellbeing and lifestyle hacks that allowed her to become more calm, present and productive in all facets of life.

Using this experience, she has spoken in front of countless people and inspired them to expand their knowledge, to nurture themselves and to live a life they love.

As a mother, Chantel believes her largest impact can be made on the future of humanity – our kids. She is working on a variety of projects to ensure that future generations are in good hands.

Work with Chantel:

Are you looking to embark on a powerful self-care journey? To learn more about the Reignite Retreat, simply visit: www.reigniteretreat.com

Connect with Chantel:
Facebook: https://www.facebook.com/selfcarewithchantel
Instagram: https://www.instagram.com/selfcarewithchantel/

SECTION 5:
SOUL SELF-CARE

INTRODUCTION

Tracey Jewel

We find it easy to look after the 'tangible' parts of our being, such as physical self-care, but soul self-care is just as important.

Soul self-care is a deeper connection to source, the universe, God, whatever you call it, as well as the deep belief we are worthy and deserving of time to look after our spiritual wellbeing.

It is the space to tend, care, nurture, correct and guide – to renew our inner beings.

There are many ways of practising soul self-care, such as gratitude, solitude, source connection through affirmations and prayer, and immersion in your 'truth' and life path.

Often it's really as simple as tuning our awareness to God/universe/source in the midst of the stress and mundanity of life.

The difference between other types of self-care and soul self-care, is that unlike 'doing the things', such as having a massage, taking a walk or journaling, soul self-care is the opposite and involves surrendering in order to create the space for God/universe/source to work through us and to be open to receiving this connection and love into our lives.

BECAUSE YOU ARE NOT BROKEN

Gavin Hyde

Every subject is two subjects:
what you desire and its absence.
– Abraham-Hicks

Energy flows where your attention goes – what you desire and the absence of it. When you are thinking of the relationship you desire, what is also active in your vibration is the relationship that you do not have.

Some beautiful paths can't be discovered without getting lost.
– Erol Ozan

My journey began when I realised I had manifested my greatest fear: my life was not how I had imagined it would be. The loving relationship I dreamed of had become destructive and toxic, I was separated from my children and heartbroken. I felt trapped in an unfulfilling job at the railways that only reminded me every day that my life was a train wreck. I tried desperately to avoid dealing with my fears, numbing my feelings with drugs and alcohol, but this only served to make me feel chronically anxious and exhausted. I was in a dark place, and even my father suffering a serious heart attack did not stop me continuing down this destructive path. I was sick and tired of feeling sick and tired. Something needed to change, but I was unaware that I was the one creating the experience I was having.

> *She remembered who she was, and the game changed.*
> – Lalah Delia

I had reached rock bottom when a good friend suggested a personal development seminar. I'm not sure what made me go that day, and I can't even remember what the presenter said, but a light turned on for me, and I decided then and there I wanted to change the direction of my life. I had a strong desire to get over my ex and meet someone new, so I signed up to the course on offer, and that is the moment my journey back to me began.

The teaching was a revelation to me. I learnt about how my thinking and my perceptions held a powerful influence over what my experience in life would be. I realised I was swimming in a murky whirlpool of anger, overwhelm, disappointment and fear of failure. And then the penny dropped, I realised that I was getting exactly what I was focusing on. I realised that I hadn't taken any real responsibility for any of the things going wrong in my life, I was just trying to run away from them.

> *Conscious thoughts, repeated often enough,*
> *become unconscious thinking.*
> – Joe Dispenza

After I completed the personal development program, I recognised my part in the breakdown of my relationship and, more importantly, that a new and more fulfilling relationship would not be possible until I found my peace with my ex. So I summoned the courage and apologised to her. By taking ownership for my part in our relationship breakdown, I was able to let go of all the anger, disappointment and feelings of failure, which allowed the space for a new loving and fulfilling relationship to occupy.

As a result of changing my mind about who I was, how I was thinking and what I was capable of, I was able to begin to fill my heart and mind with the desire to be part of a loving caring relationship, to be a present father taking part in his children's lives and to do the kind of work that would give me a sense of fun, freedom and fulfilment. I was beginning to see new and exciting possibilities for my life.

Two weeks later, I met the love of my life, she was exactly as I had imagined her in my dreams … such a wonderful feeling. I felt seen and appreciated and, for the first time, I felt accepted for just being me. This filled me with an incredible sense of my potential.

A few months later, my two sons came to live with me full time. I left my railway job. My life was no longer a train wreck, and I became the present father I had always wanted to be.

In the matter of a few months, I had turned my life around. I couldn't believe how fast this had all happened.

> *When you know what you don't want,*
> *you know what you do want.*
> – Abraham-Hicks

I was intrigued by the process I had just experienced. I was fascinated by the idea of how my thoughts and feelings create my life experience. I thought about how powerful it would be to be able to use this knowledge with awareness, and I did not want to have to endure the extreme lows to experience the extreme highs. I became passionate about the mind and how it works and the connection between the thinking mind and the feeling body.

I knew I needed to change my perceptions, but this was not as easy as I'd first thought. There were beliefs and behaviours I needed to accept and understand, I could see there were deep emotional processes I needed to address.

I took the next step. I decided to follow my heart and do something I was passionate about, I enrolled in a Diploma of Sports Therapies. This quickly led me to kinesiology, and even though it was difficult, it really sang to me. Kinesiology taught me about outdated, unwanted thought pathways and how to change them. It really worked for me.

I studied hard and became a kinesiologist and, to my amazement, I was acquiring a whole new level of skills – my gifts were emerging and my confidence was surging.

Hands down, this was my Einstein moment. I discovered the missing piece of the puzzle that had been blindsiding me from getting my life back onto the highway to happiness.

I became more and more interested in the mind, how it works, about how the mind and body communicate and the magic we can create with it. I continued to do specialised learning in all these areas.

As I went further down the rabbit hole with my studies, I completed dual diplomas in remedial massage and sports therapies, a master's degree in neurolinguistic programming and hypnosis, energetic and vibrational healing, reiki, positive psychology and so much more.

I was so grateful to finally be doing something I was passionate about and making a difference. As I began helping others, the clients I seemed to be attracting were people just like I had been – people suffering, struggling and stuck in their own life dramas.

I loved so much guiding people through their perceived train wreck. I was witnessing rapid transformations and sharing in the joy of people changing their life for the better.

About twelve years ago I was so inspired with the new direction my life was taking. I had successfully developed my own private natural health and wellness training centre in Sydney and my obsession for crafting revolutionary products and services was beginning to flip the health and wellness field on its head. I had accepted the role of head of the kinesiology faculty at Australia's premier natural therapy college in Sydney and, on top of that, I had received an invitation to travel to Luxemburg, in north-western Europe, to deliver my Magnificent Minds Learning Program to the staff at the St George's International School prior to it being implemented for all the children attending the school. For the first time I really felt like I had made it.

> *A daily ritual is a way of saying I'm voting for myself;*
> *I'm taking care of myself.*
> – Mariel Hemingway

Three Soul Care Tips

1. Always take responsibility for what is happening in your life.
2. Write down your goals and ensure that are aligned with your true values.
3. Every day be open to learn new things about yourself and your life.

The Seven Soul Care Steps

To create soul satisfaction, you need to surrender, connect inwards and make yourself a PRIORITY to allow the universe to work with and through your life.

This is the exact process I use to achieve what I am most passionate about, which is to help you heal, succeed, and transform your life.

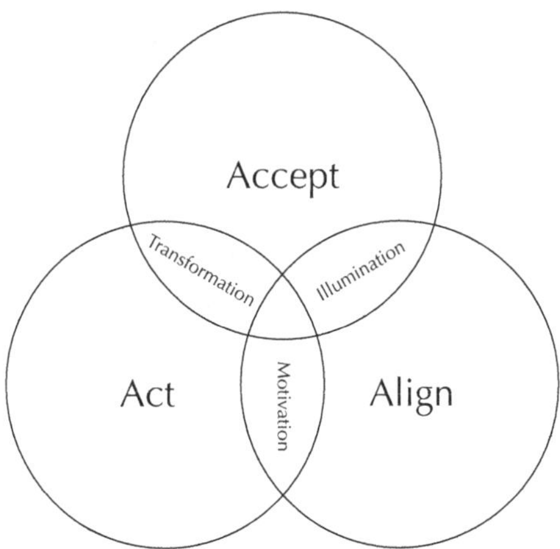

1. Breathe in, uncover the hidden power that has secretly been holding you back and ACCEPT that you are responsible for your life, breathe out the present moment and create more flow each day.
2. Listen deeply, learn to identify the difference to your behind-the-scenes real-lies self-talk and your inner voice's highest truth, so

you can reconnect and ALIGN with your authentic self, and feel fulfilled in every way.

3. Confidently pull the trigger and abundantly ACT on your intuition, allowing yourself to hit your life's big picture goals like magic and experience the freedom you deserve in your life.

When a sea captain first sees that glimmer from a lighthouse in the distance, he is reassured that he can navigate a way in through the darkness out of danger to the safety of his destination. Become the light house.

4. **Physical** – Movement is a wonderful way to move wanted energy into and around the physical body and unwanted energy out of the body. Making regular exercise a habit is necessary for a healthy mind, a healthy body and a healthy soul. It can be as simple as a walk or something more robust, like bodybuilding or power lifting. Just choose what you prefer, take action and be consistent and accountable.
5. **Nutritional** – Fuelling your mind, body and soul is also important. There is so much information available these days on the internet, so just keep it simple. Choosing to eat eighty per cent unprocessed foods, taking amazing nutritional products that fill your nutritional gaps and drinking plenty of high-quality water is a mouth-watering recipe. Take action, and be consistent and accountable.
6. **Spiritual** – Develop a daily practice combining meditation, appreciation and gratitude. Be consistent and accountable.
7. **Pursue the right goals for you.** If your thoughts and feelings are not healthy, it is impossible to create the wonderful life you desire. Always start with the end goal in mind. When we understand our true desires, the outcomes come much faster. Be consistent and accountable.

All end goals fall into three categories:

1. experience
2. growth
3. contribution.

How do you ensure you are pursing the right end goals?

Make a list under the three categories:

1. Complete the **experience** column by answering the experience question.
2. Complete the **growth** column by asking the growth questions to the experience answers.
3. Complete the **contribution** column by asking the contribution questions to the experience answers.

Experience	Growth	Contribution
Question: What amazing things do I want to experience and feel in this life?	Question: How do I want to grow as a human being into the person who is having all these amazing experiences and feelings?	Question: How can I give back and make my contribution to the world?

The biggest adventure you can take is to live the life of your dreams.

– Oprah Winfrey.

Over the previous twelve months, I have released my latest transformational training system, a revolutionary approach that is turning the personal development industry on its head: The Ultimate MindFit Method™ – a five-step process for truth seekers to learn how to turn their problems into projects and 'get good at life'.

In the past six months I have been inspired by the movement of difference-makers across the globe who are giving themselves permission to follow their passion. My own 'light bulb moment' was when I realised doing what you love is now more mainstream than ever before.

My latest project is the pinnacle of my entire life's work:

The H.E.L.P. Accelerator Success Maker

The H.E.L.P. Accelerator Success Maker is a complete educational training system combining the right pathways with practical solutions for soul satisfaction to everyday problems.

It is a road map for people who want to wake up every day feeling inspired to live on purpose, follow their hearts desires, lead an extraordinary life every single day and create a legacy of a more unified freedom for their children and generations to follow.

Heck, no matter how many times you have failed in the past, it is not entirely your fault and I will teach you why.

Because You're Not Broken

Happiness is not something ready-made. It comes from your actions.

– Dalai Lama

Bio

Gavin Hyde is one of Australia's most sought after mindset strategists, trailblazing the way, breaking new ground as a business owner, complimentary medicine visioneer, creator of the H.E.L.P. Accelerator Success Maker and five-times published co-author.

Gavin, has been turning the wellness and personal development industry on its head for more than two decades with his revolutionary approach to how people heal, succeed and transform their lives.

After a series of life-changing events that literally broke him, Gavin made a decision, against the wishes of his loved ones, that changed the trajectory his life forever.

In the pursuit to find answers, Gavin took a leap of faith and invested in his own education, which led to many years of dedication and laser-focused study. Gavin acquired multiple qualifications in the fields of personal development, complementary health and education.

Gavin's industry expertise and business success began back in the late 1990s when he founded Naturally InTouch Therapies, a private natural health and wellness training centre in Sydney. This is where Gavin's obsession for crafting leading-edge products and services that generate a deep sense of satisfaction and wellbeing for his clientele began.

Over all the years coaching, mentoring and training thousands of clients from all over the globe, he has discovered the one core multilayered problem that people face day in and day out.

We are not born with an instruction manual on how to run our minds the right way.

This effect causes us, in our deep subconscious, to create beliefs like 'I'm not good enough, smart enough or confident enough', and often at an early age we make an unconscious decision to give up following what is truly in our heart.

Gavin has an infectious passion and has since dedicated his life to focusing on providing people with the right tool kit to run their life the right way, so they can follow their hearts desire, live on purpose and lead an extraordinary life every single day.

Work with Gavin:

If you're wanting to silence some anxiety, calm your mind and feel some inner peace or you want to spark your creative genius and ride the highway to happiness, download our free training program **The Happy Mind Affect,** valued at **$157**, from: www.gavinhyde.com.au.

OR

Connect personally and experience a Free **BREAKTHROUGH** strategy call. Get everything you need in no time at all and create some rock-solid certainty in your life the right way. Valued at **$297**, book your free **BREAKTHOUGH** strategy call at www.gavinhyde.com.au.

Connect with Gavin:
Facebook: https://www.facebook.com/Thatgavguy
Facebook Groups: www.facebook.com/groups/raiseyourvibeglobal
LinkedIn: https://www.linkedin.com/in/gavin-hyde-aka-that-gav-guy-52a414b3/
Website: www.gavinhyde.com.au

SECTION 6:
SPIRITUAL SELF-CARE

INTRODUCTION

Tracey Jewel

Many people confuse the terms 'spiritual' and 'religious'. However, you can be spiritual without being religious. If you feel comfortable with a particular religion, it will certainly help boost your spiritual self-care. But don't take up a religion if you can't find common ground. For everyone, nurturing your spirit regardless of religious beliefs bodes well for a healthier lifestyle.

Anything that helps you evolve with a deeper understanding or connection to the universe is considered an exercise in spirituality. It involves looking at ourselves and finding that meaning within. What do you ask yourself about your experiences and life? Do you engage in spiritual practices that fulfil you?

Spiritual self-care can be as simple as meditating. You can pray your way to a higher power or take quiet time to reflect on yourself and the world. And yes, you can also attend a religious service if that speaks to your spirit as well. We all have something spiritual guiding us, though you may need to find what it is that works for you.

In this chapter, you'll see just how to approach the spiritual side of your self-care. Those that haven't delved into this area much before will have more work ahead, but that will open the necessary doors to free your spirit and let the harmony flow through you. Spiritual self-care means many things to many people. Turn the page and find out how you can open yourself up to the universe and receive the many blessings it has in store.

JOURNEY WITH YOUR SOUL

Robyn Jordan

By God when you see your beauty, you'll be the idol of yourself.

– Rumi

I stood high on a hill, holding hands with my creator, The All Knowing. Before me lay the many lives of my forward journey. My overview of 'a life forgotten', yet to be remembered by the unfolding of the 'perfection of the soul'. Behind me are lives appearing completed and cleared, yet trauma and potential releases remain. I witness my challenges, and know I am still magical.

I step into my next journey towards my inspiration and liberation. I see the light at the end of the tunnel. It has been a long arduous voyage in-utero, at times floating free, hearing voices and struggling to swim on. Sometimes expansive, then reluctant and reclusive. As I birthed, I was not to know I had entered another 'soul journey' in this chosen body.

Arriving as innocence in perfection, a swift entry with no turning back, I was unaware I had chosen my parents, my circumstances, my forward challenges, distress, achievements and liberation, with ultimate soul perfection for this journey and a desire to learn my soul's lessons and to travel in the catacombs of my lives forgotten – to create continuous breath to freedom. It is the ultimate journey.

There is a voice that doesn't use words. Listen.
– Rumi

I was born into an era of personal and cultural silence, combined with huge expectations of perfection and achievement. My birth offered me a mother in parental grief and father who deeply compromised the relationship and innocence of the little girl. From the outside, a picture of apparent family perfection, however, full of secrets. The innocent child with overwhelming fear in every breath, needed the courage to meet each day and take the steps alone with grief and trauma, whilst constantly searching in the journey for resilience and liberation towards the potential perfection of 'my soul' – the backdrop of a life unfolding by my soul's decision to join this earthly journey, a significant life of trauma with enlightening gifts for my evolution. My childhood is a gift to my individual soul journey and to humanity.

Not chasing a dream but following a destiny.
– Keith Urban

My life path has unveiled through interactions of family dramas and expectations of society's institutions. The parents I was birthed to have departed to continue their journeys beyond this earthly plane. They departed with their own lessons, their role as instigators of change through the unfolding of my childhood into adulthood. I have learnt forgiveness within the myriad of life's opportunities, to create and reveal my unique pathway. Enhancing my new relationship framework as wife, mother, nan, teacher and guide. I now have gratitude for those who deny me, challenge me, acknowledge me and see me. These are the many moments of falling and rising again as the Phoenix. Life is unfolding through 'all the human stuff' with the confusion, the clarity and awareness of my unique existence.

Our entry into this earthly journey is of profound significance, expressing our willingness or trepidation of being here on earth and the many combinations in between. It explores the scale of compression and shadow into expansion and light for the desire to experience our essential purity.

This is where we learn the lessons. We are discovering the self and its huge role in man's evolution. We each have an inspiring life pathway to walk, a journey of many lessons and subsequent healings. We celebrate our differences and our endless similarities, our uniqueness and our unifying human likeness. We have been taking this journey over myriad of lifetimes: all for the evolution of our soul's growth.

We all have imagination, the ability to create an 'image', to go anywhere, to be in a place instantly and travel in the other worlds that mirror this one. The purpose or value of remembering and exploring past lives is that feelings, long buried or blocked, can come to the surface and be released as our soul's unfinished business. The setbacks we experienced in one lifetime have been passed on as our soul's ongoing insights. Situations to be cleared by the newly incarnated consciousness, birthed as you return to this world with new circumstances and opportunities.

We purposefully choose life. We are not birthed as victims. We are birthed as volunteers, returning in your particular body to create healing and resolution for all we connect with, within the knowing of the circumstances of our entry, our family, and the myriad of experiences, with amnesia at a human level, to allow the unfolding to the soul's understanding to be revealed.

It is a lifetime journey within the parameters of free will. We unconsciously carry old stories that can be the driving force behind our continuous life adventures: compulsive repeating patterns that dominate our present life, karmic scripts connected to personal tragedies and trauma in a past life, traumas that deeply disturb the equilibrium of the soul, leaving parts emotionally frozen and detached, scars of the soul that carry on from one lifetime to the next. We are releasing the old stories of material loss, violence, abuse, abandonment, betrayal, scapegoating, untimely death and fears, failures and stuckness – obstructions disrupting us today.

Beyond the pain, struggle and karmic imprints of so many difficult lives, we also have memories that hold vivid stories of peaceful lives with deep love, in which we passed painlessly surrounded by loving companions – lives and times of inspiration and completion promoting healthy directions, purpose and resources for today.

Our body is temporary. It is the vehicle for carrying the soul. Our soul is constant. Past life selves are not only characters in past life dramas; they live with us now as sub personalities influencing us: Who am I? Why am I here? Where am I going? What is my soul's plan?

Past life regression accesses our subconscious or higher self, where all our soul memories are stored. We move beyond the analytical and critical conscious mind and our ego, to access our higher self, intuition and wisdom and to meet our life's lessons. The subconscious is neither critical nor analytical. All is presented as absolute truth. It knows what it knows. It will free itself from negative programming. It remembers everything from every time period. It is our sixth sense. It has all the creative solutions.

The healing of past life regression replays the old stories of the past life character, thaws the old frozen feelings, releases pains and blocked body energy, brings negative thoughts and assumptions into present consciousness, recognising their origin so they no longer belong to present life.

Once the journey through the past life is complete, exploration is through the higher dimensions of the bardo, the afterlife, the place of recognition and liberation, the safe place to be to explore and heal. We not only observe the event but include the attached emotions, thoughts and imprints and release them for integration. We relive the story by role playing to unlock the complexes, to see that we have been living a long-ago drama that no longer needs to have power over us. As shared by the higher self, the particular lesson then becomes an outworn drama played out unknowingly in our present life. Once recognised, liberation is spontaneous. We are growing as soul.

Each day I am aware of my personal journey, the practices that sustain me and my gifts, encouraging me and opening doors for me to live the truest version of myself on my human journey. With my awakening each day, I am aware of the conscious breath, the quiet inner sound only I can hear. It opens me to my journey for the day, with the trepidations and excitement. I flow into the ujjayi pranayama breath, the ocean sounding breath. It opens the front, sides and back of the body, unravels physical tension and quiets the mind. It increases my strength, vitality, enthusiasm and positive attitude for life, stimulating the healing process on all levels. In twenty minutes a day, it gives all the benefits of aerobic exercise, and I may not have left my bed.

I follow with the Svaroopa Yoga Magic 4 exercises as a daily practice: slow motion dive, crooked knee pose, lunge, reclining spinal twist releasing muscles from the tailbone, creating a domino effect of release, climbing the spine through the sacrum, waist, rib cage, shoulders, neck, skull and opens the mechanical compression of the inner organs. With less tension in the body the vital systems find their natural balance and breath is opened easily and immediately, finding the deep dimensions of your being.

My weekly connection includes sessions of Pilates, postural integration (deep tissue bodywork with emotional integration) and liquid crystals, as I am a practitioner of these magical geometric vibrational remedies. I walk alone with self and others and relax into meditation. I find humour and deep connection alone and in unison. I learn the courage to be vulnerable on the path to my authenticity.

With the depth of knowing from my journey of life I am honoured to action my wisdom through past life regression / deep memory process / psychosomatic therapy sessions. Each session begins with a face reading with photos that create full face images of the right outer masculine and left inner feminine faces, creating an awareness of the internal style of communication and the uniqueness of the present-day journey for my clients. It allows a safe, intimate first connection and acknowledgement, and it may be the first time someone truly sees themself. With exploration it brings forth the unique language leading towards the creation of an intention(s) for the session – intake questions of significant events in childhood/adulthood, messages from parents and other significant people, painful memories, fears, repeating patterns, largest defeats and disappointments and karmic scripts. Karmic scripts heard in our language are: 'I always have to do it alone', 'I will never find love', 'I am not accepted for who I am', 'I am afraid to trust', 'I don't really know who I am', 'I feel like a failure', 'people always let me down and betray me', 'I fear …', and so many more.

Entry to a past life experience occurs lying down, breathe through the body, through a guided meditation leading to entry to the past life through three doors, across a bridge, a pathway the intentions created. Entry can also occur through an injured or compromised body part or system. The 'story' is played out as if occurring in the moment, with deep expressions of reliving in its fullness the most important and decisive moments of that life.

As a past life practitioner, I hold the space moving the client backwards and forwards in that life, to meet significant moments, the depth and signature from that lifetime, to the passing moment as soul leaves body. The death transition allows the opportunity to free oneself of thoughts, feelings and pains in the after-death period. The process moves into the lower and higher bardo, the transitional planes of soul exploration between life and death, to integrate the understandings with more consciousness. It is the safe place to reside to explore and heal. Sensations may arise such as numbness, heat, cold, paralysis, tingling or shakes, all the somatic process of spontaneous release – the release of blocked energy which was associated to an old trauma. Once in present day consciousness, the insights are integrated with peace and liberation.

I create the space for you to give you back to yourself, an essential part of any intuitive guide's role. This is my commitment to humanity and the journey of life.

In essence 'regression' is here to help everyone. We all have unfinished business. Continuation on the soul's journey relies on our involvement and interaction. It is the journey to our freedom, liberation and clarity, our understanding of self and our blueprint. Who am I? Why am I here? Where am I going? What is my soul's journey? It is the pathway to finding our uniqueness.

We are growing as soul, clearing all that no longer serves us. This is ours and humanity's unique journey. As Persian poet Rumi says, 'By God when you see your beauty, you'll be the idol of yourself'.

Hold my hand and we will journey. The door is open. Step through into life.

Bio

Robyn Jordan, past life regressionist, is a guide and fellow traveller of life with you. A carer of the sacredness of the individual within humanity.

Robyn was born in Bendigo, Victoria, Australia. Her family originated from those who travelled to the goldfields in the 1880s to find their fortune and create a new life. She inherits adventure, taking a chance, disappointment and achievement.

Robyn began her career as a primary school teacher and has also worked as a kindergarten teacher and a child care facilitator. After training as a Primary School teacher at Bendigo Teachers College, she completed her Bachelor of Arts in sociology/anthropology at Latrobe University, Melbourne.

Robyn intermingled her teaching career with marriage and the birth of four sons. She is now the nan of eleven grandchildren – an integral part of her journey with innocence. Robyn is a woman who cares deeply about the innocence of children and the innocent child within each of us.

As Robyn's family matured and her forties turned into fifties, her direction flowed deeper into the care of humanity. Robyn has followed a deep spiritual path with the modalities of person-centred counselling, visionary intuitive therapy, psychosomatic therapy, liquid crystals, and her deep passion, past life regression therapy and deep memory process. The understandings of our soul journey and the awareness of our human journeys over myriad of lifetimes has become her deep passion.

Robyn's gifts of a lifelong journey of experiences and revelations of many personal lifetimes has become her gift to mankind. Connecting

the threads to awaken your true potential is the treasure.

Qualifications:

- Diploma of Primary Teaching, Bendigo Teachers College
- Bachelor of Arts (Sociology), La Trobe University
- Certificate of Person-Centred Counselling, Lux College
- Certificate of Hypnosis, Academy of Transformational Psychotherapy
- Visionary Intuitive Healing Levels 1,2,3.
- Past Life Regression Therapy, Toni Reilly Institute
- Deep Memory Process Therapy, Roger Woolger Institute/Patricia Walsh
- Certificate III in Psychosomatic Therapy 10821NAT, Australian Institute of Body-Mind Analysis and Psychosomatic Therapy
- Participant at Deep Body Immersion and Masters of Psychosomatic Therapy
- Practitioner of Liquid Crystals (Justin Moikeha Asar)
- Certified Introductory Teacher of Svaroopa Yoga

Work with Robyn:

Hold my hand and I will journey with You. Connect the threads and awaken your true soul potential.

Connect with Robyn:
Facebook: https://www.facebook.com/journeywithyoursoul
Instagram: Souljourney.robynjordan
LinkedIn: https://www.linkedin.com/in/robyn-jordan-77098055/
Email: robynjordan@hotmail.com.au
Website: https://journeywithyoursoul.com

DIVINE INTUITION: THE ABILITY TO UNDERSTAND SOMETHING INSTINCTIVELY, WITHOUT THE NEED FOR CONSCIOUS REASONING

Emma Divine

The ability to understand something instinctively, without the need for conscious reasoning.

– Emma Divine

As a psychic medium and white witch, I use magic, spirit and intuition daily. It is my passion, my job and my mission to make more people aware of the value of working with spirit and your intuition. It can benefit you immeasurably. One of the things I find myself telling everyone I work with is that the gut feelings you have, those pangs in your tummy and chest, aren't just 'gut feelings', they are a deeper knowing, a connection to something higher. Like a spiritual guide-dog leading you along your life's path, you must make friends with him, trust and follow him.

What is intuition?

Scientifically it is described as 'a brain process that gives people the ability to make

decisions without the use of analytical reasoning'. My definition of intuition is simply,

'Trust your (f******) gut!'

We all have intuition, and we all have psychic ability, because we all have the pineal gland! The pineal gland, our 'third eye', is our greatest gift, one that reminds us there is more to life than just this physical world and indeed our physical body, which I call 'a vessel'.

When you awaken your third eye and use your intuition, it brings you psychic vision, gut feelings and a more intimate relationship with God, your guardian angels and your loved ones who have passed. All this communication and 'knowing' leads to a massively strong intuition, which you can use to guide you throughout your life.

The importance of working with your intuition, your third eye, is great. When we lose touch with our naturally spiritual selves our chakras become out of line, out of sync, which leads the body to a state of poor health. We can become affected by depression, anxiety and even illness. With an open and clear third eye, we find our soul's purpose, a higher level of energy and consciousness, leading us closer to God, spirit and indeed to our best lives.

I will talk about the number of ways you can work on your intuition and some self-care rituals in this chapter, but before that I would like to share an incident that happened to me whilst performing a self-care ritual on myself. It gave me a real nudge to trust my intuition and to trust the signs I was being given.

It had been a particularly hard few weeks, I recall it being around the middle of the first lockdown in 2020. I was in desperate need of some signs from my angels that I could easily notice. When we're so low, we often miss the symbols they give us so it's important to make some time dedicated to trying to communicate with each other. I drew myself a bath, added salt and sage in preparation for my cleansing ritual. I sank deep into down, leaving my chin resting on the hot, salty water. I closed my eyes and imagined bright white, angelic light pouring over me from my head to my toes. The salt cleansing away my mental impurities and the sage adding that extra bit of magic and strength to my soul. Once I felt relaxed and had imagined the white light enveloping my body, I had a sudden explosion of bright green energy in my mind's eye. When I close my eyes, I always see colours. But this was something else, almost like I was transported somewhere heavenly. I was not scared; I was calm and surrendered to what was to come. I watched as a figure appeared and with my knowledge of the archangels, I immediately knew this was Archangel Raphael, the angel of healing. I felt tears build up, but I didn't open my eyes. I saw him coming towards me, open hands, palms facing up. The bright green energy was so intense, almost like when a camera flash goes off. Then suddenly a thud hit my chest. Still, I was not scared. I don't know what it was and I can't explain it, but with the sudden release of all my negativity, fears and anxiety, it felt like Raphael had reached into my soul and snatched away the darkness. I lay there for a moment then opened my eyes. I smiled, I cried then immediately went onto Instagram live in my towel to tell the world what had happened and ask if anyone else had experienced anything similar!?

THAT was the moment I knew my intuition was on point, I KNEW I was going to be okay

because he had shown me so.

You see, never disregard your intuitive thoughts and feelings, they've been put there for a reason. You ARE right.

I think there is something we all have to learn, and that is to have complete trust and faith in ourselves, always go with our 'gut' and to have the power to know that we, as human beings, have immense knowledge of what is to come if we look deep enough. For we are angels in a physical body vessel, moving through this life until we reach home again.

How can I improve my intuition?

The key here really is trusting yourself, having more faith in yourself and having confidence in your decision-making. Once you overcome those barriers of self-doubt, you will see yourself grow in ways you never imagined. With self-acceptance, comes freedom. Raising your vibration is an integral part of strengthening your intuition. Why? Because, as I said earlier, intuition isn't just a gut feeling, it is a higher knowing, it is our soul and spirit working on a higher level. We are all-seeing, all-knowing creatures. We all have a psychic ability within us and we can all work on our intuition so that we can use it in our everyday life or in times of need. We are all guided, we just have to trust those messages within us and work on trusting ourselves again. After all, we were not born with doubts and insecurities, hey?

Mental blockages that disrupt our intuition can stem from many things, be it trauma, anxiety, maybe being bullied at some point in our life plays a role too. There are so many contributing factors. My lack of self-belief came from a long string of negative events in my life. I won't go into those now, but let's just say they knocked me down, brick by brick, until I was a shell of my former self. Fast forward some years and I took back the reins. I focused on my gift and built up my intuition by learning to trust myself again. THIS is how I am where I am today. I am eternally grateful that somewhere inside me is a burning fire, an energy so strong that it will not let me get past a certain 'bad point'. I KNOW I have great things to do; my intuition tells me so.

What are some things I can do to help me along the way?

So, I love meditation, and this is the first thing I advise people to do when they come to me for advice on, well … almost anything! That time away from our daily lives, negative influences and uncertainty really puts things into perspective. You see things from a higher level, a higher consciousness. Meditation gives you clarity and allows your mind, body and soul to take some much-needed time out in which you can regain your power and take back those reins.

There is no right or wrong way to meditate. It is personal to you so just do whatever feels right, whether that's sitting quietly in nature, lying in the bath or lighting candles and sitting in the lotus position! Personally, I like to lie in bed and use guided meditations on YouTube. My mind tends to wander so I like the spoken guidance!

I also love to use crystals; they have such a beautiful vibration and energy that can speak to our souls. They're a lovely, gentle stepping-stone into this world of spiritual self-care. There are thousands of different crystals, so you are sure to find a number of stones that speak to your heart. My best advice here would be to take your time, feel them and hold them, see how you connect with each stones' energy to find your perfect match!

I talk a lot on my socials about rituals and how wonderful they are, and also how simple they are. I honestly believe they are needed, more than you would realise. The ritual I mentioned in the beginning is so simple and is one of my favourites. We all have a bath or shower, and it is something we do every day without even thinking about it, right? So why not use this time to regroup and realign. Get the salt out; it's so simple!

Another thing I think is so important, even when we feel low or stuck, is that we make sure we continue to do the normal things like brush our teeth and brush our hair. These daily routines can become a ritual if you allow, which in turn becomes a tool you can use in building your trust and love with yourself. It all comes together in a beautiful manifestation of your best you. It is so important to get up and show up. Treat yourself like you would treat others. Give yourself that time and respect.

Intuition isn't something to be ignored. It is inbuilt in us for a reason. Some of us just need to rebuild that trusting relationship with ourselves and allow ourselves to open up and get back to the naturally spiritual mindset we were born into this physical world with.

Here's some questions for you to think on:

- What will I do today to look after myself?
- What tool(s) can I use today to increase my awareness?
- What do I need help and guidance with?

Then at the end of your day, think about these…

- Did I look after myself today?
- Did I make time for small self-care rituals? If not, why not?
- Did I take notice of the signs I was given today?
- What can I do differently tomorrow to further strengthen my intuition?

You have the power to make your life exactly as you want it, you really do. So, I challenge you to take back control, release those blockages that stop you moving forward and promise yourself you will take care of YOU.

I want you to come back to me in a week, a month or even a year and tell me the steps you took to improve your intuition and tell me the rewards you then received! Because I promise you, whoever you are, whatever you do, wherever you come from and no matter what you have experienced in the past, your intuition is guiding you from this point on to your best life. It's telling you right from wrong. It's telling you your next steps. You have now taken the reins again and you're ready to explore your higher consciousness.

Emma Divine xxx

Some of my favourite quotes!

Create a life that feels good on the inside, not just one that looks good on the outside. – Fearless Soul

Follow your intuition, it will always lead you to the right destination. – Fearless Soul

I am not in control of what happens around me, but I am always in control of what happens within me. – Fearless Soul

Realise deeply that the present moment is all you have. Make the NOW the primary focus of your life. – Eckhart Tolle

Don't gain the world and lose your soul; wisdom is better than silver or gold. – Bob Marley

My intuition is my guide; I will follow it and embrace it no matter what life brings. I know I am protected and I know I have happiness ahead. My intuition is always right, why? Because it is my link to the universe, my angels and my guides. – Emma Divine

Bio

Emma Divine IIHHT MICHT is a psychic medium and white witch, practising divination and giving psychic readings daily.

Born in Cardiff, UK, Emma studied holistic therapy and under that umbrella, qualified in holistic massage and healing, reflexology, aromatherapy, Indian head massage, anatomy, physiology, nutrition and chemistry! She had previously studied business management. She is planning to start her master's degree in late 2021, studying astrology and astronomy. The stars and universe are of fascination to her, and undertaking this course will also allow for a wider scope of services offered to clients.

Emma has always been spiritual, with her first memory of the like being before she was born! One to ask her about! Emma prides herself on her honest and open readings, connecting to spirit and using oracle cards to provide psychic insight into the future. With all of her work, Emma's aim is to inspire others to lead a calm and spiritual life. Her love of all things spiritual and magical comes through in all areas of her work, gently guiding clients, friends and strangers alike, into knowing they're not alone and coaching them in the ways they can use spirituality in their lives too. With her earliest memory being of when she was in her soul form, Emma has her whole life's worth of experience in these fields, making her a true and honest leader and coach in spiritual and magical guidance.

Work with Emma:

Join Emma on Facebook and Instagram for free weekly guidance and spiritual messages.

Connect with Emma:

Facebook: Emma Divine Psychic Medium (Group)

Instagram: @emmadivinepsychicmedium

Contact: (+44) 07398 101 133

GOOD VIBES: SELF-CARE FOR CONSCIOUS ENTREPRENEURS

Amanda Bazi

Love is patient, love is kind. It does not envy, it does not boast, it is not proud. It does not dishonour others, it is not self-seeking, it is not easily angered, it keeps no record of wrongs. Love does not delight in evil, but rejoices with the truth. It always protects, always trusts, always hopes, always perseveres.

– 1 Corinthians 13:4-7

Dear Amanda,

Thank you so much for being so brave and embarking on this exciting journey. I know that you doubt yourself at times, and you aren't really comfortable with not knowing what happens next … but I promise you … everything will turn out far better than you could have ever imagined. I know the desires of your heart, the purity of your soul and the strength of your will. I love you; I honour you, and I thank you for all that you are doing and all that you have become.

I am here with you, guiding you always.

I love you unconditionally and eternally.

Love,
Amanda (Your higher self)

My name is Amanda and I live in Sydney, Australia. It is May 2021, and what an amazing ride it has been to get to this point. As I reflect on my life and what it has taken to get me here, I am incredibly humbled and filled with so much joy to be able to share a little bit about myself and a few self-care tools I have learnt along the way. Thank you for being here and showing up for yourself!

Since birth, my initiation has been wild to say the least. Everything I have experienced and overcome has made me stronger and built resilience within me. In saying that, I wouldn't be half the woman I am today without my mother. She has been my guardian angel and protector. She has been by my side my whole life, loving me unconditionally, encouraging and supporting me all the way. She blessed me with the gift of unconditional love, kindness, compassion, freedom, integrity, loyalty, faith and inner strength. These became my highest core values, which I hold close to my heart and that I aim to share with the world and pass on to my children one day too.

In my life, I have directly or indirectly experienced and healed through domestic violence, childhood trauma, bullying and racism, toxic relationships, addiction, suicide, anxiety, depression, psychosis, post-traumatic stress disorder and most recently a toxic work environment. I have overcome painful emotions such as fear, anger, shame, betrayal, sadness, loneliness, low self-worth and so much more. But I allowed myself to *feel* which then allowed me to *heal.*

My self-healing journey began back in 2019, when I decided to take my life back and put an end to my own suffering. I was extremely unfulfilled working in the nine-to-five corporate world. I was completely out of alignment – mind, body and spirit – and knew that this was not my life. I innately knew I was destined for a higher calling. After working myself to my absolute limits, I was drained of my energy in every way possible. Mentally exhausted, in physical pain, emotionally depleted and crushed in spirit. All my passions and the things I used to love doing when I was younger were no longer present in my life.

I had graduated in psychology and was a volunteer Lifeline Crisis Supporter because I wanted to make a difference in this world and in people's lives. How did I end up in an office job, running around stressed out every day? This was not making a difference to me. This was not the impact I wanted to leave on the world. This is not what I had set out to do in life.

I lay down one night in tears, drained of all energy, after what would have been another day doing something I did not love wholeheartedly. I was intuitively guided to go to YouTube. I typed in 'music for healing'. Immediately, thousands of videos popped up. I selected one and let it play for hours as I just lay in bed and cried and cried and let it all out. I played different ones every day. The frequencies and sounds were soothing, calming and gave me a sense of clarity and peace. The peaceful music allowed me to shut out the outside world and just go back to basics. Back to myself. Back to my inner knowing. Back to my inner child. Back to innocence and a return to my inner sense. The only way out was to go within.

This lifechanging practice truly was the gateway to a whole new world for me. I started learning how different frequencies and vibrations affect us on all levels – physically, mentally, emotionally and spiritually. I couldn't believe I had never heard about this before. After years of primary, secondary and tertiary education, I had not once come across any literature that even remotely addressed the power of sound healing, frequencies and vibrations. I thought to myself 'What else don't I know?' That's the thing, when you're living unconsciously, you don't know what you don't know.

After working in a toxic environment for so long, I had become a negative, unhealthy version of who I truly am. I have always been happy, positive and laughing throughout my life, no matter what came my way. I had turned into a depressed, sad, person with negative self-talk. It wasn't the true me, and so I knew if I wanted to reclaim my life, I had to start by reclaiming my mind. I listened to all different videos with positive affirmations to reprogram my subconscious mind. I started with self-love. Self-love is the greatest and most transformative gift you can give yourself. No matter your past or your current circumstances, you have the power to love yourself unconditionally. I was very consistent and committed to my self-healing. Gradually, I started to develop new, positive thoughts, which then led to new unlimited beliefs, which inspired new positive emotions, that reignited the passion in me to take new action. This, ultimately, led me to co-create and manifest a whole new life.

I found the courage to break away from the outdated nine-to-five system and put all my time, energy and effort into myself and into discovering my highest purpose. I left the corporate world late in 2020 and decided to pursue my original passion for helping others. After some serious soul searching, I rediscovered my inner knowing that I am a healer. As a Divine Energy Healer, my mission is to support the healing of humanity on a physical, mental, emotional and spiritual level. I set up a private healing space in my home and feel grateful that I have the opportunity to be in service and to do something I love for others in a way that is authentic to me. I'm also so grateful that I now have so much more time to invest in my family, friends and myself and my own self-care as a conscious entrepreneur. As a way of giving back and showing gratitude for all my blessings, I will be sharing some of my main self-care tips that I hope you will find helpful and are able to easily incorporate into your day.

Daily self-care practices

In my daily self-care practices, I like to incorporate the elements of earth, air, fire and water. We are made of these elements, so when I feel out of balance, reconnecting with these elements is what helps bring me back to a state of harmony and peace.

To connect with the earth, the options are endless! One of my favourite practices is walking barefoot on grass. The free electrons from the earth transfer to the soles of your feet and this grounding effect is one of the most potent antioxidants that we know of. The earth is 'recharging' us with energy so to speak. Walking barefoot on grass, sand or soil, plants and roots us in direct contact with the electromagnetic healing properties of the earth. Doing this for just ten minutes a day relieves stress, improves sleep and overall health and wellbeing. I also love connecting with nature through cooking. Just washing fruits and vegetables is a meditative practice in itself as we are connecting with the produce of our earth as well as the element of water. As a new homeowner, I am also slowly but surely getting into gardening and loving it!

As a Leo, I am a fire sign and naturally drawn to the sun and fire. I sit in the sun almost every day for at least twenty minutes as that is all it takes to trigger your body to release over 200 microbials that fight fungi, parasites and viruses. How amazing is that! If the sun is too strong for you, try finding a spot in your home or office where the sun filters through and try laying or sitting in that instead. To connect with fire, I love lighting candles around my house and gazing at the flame. Flame gazing is such a simple, yet effective, meditative practice to calm your mind and promote inner stillness and relaxation. During wintertime, I love a good fireplace or bonfire at my brother's house. There is such a soothing ambience created by a crackling fire and a warmth that envelops you from within.

Another extremely important element to incorporate into your daily self-care practice is air. It is through breathwork that I connect with air. There are great breathing techniques out there. One example is the Wim Hof method, which helps regulate emotions, trauma, boost the immune system and so much more. In fact, breathing expels seventy per cent of our body's toxins, therefore, completely unrestricted breathing is essential in regulating our entire being and maintaining cognitive function. Going for a brisk walk and breathing in fresh air does wonders for the mind, body and soul. When you are feeling stressed, give yourself some time out of the external world and some time-in to reconnect with your breath and breathe in as slowly or as fast as feels natural for you. You will find a rhythm that is unique to you. Personally, I like to slowly breathe through my nostrils for as long as I can as my stomach expands, then allow the same breath to travel to my lungs, all the while my tongue is locked on the top of my mouth. I pause at the end for as long as possible, then unlock my tongue and exhale slowly out of my mouth. Repeat for as long or as little as you like.

Exercise is a great tool for self-care as it is a means of forced breathwork and a natural anti-depressant. Getting a good night's sleep is crucial and extremely restorative as it is long, uninterrupted breathwork. Take a moment now to take a few deep breaths in. Inhale and count to yourself one … two …three …four … and exhale one … two … three … four … and repeat.

As an empath, claircognisant and clairsentient being, I am very in tune with the energy of people. I actually feel what others are feeling in my own body at times. If you're anything like me and you really feel things to your core and are sensitive to others, I highly recommend cleansing your energy with water. My go-to energy-clearing self-care practice is a nice hot shower or bath. It dissolves any tension I've been holding onto and washes away the negative energy I may have circulating in my energy field. In the morning, a cold shower is the quickest thing to energise you and wake you up. The hot water is a completely different experience; rather than energising you, it relaxes you. Depending on your needs at the time, a hot or cold shower is a great self-care practice. I also regularly do shower meditations where I concentrate on the sound of the water and the feel of it on my skin. I visualise the water rapidly washing away all the tension I have been holding onto and envision it wash away down the drain. Give it a try and see how you feel!

Swimming in bodies of water in nature is deeply purifying and cleansing. I love going to the beach and swimming in the ocean. It is one of my happiest places to be! You can swim in lakes, ocean pools, rivers, springs and so much more. Discover what practice you are most aligned with and have fun with it!

Staying hydrated with clean, non-toxic, structured water is also an especially important part of looking after yourself. We are, on average, seventy per cent water, and approximately ninety per cent of our blood is water. Scientist Masaru Emoto has proven that water is conscious and can be programmed through human consciousness, which has a direct effect on the molecular structure of water. What does that mean for you? It means that your own thoughts, intentions, meditations or prayers can change the structure of water too! This means you can change the structure of your cells in your body directly through your consciousness! That is why positive self-talk is so important as our subconscious mind and body is listening to everything we think and say about ourselves.

Moreover, I am a very strong advocate for free flow and creative expression as conscious self-care practices. These can be anything from singing, dancing, writing, painting, yoga, exercise, stretching, fluid movement and creative design. These are just a few ways to tap into your inner self and allow the creative side of you to flow unrestricted, allowing any stagnant energy or emotions to move through you to be felt and released.

As a healer, one of my daily rituals is cleansing the energy of myself and my home. I cleanse my home by burning frankincense rocks, palo santo or white sage and going through every room in my house and blessing the space with my intentions and prayer. I also air my house out and let the sun shine in. I fill the home with peaceful, calming music and ensure I declutter my surroundings for mental clarity. In the words of feng shui master Marie Diamond 'your living space is your 3D vision board'.

One of the most powerful daily rituals I have been practicing as far back as I can remember is prayer. To me, prayer is sacred, divine communion with myself, my higher self and God. Just like your inner child is always with you, your higher self is also with you at all times, divinely guiding you. Do you ever have those profound moments of realisation or sudden epiphanies or even just having that real sense of inner knowing? That is your higher self-communicating with you!

Another daily ritual I recommend is sun gazing which is gazing into the sun at sunrise and sunset when there are zero UV rays. There are a multitude of health benefits of sun gazing, such as stress relief, increased energy, pineal gland activation, increased production of serotonin, increased melatonin for better sleep and so much more!

Lastly, I truly believe love and laughter is the best medicine. Have fun with life, let your inner child run wild and play!

As this chapter comes to a close, my message to you is to keep exploring your inner self and discover which daily practices and rituals light up your world. It is so important as a conscious entrepreneur that you fill your own cup and put all that love and energy back into yourself. Your mind, body and soul will thank you for it!

Written with love, from my heart and soul.

Love, Amanda

Bio

My name is **Amanda Bazi**, and I am thirty years old. I live in Sydney, Australia. As a psychology student, I learnt about human behaviour, cognitive functioning, mental health and so much more. As a volunteer Lifeline Crisis Supporter, I undertook Applied Suicide Intervention Skills Training (ASIST) and was trained in mental health counselling. I have volunteered in youth and aged care facilities such as Uniting Aged Care and Marist Youth Care. I graduated in psychology and have been using my skills working in a global fast-moving consumer goods company for the past eight years across sales and marketing.

In October 2020, I decided to do some further study and reignite my passion for helping others. The nine-to-five dream I was sold was completely unfulfilling for me, and I knew I was destined for a higher calling.

I attained qualifications in neurolinguistic programming (NLP) and Time Line Therapy® and also trained as a hypnotist and life coach. I still felt, after all the education and experience, that there was a crucial missing element in everything I had studied. It was the unseen force driving us and the planet – ENERGY.

I felt so aligned with energy healing and took an angelic reiki course. I finally felt like I was in the right place in divine timing. Although, I did not feel aligned channelling spirits or ascended masters or using my body as a vessel for anything outside myself. I never have, so it did not resonate. I have always had a divine communion with God since I was a little girl through prayer. Through prayer, I received my message to connect straight to God when performing my healings.

I have since created my own method of energy healing called Divine Energy Healing where I connect straight to God and one's higher self when I lay hands healing others. This is my divine gift to offer the world.

My mission is to heal humanity through healing past trauma and connecting with one's higher self, to remove density from one's body and dissolve any fallen architecture, negative programming or fallen beings in one's energy field, activating one's organic divine blueprint and bringing organic light back into the body, empowering others to live a life that is authentic to who they truly are and coming into complete alignment – mind, body and soul.

I feel so grateful and blessed that I have come to this point in my journey, and I am incredibly humbled to be able to offer my gifts to the world and YOU, the lovely person reading this!

Work with Amanda:

If you would like to book a Divine Energy Healing session with me, I am available over the phone, video call or in person in my healing space in Sydney. Special offer of 10% off all services for readers.

Connect with Amanda:

Facebook: GOOD VIBES Holistic Healing

Instagram: @goodvibesholistichealing

Email: goodvibesandcoau@gmail.com

Website: www.goodvibesholistichealing.com

The only way out is in.
-Amanda

SECTION 7:
ENERGETIC SELF-CARE

INTRODUCTION

Tracey Jewel

The energies of the earth and the universe swirl around us constantly. At any given moment, this energy is surrounding us to bring support to our physical, mental and emotional needs. When this energy is misaligned, it can make everything feel unbalanced.

That energy though is the key to unlocking our greatest potential. The meridians of energy are running through every fibre in our bodies and connected to all our organs. Human beings are naturally built for prime balance, but those energetic imbalances can scramble the signals and compromise your wellness as well as your quality of life.

The good news is, you can learn how to correct these imbalances and set things on an even keel once more. Energetic self-care helps you learn to breathe and channel that energy the right way. In this chapter, we'll learn how to restore balance to the nervous system and set harmony among the entire body for the best results.

Think of it like physical self-care except on a more internal scale, focusing on all those parts of the body that make it run like the finely tuned machine it was designed to be!

RECONNECT TO THE FLOW OF ABUNDANCE THROUGH ENERGY HEALING

Keryn Rose

Abundance is not something we acquire. It is something we tune into. – Wayne Dyer

'You've got cancer, Keryn.'

These were the words I said to myself as I looked in the mirror on the morning of my hysterectomy surgery. I was only forty-five!

'But you're going to be okay.'

Somehow, I 'knew' I had cancer. And somehow, I also 'knew' I would be okay. The surgery went ahead as planned, standard pathology tests were done and as it turned out, I did indeed have cancer.

I found out that morning how powerful my intuition can be. And I sit here sharing my story with you as a cancer thriver and surfing the flow of my abundant life. That moment in front of the mirror was a beautiful and well-timed reminder of the gift of intuition and flow of abundance that I had always had access to, but which I had somehow become disconnected from. It also reminded me of the importance of trusting and believing in myself. This experience fuelled my desire to help others reconnect to their own intuition and stay fully connected with the flow of abundance.

Being 100 per cent connected with yourself and your intuition allows you access to a better understanding of yourself, which opens up the space for you to experience your unlimited potential and uniqueness.

Society appears to easily accept that mothers can sense or feel when there is something not quite right about their kids. It's called 'mother's intuition'. I was reminded of this when, sitting with my sixteen-month-old son three days after his open-heart surgery, I sensed something wasn't right. His energy lacked vitality. I could 'see' him drowning. I called the nurse over and, on listening to his chest, a flurry of activity broke out. He was whisked back into surgery to drain fluid from his little lungs. These days, every time I see all six feet and two inches of him, I am grateful for what I 'saw' that day.

Intuition is something you are born with. It is your very own personal guidance system, and it becomes more powerful when you are fully connected with yourself. It is my wish to help you learn to feel comfortable using it, opening up access to the flow of abundance that is rightfully yours.

I love the sound of the word abundance. There is a certain richness about it. It is not often I see a colour when I hear a word, but when I hear the word abundance; I see the colour purple: a beautiful deep rich purple.

Your connection with the flow of abundance is directly linked to your connection with yourself. I do not believe you can be fully connected and in the flow of abundance without being fully connected and in flow with yourself. Are you fully connected to your flow of abundance?

I would like to ask you three questions:

1. Would you describe your relationship with your finances as abundant?

2. Would you describe your relationship with your health and wellbeing as abundant?
3. Would you describe your relationship with others and, more importantly, with yourself as abundant?

How did you go? Were you able to answer 'Yes' to any of these questions? I have asked these questions many times, and I have discovered the majority of people feel a lack of abundance in their lives, whether it be financial, health and wellbeing or relating to others and themselves. I truly believe this is a reflection of a lack of connection with themselves.

So, how do you become disconnected from yourself? It happens very slowly as you live your life. My most memorable point of disconnection was when I was a business owner, mother, wife and daughter. Even just writing it stirs up feelings of overwhelm. It was at this point I was diagnosed with uterine cancer. It was a universal wake up call for me. I didn't realise just how disconnected I'd become from myself. Twelve years later I continue to learn of the abundant healing power found in staying fully connected with myself.

In my work as an intuitive energy healer, particularly as a certified body code practitioner, many people I work with feel stuck in their lives. They just don't feel themselves. Their life lacks real purpose and they're searching for freedom. A common thread running through their stories is a lack of vitality and flow! It's like a dimmer switch has been turned down on their awesomeness, and they can't remember where the dial is. For these people there is a real lack of connectedness with themselves. Together, through the power of energy healing,

we work to reconnect them with themselves.

For an abundant relationship with your health and wellbeing, I work with you to give your body full access to its healing power. Working together we unleash your body's natural healing power by freeing you of limiting beliefs, patterns of failure and self-sabotage that may be hiding in your body as energetic imbalances. For an abundant relationship with others and, more importantly, with yourself, I work with you to release the negative energy of past painful experiences related to love, relationships and family ties, opening you up to receiving true and lasting love of all kinds. For an abundant relationship with your finances, I work with you to unlock your potential for wealth and abundance by releasing the imbalances that cause money blocks and other limitations.

With all that is happening in the world at the moment, you may be wondering how much control you have over yourself and your life – if any! The awesome news is that while you have no control over what is happening around you, you have 100 per cent control over how you respond to it. Chances are, you are so connected with what is going on outside of you, that you have become disconnected with what is within you! For you to be able to optimise your awesomeness, it's important to set aside time every day to stay fully connected with yourself and to grow your relationship with yourself.

End your day

Here are three gentle ways to unplug from the outer world at and reconnect with yourself at the end of your day:

1. Imagine the transition from workday to your time: Visualise yourself moving out of your 'day' and into your inner sanctum. See yourself walking through a door and into a space that takes you deep into a feeling of peace and relaxation. One of my favourite places is sitting on a beach, watching the sunset.
2. End your day with an attitude of gratitude: Find three things to be grateful for today. The powerful energy of gratitude will flow

through you, flooding your body with positive vibes. In a world that can easily be seen as negative, being grateful for something shows it is important for you and reflects a sense of worthiness to you.

3. Say 'I Love You' to yourself: Say the words 'I love you [your name]' out loud to yourself. When you give yourself a gift of love, you are actively engaging in the most important relationship in your life – your relationship with yourself. The ability to show yourself how important you are to yourself is the foundation on which every other relationship you have will be built.

Start your day

Here are three beautiful ways to reinforce your connection with yourself before engaging with the outer world:

Create your day: There is something very precious about mornings. It's a new beginning, and a powerful time to create. When you wake up, before you get out of bed, set some intentions. Visualise your day unfolding as you would like it. This practice engages you with your day on a conscious level and gives your day framework.

1. Start your day with an attitude of gratitude: It's so easy to overlook the little things that create your world. I love acknowledging the fact I'm alive when I wake up, knowing there are people in the world that won't be experiencing that today. An attitude of gratitude reinforces joy and positivity in your daily life because it focuses a light on what is resonating with you.
2. Do something today that makes your heart sing: Create a list of things that make your heart sing. Those little things that fill your heart with joy. I love watching the sunrise as I walk along the river. I love watching the sunset over the ocean. What makes

your heart sing? Snuggled up on the couch with a good book? Soaking in a warm bath? Enjoying a good coffee in your favourite café? Once you have created your list, make time each day to do at least one of them.

There is one very special person that came into your life with you and will leave this life with you. That very special person is you! You are the central figure in your story. You are also the writer, the director, the star and very often the critic of your story. It is all about you, and it all starts with you. Every day you are given a new opportunity to be the best you that you can be and surf your unique flow of abundance. Make time to fully connect with yourself every day.

Investing in yourself is the best investment you will ever make! Every little bit matters because you matter! Do you believe you matter? Do you feel you are worth taking care of? Are you ready to experience greater levels of abundance in your life?

I can help! I offer a FREE, no obligation thirty-minute discovery call designed to give you clarity and guidance on how you can experience greater abundance in all areas of life through connecting to the powerful healing power within you.

Bio

Keryn Rose is an intuitive energy healer. As a young child, Keryn knew there was more to life than what her physical eyes could see. She could feel it. It was on the morning of her hysterectomy surgery when she looked into the mirror and told herself she had cancer, which turned out to be true, that Keryn realised the power of her gifts. Now she combines her intuitive gifts with an energy healing modality known as the Body Code, assisting people all over the world to find harmony and balance, relieve stress and support their body's natural ability to heal.

Qualifications:

- Student of the University of Life (current)
- Certified Emotion Code practitioner 2012
- Certified Body Code practitioner 2015
- Reiki Level 1 2019 (Intuitive Reiki International)
- Reiki Level 2 2020 (Intuitive Reiki International)

Work with Keryn:

Are you curious about how energy healing can help you to reconnect with the abundance and freedom that naturally flows within you? Using the link below, you can claim a FREE, no-obligation discovery call with Keryn, and discover for yourself the profound healing power that lies within you. Go to this link to book your session now: https://calendly.com/keryn-4/30-min-discovery-call

Connect with Keryn:
Facebook: https://www.facebook.com/kerynrose.com.au/?modal=admin_todo_tour
Instagram: https://www.instagram.com/kerynjrose/
LinkedIn: https://www.linkedin.com/in/keryn-rose-98a5ba1a1/
Website: www.kerynrose.com.au

THE VICE OF SELF-SACRIFICE

Dani Alkhemi

Self-care is never a selfish act it is simply good stewardship of the only gift I have, the gift I was put on Earth to offer to others.

– Parker Palmer

Self-sacrifice has long been packaged and sold to us as one of the noblest virtues one can possess. And we have bought it. Little wonder really, for we see sacrifice being glorified over and over again in books, movies and on Netflix. For millennia we have heard about the tenets of martyrdom through religious doctrines. We have heard countless stories told and retold by family members that leave us with a type of reverence for sacrificial acts, subconsciously taking it upon ourselves as our duty to uphold the standard. We even include tales of sacrifice whenever we connect with friends or colleagues, as though we should be sporting a badge of honour for our efforts.

But what if self-sacrifice is costing us more than we realise? What if this whole notion that has been sold to us as a noble virtue is undermining our quality of life? What if self-sacrifice is a symptom of something else much more problematic? I learnt the answers to these questions the hard way.

During my early thirties, I returned to contracting at my favourite company. I was thrilled at the prospect of being back with a team that felt like family and a brand I was passionate about. However, not long after I returned, the privately-owned company was sold to a publicly listed company.

In the initial stages, I loved it. But a few weeks later, I felt more like a machine and less like a human. Everything kept expanding at a chaotic speed as if we were caught up in a relentless business hurricane. Those of us with greater responsibilities as managers became more and more stretched as expectations for ever-higher performance and the mantra of more, more, more came bearing down upon our shoulders like invisible wooden yokes, two sizes too big.

As the business kept growing aggressively, there was an unspoken expectation to just grin and bear it, to keep pushing without compromise until results were achieved. Six days a week, day after day, I was doing a job designed for two people.

Night-time brought little respite. I went from being a sound sleeper to waking in the early hours thinking about things that were blowing out of control, only to fall asleep and reawaken with a new problem dancing around my mind. Or worse, I would spend the whole night dreaming about work!

Unable to disconnect, I would wake up feeling like a zombie and drag myself through the day jacked up on coffee and adrenaline. Lunch breaks morphed into snatching whatever food I could shovel into my mouth in between customers and sales staff so that I could be ready to make deals happen at short notice. My weight crept up with poor food choices and chronic stress. In small moments between dealing with floods of people, I noticed my breathing was shallow, rapid and choppy. Sometimes my heart rate would speed up like an engine revving for no obvious reason.

In my home life, my relationship was also being negatively impacted because I did not have the bandwidth to go anywhere or spend quality time together. All I wanted was to be left alone, in my own space. I was irritable and wired, and at times not the nicest person to be around. I craved stillness and silence, which caused heated arguments. Tension in my jaw and pressure on my shoulders increased daily, bit by bit, so I felt like I was stuck in a vice. Still, I kept pushing harder and harder, until I couldn't bear it anymore.

I finally hit the brick wall at the end of a chaotic Friday filled with the usual month-end drama. Nothing was going right. I was sprinting from one fire to the next, torn in twenty different directions at once, with people pulling and clawing at me. My only respite was going to the restroom to catch my breath just to be left alone for a minute or two.

Then it dawned on me. It felt like I was battling an avalanche every day, and I realised a part of me was scared of slowing down in case I would not be able to get back up to speed again. Being so tightly strung I felt like I might explode if I breathed too deeply. I felt foggy and heavy. My brain kept short-circuiting. Bone-deep sadness washed over me. I looked in the mirror and thought to myself: *This is not right. This is not how life is supposed to be.*

When my manager called me into the office, I was on the verge of a meltdown. Just the act of stopping and being for a moment to catch my breath was enough to crack the façade I had worked so hard to project. Tears threatened to fall. Intense anger welled up from deep inside me. *How could I be so stupid?* Here I was showing my weakness to everyone. My inner critic screamed at me to toughen up. Then I caught sight of my main manager looking at me with a mixture of empathy and curiosity as if to say: *Are you okay?* I looked away and tried to focus on something mundane on the floor. A scrap of paper caught my eye, but it was too late. The dam had already burst its banks.

Tears flooded out of me like Niagara Falls. The more I tried to contain myself, the worse my sobbing became. I gasped for air like

I had been winded. All three managers instantly stopped what they were doing, stared bug-eyed at me and exchanged awkward glances. I felt like a blubbering fool, and yet the torrent of tears would not stop. Months of having relentless pressure to over-perform without enough support had finally taken their toll and were now laid bare for all to see.

That was a turning point for me. I made a list of demands that were non-negotiable. All of which were accepted on the spot. Over the next few weeks, better systems were put into place and everything was running shipshape with less stress. I focused on rebalancing my health and wellbeing, invested time and energy back into my relationship and went back to sleeping peacefully at night, vowing never to play this game again.

Whilst my story of self-sacrifice ended well, others are not so fortunate. The Harris Poll, an online survey, found in 2020 that more than three-quarters (seventy-six per cent) of employed Americans report they are currently experiencing worker burnout, and employed women are more likely to report they are currently experiencing worker burnout than employed men (eighty per cent versus seventy-two per cent). Worryingly, nearly one in ten American employees (nine per cent) say that nothing would help them avoid or reduce experiencing worker burnout.

When working in a fast-paced, high-performance environment or running a business with a big vision, self-care is often the first thing put on the backburner. Why? Because there's a belief that in order to achieve the big important stuff, you must be prepared to sacrifice yourself, and to do so is noble. Not only is this concept flawed, outdated, and unsustainable, it is not even aligned to the way we were actually designed to operate.

Because we have made greater success synonymous with hustling harder, pushing through and overloading ourselves, we have paved the way for an inevitable crash and burn. We value self-sacrifice over self-care so much, we ignore the many red flags before trouble strikes. It is only when burnout, depression, anxiety or adrenal fatigue start showing up that we recognise something is wrong. Yet sometimes even this is not enough to wake us up, and we make the mistake of brushing the symptoms off as a passing phase.

We then seek the convenience of a quick fix, using methods that lull us into feeling better but are temporary at best, and sometimes even more destructive. We end up popping pills, consuming too much sugar or fatty foods, and increasing or adopting addictive behaviours, loading more stressors onto ourselves. Or we book a long weekend away and cross our fingers in the hope that it will all get better given enough time and a little rest.

But the problem is the underlying issue has still not been resolved, so it is a matter of time before the symptoms make their reappearance – usually when we least expect it. Surface treatment of problems will always get us shallow results. The truth is, illness is always a symptom of dis-ease within oneself. So, in order to shift things for good, we need to address these issues at the level they started, not the level they are presenting.

In the symptoms mentioned above, it is the belief of self-sacrifice that is the driving force behind the behaviours that lead to the symptoms. For example, burnout is about sacrificing one's total wellbeing and often one's boundaries in order to get results, achieve and perform.

Now, let's go one layer deeper. What is sitting beneath that destructive belief, driving someone towards self-sacrifice? Well, sacrifice means to give something valued up for the sake of other conditions. In this case, we could say that someone is sacrificing themself for the sake of their job/title/business/company/results.

Why would they do that? The truth is they do not value themself. Deep down they believe, feel, think, experience, and see themself as being unworthy. And that energy of unworthiness is the real culprit that's fuelling the behaviour which creates burnout. Something I call a 'power block'.

What are power blocks?

Well, if anything before this point has resonated with you, then you have them. Power blocks sabotage you on multiple levels and cost you a great deal because they are kind of like hidden success gremlins. Power blocks are multifaceted and multidimensional in nature so they can impact you mentally, emotionally, energetically, spiritually, physically and financially.

Why are they so disruptive? Because they are making everything much harder than necessary, which means the amount of effort you have to exert to achieve what you want is exhaustive. So, you will feel like you are always having to bulldoze your way to greater success, usually at the cost and sacrifice of something else, be that your health, happiness, impact, energy, relationship or yourself – maybe even all of them.

In a nutshell: Power blocks stop you from reaching your highest potential.

Don't worry, there is good news too. First of all, if you recognise you have some power blocks, it's not your fault. Mostly power blocks sit at an unconscious level as they have been created through traumatic events in both this lifetime and other lifetimes (yes you are a multidimensional being). They are also caused by intense experiences during our formative years and even get passed on by our ancestors.

Second, there is a massive upside to having power blocks because when you get to the heart of the matter and alchemise them, greater success becomes much easier for you to achieve. As your hidden power is liberated from these blocks, the drag and resistance they used to create will turn around to streamline your efforts, which means you'll blast past the stratosphere with ease. Like you see on the graph, the best part is all this is done from a place of authentic power and self-care. Now doesn't that sound a whole lot easier and nicer than sacrificing yourself to get results?

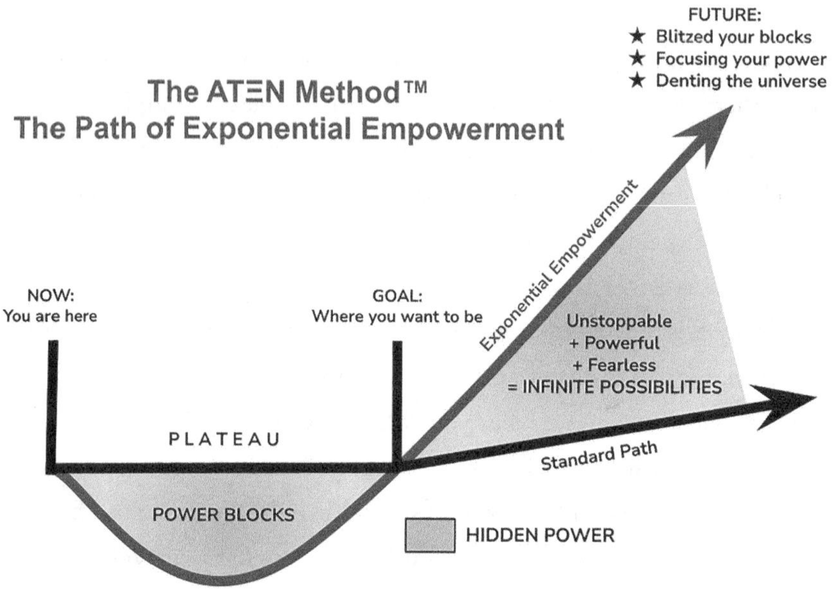

Practical Power Tips for Transforming Self-Sacrifice into Self-Care:

Unblock your throat chakra! Speak up and ask for what you need. Express yourself. The worst you will get is a 'no', and then you can decide what you want to do next. Always honour yourself, no matter what.

If you are running your own business or team, make sure there is enough support for you and your staff members. Do a weekly check-in to gauge stress levels and share creative ideas and solutions to ease the load.

Ask staff, friends and even family members what they think would make impactful and easy to implement self-care tools so that it doesn't fall on you to think of everything. Often genius ideas will come from outside of your work realm.

Implement and rotate new non-negotiable self-care rituals like daily meditation (seriously, ten minutes is better than nothing!), fasting, juicing, regular massages, yoga, tai chi, going to bed earlier, plus digital and social media detoxes on your days off.

Turn your phone on flight mode when sleeping and get it away from your head, or better yet put it in another room for the sake of your brain and wellbeing (just looking at your phone during the night can overstimulate your brain and have you wired for hours after).

Download apps that help to keep you accountable and track your wellbeing, sleep quality, stress levels, food choices and daily exercise so you can track and measure your progress.

Commit to becoming a Wellness Warrior and buddy up with a reliable friend or a network of like-minded people to check in daily with your wellness wins until it becomes second nature.

Look into purchasing high-quality EMF (electromagnetic field) protective items that you can wear and place at your desk and in your home to offset wi-fi, mobile networks, Bluetooth and everything else technology-related that continually wreaks havoc on your body, bio-field and immune system.

Salt lamps are a great investment because they produce negative ions which have the same impact on you as walking along the beach when the waves crash upon the shore. If you cannot have them at work, then get some at your home in places where you can leave them going 24-hours a day, like the living room. The beautiful soft glow emitted is soothing to look at too after a stressful day.

Ask yourself the question: 'Is what I am doing worthwhile?' If you don't like the answer, dare to do something about it.

Contrary to what we have been led to believe, self-sacrifice is not the answer and never will be. Greater success should never come at the expense of one's health, happiness or self. Radical change can only happen when self-care is normalised as part of everyday business ethos and by us as wellness-respecting individuals. If we are to truly thrive and succeed at higher levels, then self-care must become non-negotiable.

If nothing else, please remember, your true value has nothing to do with your job title, business achievements, income, results or what you are prepared to sacrifice. You, precious one, are valuable beyond measure. To prioritise your happiness and health is to prioritise yourself. You are your single greatest asset. Aren't you worth investing in and protecting?

Bio

Dani Alkhemi believes you are more powerful than you realise, and you shouldn't have to sacrifice yourself, health or happiness to achieve the big, important stuff.

Born with incredible spiritual abilities, which have been refined over her lifetime, Dani is passionate about using her unique gifts to help the top one per cent of conscious leaders unlock and activate their highest potential so they can live and lead from their next-level greatness and unleash their most audacious vision.

After a decade of working in a high-performance environment, where hustle reigned supreme, success came with personal sacrifices and burnout was standard, Dani realised she was meant for greater things.

Despite a healthy six-figure income, results ranking in the top percentile nationally and $100 million in sales to her name, deep down Dani knew she was secretly selling herself short by not living to her highest potential and making the best use of her gifts and talents.

So, Dani quit her job and booked a trip to Egypt to do some serious soul searching. While exploring inside the King's Chamber of the Great Pyramid, something extraordinary happened. As a result, Dani's innate genius and spiritual gifts became more potent and honed, while an ancient key of power was reactivated – a secret key traditionally reserved for helping Pharaohs flourish.

What took mere minutes forever transformed Dani and sparked an epic, nine-year quest focusing on the principles of power, harnessing untapped potential and the importance of purpose.

From here, Dani created the ATΞN Method™, a dynamic fusion of ancient Egyptian alchemy and The Three Codes of Power, which transforms conscious leaders into fearless leaders so they can blitz their blocks, focus their power and dent the universe.

Now this no-nonsense Rebel Warrior Priestess is on a mission to exponentially empower her clients to become fearless leaders who embody their truth, power and greatness unapologetically so they can disrupt the status quo, transform outdated, misaligned systems and collapse fear-based paradigms that are currently keeping the masses stuck, suffering and struggling.

Live Courageously. Lead Fearlessly.

Dani's Gift to You:

Discover your fearless leader archetype – Do you know your unique 'power avatar'? Access Dani's special profiling tool designed for mission-driven conscious leaders. Take the test to discover your fearless leader archetype and reveal your unique power avatar, signature leadership style and the famous Pharaoh who embodied it best. Plus, you'll get free bonuses when you download your profile. You can take the free test at: danialkhemi.com/flq

Connect with Dani:
Facebook: facebook.com/DaniAlkhemi
Instagram: @danialkhemi
LinkedIn: linkedin.com/in/danialkhemi
Website: danialkhemi.com

ANXIETY AND OVERWHELM: KEEPING IT REAL

Meagan Kerr

It's about living real, and living with joy.

– Meagan Kerr, The Real Living Movement

Overwhelm

Drowning, not waving … Can you see I am smiling? … I'm not smiling … really!

A personal story of the experience of overwhelm in the life of a happy and successful mum

and practitioner who faced life, work and raising kids.

This is a story of BIG emotion. It's big because it is never an emotion that comes along alone. There are BIG emotions that arrive all on their own accord, like grief or fear, for example. That single emotion is all consuming. You feel it with every inch of your being. And, understandably, it can consume your thoughts, your wellbeing, and be expressed in how you speak and think. It's like saying, 'I'm consumed by grief' or 'I'm stricken by fear'. These are clearly BIG emotions. But what I am talking about is the BIG O. It's Overwhelm. It is not a single emotion, it is so much more, and never arrives on its own.

Overwhelm is an emotional experience of an intense set of feelings or sensations that is bigger than stress and is compounded. It's a layering effect. Much like the layering of blankets when the cooler autumn nights start after the solstice each year. They increase the comfort, they increase the warmth and the feeling of safety or nurture. But the emotional layers of overwhelm increase exponentially the discomfort, the pressure. They smother and make us struggle every single day. You are stuck. Stressed. Anxious. You try to go about your day, stick to the routine things you need to do, but there are moments you just feel that you can't. They may take you by surprise, but they will infiltrate every area of your life and not go unnoticed. You may hear it in the tone of your voice, in your snap at your partner, the increase in your yelling, the experience of tears rolling down your face when you are driving to work or listening to the radio and the overthinking of the simple stuff. A trip to the supermarket becomes an event. The phone rings and you can't pick it up as you feel like you might vomit. There's the nausea, the lack of emotion you show when your child tells you about their day, the panic evoked, the anxiety rush that you feel over and over … and this happens all at the same time.

The immensity of overwhelm is on the increase in our society. A 2014 study reported in

forbes.com stated fourteen per cent of people reported they had experienced the feeling of overwhelm. In 2018, Mentalhealth-uk.org reported seventy-four per cent of people have experienced overwhelm. Although these are unrelated studies and on separate communities, what it does highlight is the collective experience of overwhelm has significantly increased, and the experience is not limited to a segment of community, but it has a global reach.

In my own clinic-based practice, over the past decade I have seen an enormous increase in the experience of overwhelm. Where, many years ago, clients more often came to work through a BIG emotion, a life event or a specific issue. This has completely changed. Now people come with the main reason being overwhelm. What is more alarming is the age range of this experience. There is no age group, sex or socioeconomic measure that excludes you from this experience. None.

These are all ways the experience of overwhelm have been described to me by many, many clients over the years. It is also my personal experience.

My Story

My own experience of this most intense set of experiences – emotional, physical and mental – the fear, the anxiety, the nausea, the panic, the brain fog, the fake smiles, the screaming from the inside out, the coping, the not coping … all started for me when the youngest of my four children began having seizures, which led to the eventual diagnosis of a genetic disorder called cerebral cavernous malformations (CCM).

She was eight, having multiple absent seizures a day – enough fear to stress out any parent, but, as a practitioner, I felt I had the skills and experience in health to deal with what she was going through, support her and get the best help possible for her. Yet, I felt moments of absolute overwhelm. We had also just sold our family home and moved, and I had to find a new clinic location. I had left my financially stable job to follow my passion full-time of working as a healer, my three other children also had various changes to navigate including new ways to get to school, a move and stuff teenagers have to negotiate in life. My hubby had also changed his job, and with our move he was further away from home every day. Despite this, the daily tasks we as high functioning women just seem to do continued.

I started to seek research for the rare condition, I still waved at the familiar faces at school pickup and drop off, I smiled, I cooked meals, I cleaned, I did the washing, I drove children to school and after school activities, I ran a business, I paid bills, bought groceries, and, after about six months or so of this, inside I was screaming. I had these random moments where I would drift to other parts of my consciousness – a daydream that was more like an escape. There were moments where tears just ran down my face, where they were actually annoying, like I had a leak. There were times in the shower where I sobbed, times where it was the only place I felt I could think. But, overall, I was turning off, swallowing emotions like lollies, holding it in. All while I logically knew I had a lot to cope with.

I found myself doing the weirdest behaviours that just weren't me. If the phone rang with a no Caller ID, I would get the massive physical sensation of my heart and stomach all falling from a great height. It made me want to vomit. *Like, what the …? Answer the phone, woman. It's probably a new client!* But I felt that at any moment I might just physically turn into the crumble topping on an apple crumble dessert and literally fall apart: the type of falling apart that was not going to be a short fall; it was going to be so far away from me that it too felt overwhelming. Sometimes you have a lot going on in life and you just need to have a good chat, a good cry and you know you will feel better. Then you gather your resources, or as I like to say, you put your big girl boots on and off you go! It was so not like this. This was overwhelming.

As a very logical person, I almost wanted to slap myself. I am a practitioner! I had skills and experience that had helped many people through the exact same stuff. I pulled some of these out of my back pocket, I tried to do them, I had moments of feeling a bit better, a bit like progress. That was all until that one day.

That one day, I had gotten the four children off to school. A mother's joy, a day off without anyone else at home. I was looking forward to it … although also unnerved by it. My youngest, despite being unwell, loved her new school and friends and had the most beautiful soul as a teacher. She let her be there and cared for her and called me if needed, as I was literally a three-minute drive away from school. But that day, my happy and inquisitive second grader asked me a question on the way to school, as kids often do when they have you alone in the car. She had been told that one of her 'get better' options was surgery. As anyone would, faced with this as an option, she asked all types of questions, like, 'will it hurt', 'when can I go back to school', and so on. But this day, she asked me, 'mum, can angels have babies?' I took a huge breath as I looked at her in the rear vision mirror, and calmly replied: 'I don't know sweetheart, but I would hope so because little angels would be super cute'.

I got back to the car after taking her to the classroom, took the three-minute drive home and, as I pulled up to the gate, the tears started again. But this time, as I stopped the car to go and open the gate, I couldn't move. I was stuck. My limbs had become instantly heavy and weak. The tears intensified. I couldn't take a breath. Was I going to die? Holy crap, breathe, I thought to myself. So many tears, I could not see. So much pressure and weight in every cell of my body. I was still stuck. My inner voice screamed at me: Take a breath! I panted, much like a dog. I still could not see a thing, or move. The physical sensation was painful, heavy. More panting. This calm inner voice was saying: 'Hey, this is an experience a client told me about – something I had only ever read about – this is intense! It was like part of my being was outside my body, still analysing, commenting and talking me through what to do. It told me to put the car into park, put the hand break on and try to reach for my phone in the centre console because 'girl, you need help'.

I think I sat in that spot for about three hours. I lost track of time. Somewhere in the process I managed to call my parents. When the phone rang, I really wasn't sure I would be able to talk. Between the panting, I said something my parents understood and, as the panting and tears continued, my mum's voice just said: 'It's okay, we are on the way; we are on the way'.

Outer me knew they would be forty minutes to an hour. Hubby was one-and-a-half hours away, so I next tried to contact him. I focused on the panting breath. That was enough. Just breathe.

It was all those layers, absolutely crushing my soul. This was the crumble I tried to avoid. The intense heaviness coupled with my lack of self-care along the way had all compounded to that moment. That scary, uncontrollable, emotion filled every second. I spent the rest of that day telling my husband and parents all that was on my mind, every single part, everything I was holding onto, all the unsaid words, the songs that triggered me to cry, the worries of everything that we were experiencing. And we discussed in-depth what help I needed.

Worst of all, despite the catharsis, I also knew it was only the beginning, because really nothing going on in life had changed. But I had. I now had the amount of relief I needed and the kick up the butt to make me make the changes I needed and get help.

I was very lucky in that I was able to turn to a mentor, another energy practitioner, to support me. And my family understood that this type of healing would help me.

We are amazing beings capable of more than we could possibly know. This life experience, the years of study, my own interests in energetic development of our nervous system, coupled with my soul awareness of the reason I am here and my life mission to share the understanding that energy is at the centre of everything – every emotion, every cell, every breath – made me the successful person I continue to be.

Energy is the source of our function, our being, and if we ignore any of it, it will consume us with its power. After that day, I vowed to not ignore this knowledge, the tools and techniques that come with leading a life of health with energy awareness. With support, I engaged in a self-care routine, and we found care for my daughter to not only address the medical definitions and awareness of this rare disease, but also an energy team who would continue to work on potential – the limitless possibility, which she absolutely is.

Self-Care Advice

Self-care with energy awareness can be as simple as spending time writing in a journal. This could be to acknowledge gratitude – what you are thankful for each and every day – or it could be to tell your story – sort your thoughts, write your wins and your challenges – as a type of narrative to re-read as a reward for yourself for your achievements. Or it could be a different type of writing, where you do not think about the story, the structure, the spelling or the grammar, you simply write. You might like to set a timer, say for four- to ten-minutes, and just write. Release all you are thinking or holding on too, absolutely anything that pops into your awareness. Get it out, release it, then, when the timer goes off, don't re-read it, just throw it away. You do not need to hold on to any of it. It is done. So be it.

To move from anxious, stuck, and stressed – the ASS place – to fun, freedom and fulfillment is absolutely the best move you will ever make! My signature methodology, developed from real life, clinic work and personally working with many people, sets the pathways allowing you to be able to REST, RESET and RESTART in your REAL life.

My life's purpose, what I am really passionate about, is ensuring more people have the awareness of energy-based tools and techniques that are capable of creating infinite energetic potential for us all. Changing lives, empowering souls, producing joy. I want to ensure that, as leaders within our families, we don't just understand this concept, but that we use it, speak it, live it, share it with our friends and pass the tools and understandings on to the next generation.

I would love to start this with you. Connect with me, or listen to my podcast 'Daggy Mums. LifeUnstuck' and let me show you how to get into REAL living.

Bio

Meagan Kerr is a gifted energy healer and registered specialised kinesiologist, among many other things. She is an avid learner, with a special interest in neuro development and quantum medicine. She is owner/practitioner at One Health and Wellness Clinic and is the creator/mentor at One Health College for Energetic Wellness and the RSA Method. Born and raised in Sydney and residing in the Hawkesbury district, she enjoys time with family, sunny days and swimming.

Meagan initially studied a Bachelor of Arts degree majoring in psychology and computing. She applied her skills in IT and people management in the manufacturing and finance industries. She returned to her love of understanding healing from a pure holistic viewpoint retraining as a kinesiologist. After running her clinic for a decade, she decided her unique approach and methodology needed to be shared and taught to all households as a set of tools to enhance communication and connection. This mission led to the birth of One Health

College, the only place where you can learn about her unique Real Self Alignment method. Her journey continues with the next collaboration on this authoring journey.

After being witness to a large increase of stress and anxiety related issues in her clinic clients, and even in her own life, Meagan has formulated a set of tools for all to use. Many people know they have to reduce stress and that they need their anxiety to melt away. And just as many people have no idea how to do it or who can help them.

The Real Self Alignment method is a set of tools, utilising a simple three-step process, to get clear, be connected and into REAL living.

Work with the Ultimate Daggy Mum:

Join my VIP club for FREE or check out The REAL Start program. You will find free tools and monthly access to low cost support online at www.DaggyMums.com.au.

Listen to my podcast 'Daggy Mums. Life UnStuck' for insight and awareness into the lives of women, supporting women.

Check out my clinic based services and online learning programs through One Health and Wellness.

Connect with Meagan:
Facebook: One Health or Daggy Mums.Life Unstuck
Instagram: @OneHealthandwellness or @ Daggymumunstuck
Website: www.onehealthandwellness.com.au or www. Daggymums.com.au

SECTION 8:
FINANCIAL SELF-CARE

INTRODUCTION

Tracey Jewel

What goals do you have for your money? Have you saved anything up yet? What will you do with it? Financial self-care is all about fine-tuning your habits with money to reach your goals. Through budgeting and managing debts, you can take care of this important part of your life.

You may put this to the side as you look after your family and loved ones, but this act of self-care prioritises your finances so you can manage your whole wellbeing. When you neglect your finances, nothing good can come from it. Feeling upset about debts or lack of savings will result in greater anxiety, guilt, shame and relationship stress.

Ignoring the elephant in the room won't make it vanish away. You've got to confront overspending habits and find new solutions or you'll impact your mental wellness. Those who have financial woes they ignore often socially isolate and feel dissatisfied with life.

It's time to take the power back by prioritising your finances and getting into a healthy money mindset. When you start thinking about how you're improving your financial future for yourself and your family, you take the control back. And that control will leave you feeling empowered and able to create a balanced and fulfilling life.

Learn how to manage your financial self-care now and build up to the things you've been dreaming of doing with your life!

FINANCIAL PLANNING: USE YOUR WEALTH TO LIVE AN AUTHENTIC LIFE

Jodi Escudier

It's not how much you earn but what you do with it that counts.

My relationship with money changed forever the day I started work at an investment bank in London. Growing up in a working-class family, I was familiar with the phrases 'money doesn't grow on trees' and 'I'm not made of money' – subliminal messages that were unconsciously fed to me through my childhood that money was scarce, should be guarded and its primary use was to get us from one pay cheque to the next. This new environment I found myself in was fundamental in its impact on my perception of money and wealth because I could see how money was being used as a tool to reach goals, make progress and live a more authentic life. There was direction and purpose and a pull towards reaching financial freedom. Instead of living pay cheque to pay cheque and treating money as a taboo subject, I could see money being used by people to live a life that was more authentic to them. What do I mean by this? Think of it this way: if money was not a restraint, how would you live your life differently? Would you do a job that was more meaningful to you? Would you travel to places that you connect with spiritually? Would you volunteer to do charity work in a third world country? Take away the money constraints and you will reveal dreams, goals, and expose a life that is more authentic to who you are and ultimately how you would choose to live if you had financial freedom.

It is well documented that money and finances play a huge part in people's mental health, stress levels and relationship success. Negative emotions such as fear, guilt, shame, conflict and envy are often associated with money and finances – the need to 'keep up with the Joneses' instead of focusing on our own financial journey and goals. What if keeping up means burying yourself in a mountain of debt? Is it worth sacrificing your own mental wellness for a life of trying to keep pace with others? Your own finances are just that, your OWN, and no one else will care about them as much as you should. If you are taking actions that have a negative impact on your own financial journey, the only people this behaviour is affecting is you and your family. Why would you sacrifice your own financial wellbeing for that? Surely it is better to have your own goals and a path to financial freedom to keep you focused and on track, and use your own financial position to make positive progress?

Financial distress and discomfort are caused by a lack of control or knowledge when it comes to our finances and the money that supports us to live life. This can result in depression or divorce, children hearing arguments about money and overall negative energy around money. It therefore has a damaging impact on our own wellbeing.

When managed properly your money can be used as a tool to provide you comfort and certainty. Having a plan to financial freedom in place can give you the peace of mind that comes from having a financial safety net should you need it. You can grow your wealth so that you can have the options in the future that wealth provides – options over where you live, the work you do, the type of medical care you have access to and a path towards financial freedom. Live a freer life by repaying debt sooner to become debt free, and direct surplus cash into things that bring you joy.

How can we use wealth as a tool to enable us to reach a more authentic version of ourselves, to strive towards financial freedom and live a life of truth and happiness? First, we must get over the notion that money is bad, evil, scarce or something to be avoided or ignored. You do not have to be wealthy to improve your cashflow, but you do have to be better at managing your money. Often, we have been taught all our money lessons from our parents. These parents were taught by theirs, and this is a generation that may have lived through a war, when money was something to be closely guarded and never discussed or attributed to goals or progression. Think about your own family's attitude to and handling of finances. How has this impacted you, both negatively and positively, about how you handle your own money and cashflow? Fortunately, your family's beliefs towards money do not have to be your own. From right now you can choose to change the story, to implement better money management strategies, and adopt a positive, goal orientated approach to your finances that will improve not only your own but your spouse's and children's money relationships in the future too. We have every opportunity to use the money we have to live a life of abundance, growth and authenticity. Let's normalise talking about money with our family and friends, to dispel the fear that often silently accompanies finances. Notice how inner peace and certainty lends itself to those who have a handle on their finances (not those who are 'richest', but those who are in control of their money) and have a plan in place to make progress and reach goals.

So, what does financial freedom mean to you? What does a life of financial freedom look like for you? Where would you go? What would you do? How would your life be different?

Here are some steps you can implement today to help you get there:

Adopt a Positive Money Attitude

Be conscious of the self-talk you have around money. Phrases like 'I'm no good with money' or 'I'm bad with handling my finances'. Is that actually the truth, or do you simply have a gap in the knowledge needed to confidently manage your finances?

If you are not in piles of debt and can afford your lifestyle, that means you are doing something right, right? Wrong! Keeping afloat and avoiding / ignoring your finances is not managing your money and not taking you on the path of financial freedom.

Adopt phrases like: 'I am learning how to improve my finances and get better every day', 'Managing my money brings me financial wellness' and 'I am on a path to financial freedom'.

What does Financial Freedom Mean to You?

Use your money as a tool to live the life you want, have purpose and direction and make financial progress. First you must decide what goals you are striving for. What does financial freedom mean to you? What do you value in life and want more of? Write this down. Next list some short-term, medium-term, and long-term goals that will help you get there.

Example: Financial freedom means starting my own business. Why? This will bring me joy doing work that I love and not being tied to paid employment. Short-term goal: Get current expenses under control. Direct surplus into repaying credit card debt. Investigate overheads for new business. Medium-term goal: Save one year of expenses and a financial buffer, work part-time and start business in free time. Long-term goal: Transition full-time into own business, enjoy financial freedom and wellness.

Know Your Numbers

You cannot manage what you do not measure. Know how much it costs you to live your life, then direct the rest towards living the life you want to live. If you do not have enough money, find ways to make more – sell unwanted items, take on a side hustle. There are always opportunities if you actively pursue them.

Yes, this does mean taking note of your numbers. What do you have coming in and what do you have going out? These expenses can be broken down into:

- core expenses (necessities for everyday life)
- discretionary expenses (clothes, technology)
- lifestyle expenses (holidays, entertainment)

Spend less than what you earn (avoid lifestyle creep and keeping up with the Joneses). Direct surplus cash towards goals to help achieve financial freedom. After you have covered the above expenses, what you do with the surplus income is what you can use to change and enhance your financial position. The direction of your surplus cashflow is the **one** factor that will make the biggest difference to your overall wealth position and your success in reaching your financial goals and freedom.

Implement A Plan

Now you have identified your financial freedom and what goals you need to achieve to help you get there, you have to implement the plan and (most importantly) stick to it. Write down your spending plan (use good, old fashioned pen and paper, a spreadsheet or a fancy budgeting app). Be conscious of your spending and review it as often as you need in the beginning to make sure you are staying on track. Once you have control over this, review it monthly. Direct surplus cashflow into one of the goals to help you achieve financial freedom. Check off goals once achieved and celebrate small wins.

Have a positive relationship with money, control over your finances, make financial progress and achieve financial wellness.

Financial freedom is achievable if you put a plan in place to reach it. Your goals must be smart and realistic. This will give you the best chance of success. Once you can see your money as something to be used and managed for a greater purpose, you will have motivation to improve your money management, stick to your plan and ultimately achieve financial freedom – whatever that means to you.

Bio

Jodi Escudier has been a financial adviser to individuals and families in Australia since 2013. Jodi provides positive, strategic advice to help Australians save, protect and grow their wealth in a way that aligns with their own financial goals and beliefs. With a down-to-earth communication style and ability to hold meaningful conversations, Jodi builds valuable relationships with clients that see them fulfil long-term goals and provide financial security for their family.

Jodi has a particular focus on educating women in financial literacy so that they may empower themselves to build wealth and make positive financial decisions for their future. She frequently holds financial education workshops for women, regularly blogs on this topic and shares general information and tips on Instagram.

Outside of work, Jodi is a keen reader and runner and drags her young family to the beach as often as possible.

Work with Jodi:

Jodi is a Private Client Adviser and Representative at Boutique Advisers Pty Ltd, AFSL 520405.

Connect with Jodi:

Instagram: www.instagram.com/the.womens.wealth.coach

LinkedIn: https://linkedin.com/in/jodiescudier/

Website: https://boutiqueadvisers.com.au/

COMMUNICATE YOUR VALUE WITH CONFIDENCE SO YOU GET PAID WHAT YOU'RE WORTH

Jessica Osborn

Your value is decided by you, and you alone.

– Jessica Osborn

Money – it's a little word, but it's tied up with so many complicated feelings. We don't just need it to live, it has somehow become, for many, a measure of our professional worth. As business owners, service providers and even as employees, that's where it can all go so wrong for us. We put our 'worth' into the hands of the market – an employer or a customer – when we should be proudly championing our 'value'.

In my experience, it's a problem that affects women acutely. When I talk to clients about limiting beliefs – the things we internalise that hold us back from achieving goals – money raises its head time and time again. That one little word can hold so much sway over our sense of self.

We need money to survive, but many of us are deeply uncomfortable talking about it. Unfortunately, the pain doesn't stop with that awkwardness, it continually limits our earning potential – and it's all on us! And I say that having been the woman who resented being paid below market rate while delivering insane results for ASX-listed companies. I looked to career moves to right the wrongs, until the day I decided to take charge. I got clear in my own mind on my value to the organisation, and then I did the uncomfortable thing and stated my case. From there, earning the wage I deserved became much simpler.

But I began to realise that it wasn't just 'my' problem, it was an epidemic! As I recruited incredible women, I noticed how often we negotiate DOWN at the interview table, how frequently we ask a prospective employer to tell US what we deserve to be paid, and how rare it is that we stand up and ask for the raise we deserve. And that experience isn't limited to the corporate world – it permeates and stunts small business.

Today I'm a marketing coach, surrounded by talented female business owners whose biggest failing is usually the fact that they don't recognise their own worth. And I've been there too! I came out of a stellar corporate career and started charging at 'newbie' rates because I immediately discounted all my experience. I've had to train myself out of that habit, and you can too.

So, let's get real. We deserve to be appropriately compensated for our skills and our time. I don't think anyone would disagree with that statement. But who decides what 'appropriately' means? You do. If that sounds counter-intuitive, then believe me when I say, this chapter was written for you!

As women (and this is of course a generalisation, but not without foundation), we have a tendency towards people-pleasing. We want to be liked and we fear rejection. So, when it comes to dollars and cents, we avoid talking about it. We struggle to ask for money we're owed, to pitch for higher wages, to set or negotiate rates. Instead, we look to others to tell us what we should be paid, both by analysing the market or even letting the customer dictate. Sound familiar?

Now, here's the reality: If you ask someone what they'd pay for something, their answer will invariably 'as little as possible'; so, when you look to the market or your customers, you're never going to get the answer you want and need. Instead, you'll get a lowball figure that just confirms your worst fears about your perceived 'worth', and your confidence drops further. An insidious, crushing spiral to the bottom of the pay scale.

But it doesn't have to be that way. Here's what to do:

Get clear on your revenue goals

You know the income you need to generate and the time you have available to do it in. So, the trick is to understand what you need to charge in order to meet your financial targets. It sounds very simple, but that's actually the place you need to start.

Rate setting begins with the question: 'How much money would make this project worth my time?' It's not about how much money you can squeeze out of a prospective client, nor should it be done in fear of what might scare them off (you actually have no idea of their true price tolerance!). It's NOT – and I cannot emphasise this enough – greedy to expect to be compensated for 100 per cent of what our time is worth. Your time is finite and you need to leverage it to generate income (without sacrificing your family time, me time or sanity!). You control your time, and you control your earning potential.

Ignore the competition

Your competitors are only truly competitors if they 'out-value' you. Matching them on price only ever results in a race to the bottom and one winner – the client (or employer). Of course, budget is a consideration, but setting your rates in step with others will only limit your income and obscure the big picture of pricing, which is about showing your own true value.

Articulate that value

When you're selling a service, you're selling more than your time – you're selling results. The customer isn't interested in how long it takes you to do what they're asking; they want to know how it's going to benefit them. It's absolutely critical that you stop trying to sell them Pilates classes and start selling them a healthy body and mind. Look at what you have achieved, the difference you make and the impact you have, and start talking about it. Ask yourself questions like:

- How much money will your service help them make?
- How much time will you save them?
- How much easier will you make their life?
- How much happier, healthier or fitter will they be after working with you?

Carry out an honest assessment of how you're showing up for your clients, your experience, your skills and your value-adds – the whole picture of what you bring to the table. Make the 'price' secondary to the 'value' in your own head as well as in your communication, because it actually isn't about the time or effort you put into the job, it's all about the benefits that your work brings to your clients.

Stop working for free

Any time you feel like offering your services for free, be very clear about the reason you're doing it. The reality is that 'freebies' rarely achieve the results you want, because when someone gets something for nothing, they don't value it. I once gave someone a six-month membership to my group coaching program and they didn't even join a single call! Even though they wanted it at first, they had no commitment to it – because it was free. Conversely, when others pay $5,000 for the same program, they turn up every time, they put in the work and they get the results.

Furthermore, when you choose not to charge, it sends a message that you're not confident in the value you bring. So why would a prospect have confidence in your ability to deliver? Underpinning the 'freebie' conundrum is usually a fear of rejection. But think of it this way, all you're likely to do is exchange 'rejection' for 'resentment' when you're stuck doing something for nothing for a 'client' who doesn't really appreciate what you're delivering. Charge for it! You know you're worth it (and they do too.)

No more undercharging or discounting to win the work

That same fear of rejection, combined with the fear that the other person won't see the value in our work, leads us to pitch ourselves low. However, if someone thinks you're too expensive – they're not your ideal client. If someone wants you to work for less than what you're worth – they're not the ones for you. Let them go, make space for the ones who are the right fit.

How many times have you won the job and then looked miserably at the invoice, wondering why it seemed so important to 'win' such a small victory? If you don't know your worth and value it accordingly, you're leaving yourself open to stress, resentment and a big attack of 'why, oh why am I working for buttons?' When that happens, you don't do your best work anyway!

Position yourself in your market

Achieving your income potential also means attracting your ideal customers. That means the type of person or business you can get the best results for and who values your specific skill sets and experience. You need to:

1. Understand their pain points, and how you can solve them.
2. Identify the results they need, and show how you can deliver them.
3. Differentiate yourself from the rest of the marketplace.
4. Make it easy for them to see themselves as your customer and feel confident that you're the right choice.

When you've ticked all these boxes, take a breath and look at how far you've come! There you were, staggering along in the pricing wilderness, quoting with eyes closed and breath held, watching your competitors with a mixture of envy and self-doubt. Now look at you, a service provider with a clear sense of your own value and a direct line to the clients that fill your heart and line your pockets.

If I can leave you with one message, it's that whether you believe your skills are worth a little or a lot, you're always correct. Beliefs are the things we hold to be absolute truths deep down, and they dictate how we show up in the world and what is delivered to us in return. Believe in your value, and set your price. You're worth every penny.

Bio

Jessica Osborn is a business coach and marketing specialist, who supports female entrepreneurs to realise their potential and command their worth.

Drawing on a twenty-year corporate marketing career and her experience as the founder of two thriving online ventures in the last ten years, Jessica empowers women to leverage their unique value to create differentiation in the market, attract their dream clients and build profitable, scalable businesses.

Jessica specialises in helping coaches, creatives and professionals to go from overlooked in a crowded market to in-demand and profitable, without succumbing to the hustle mentality.

Having helped many clients achieve transformational success with up to 500 per cent increase in profit in the space of a few months, she's passionate about seeing more women overcome their limiting beliefs and create a lifestyle of freedom.

Jessica is degree qualified in business (marketing and psychology) and offers access to her proven growth frameworks for service-based businesses through her popular online programs, Business JAM and The Momentum Club, and through limited private one-to-one coaching spots.

She is currently working on developing a high-level mastermind and business retreat for women ready to scale their business from six to seven figures.

Qualifications:

- Bachelor of Business Studies (marketing, psychology)

Work with Jessica:

Join me in Business JAM and receive a personally recorded in-depth website review to help you attract the right prospects.

Special Offer – I am offering readers a complimentary thirty-minute business strategy session for women ready to take action on reaching their business goals. Book your session here.

Connect with Jessica:
Facebook: https://facebook.com/jessicaosborn.bxcoach
Instagram: https://instagram.com/jessica.osborn/
LinkedIn: https://linkedin.com/in/jessicaaosborn/
Website: https://jessicaosborn.com

SECTION 9: PRACTICAL SELF-CARE

INTRODUCTION

Tracey Jewel

Many times, our self-care practices feel out of sorts because of a lack of organisation. That's where practical self-care comes in, to maintain a sense of order and create a clear path ahead.

Is your desk cluttered and chaotic? What about the rooms of your home? Even having a messy closet filled with clothes you haven't worn in a decade can lead to an overwhelming feeling looming over you like a dark rain cloud.

Perhaps you're worried about finances and how to move towards your dreams of owning a home, buying a new car or even taking a vacation. There are many things you can do to engage practical self-care and bring these things into fruition.

This chapter will help you fill in those gaps and clean the closet in your room as well as in your mind. Learning key organisational skills gives you a liberating feeling and sets you free. After building these habits, you'll be able to take the steps forward without any hindrances.

It's time to discover how a little practicality in your life can move those obstacles and make your visions come into clear focus. Set yourself free by engaging in practical self-care practices that allow you to streamline your life and make a plan for the future.

NEW BEGINNINGS START WITH YOU!

Ruth Morgan

The future belongs to those who believe in the beauty of their dreams.

– Eleanor Roosevelt

I was a shy little girl, about six years, old hiding behind my mother's skirt as she chatted outside church one Sunday morning. A lady from the congregation peered behind her, curiously looking down at me over the rim of her brightly golden spectacles and asked:

'So, my dear, what will you be when you grow up?' Having never been asked that before, I timidly replied 'a nurse' and quickly hid again.

I didn't know then that those two words would begin my vision, purpose and journey in life. Upon reflection, it does make sense though because I frequently enjoyed playing doctors and nurses with my teddy bear and dolls. Also, I was often home from school with tonsillitis, feeling listless and feverish with a very sore throat and surviving on red jelly, water and thick, sweet, chilled antibiotic syrup. I would always feel disappointed when I couldn't swallow the bubbly fizz of the lemonade my mother expectantly served me.

More seriously, I vividly remember when I was ten, curling myself up on the carpet in the hallway with the sharpest most agonising abdominal pain ever. Some days later, I was in hospital having my appendix removed. And I can remember an urgent wave of groggy nausea upon waking from an anaesthetic after having my tonsils out when I was thirteen. My excruciatingly painful sore throat was burning like acid, which made it harder to swallow than I could ever remember. I was supposed to be better.

Those two hospital experiences gave me a deep insight and awareness about the invaluable need for kind, caring and friendly nurses. The hospital 'sisters' I had encountered were unfortunately for me a cold, disciplined, harsh, military style, who made me feel uneasy.

On a brighter note, I remember feeling positive and adventurous after watching *The Nun's Story*. Imaginary stories consumed my mind about what it would be like to be a compassionate nurse in a distant, primitive and foreign land. Back in reality after arriving home from high school, I would curl up on the sofa and eagerly watch the next episode of *The Young Doctors* on colour TV.

Despite my desire to be a nurse, I impatiently left school in Year 11. Upon my father's insistence, I completed secretarial college and worked as a stenographer. Unfortunately, I didn't like it very much, and so I resigned. Excitedly, I commenced general nurse training in 1981 and successfully graduated in 1984. Three years later, I married. I gave birth to three children, all two years apart, then sadly, after thirteen years of marriage, I divorced.

As a single mother, I remained committed to my career, juggling hospital work and family. Being a high-achiever, I was inspired, guided and motivated by creative goal setting. Contrary to the single parent 'norm', I continued to gain post-graduate qualifications in intensive care nursing and diabetes education and management. For work-life balance, I split my hours between clinical hospital duties and patient support office work. Over the years, I've eagerly helped to support and heal thousands of people across multiple disease states.

Looking back on my life, I realise how my experiences of illness have shaped who I am. I learnt to place a high value on wellness. In fact, every day I aspire to be well and I want to help others feel and be well. I've developed several strengths as a result of my journey. I am honest, loving, appreciate beauty and excellence, can self-regulate my behaviour and I am kind. These attributes enable me to thrive, flourish, care for myself and to serve others well.

My passion is health, wellness and living life 'in flow'. With forty plus years of nursing experience, and after reflecting on what went wrong for many patients, I've gained deep insights into how people 'fall off their tracks'. While some situations are fate and others 'luck of the draw', in many other circumstances stress, disease and unwellness may be pro-actively delayed, prevented or need not occur at all.

My vision continues to evolve. As a health, wellness and 'life in flow' coach my 'why' is to interrupt the usual human trajectory of non-aligned, unbalanced and unhealthy behaviours and assist others to positively transform their lives. My contribution is towards a mission much larger than myself – global wellness.

People I serve are career driven professionals who want to master behaviour change to achieve their no. 1 health and wellness priority. Coaching sessions I deliver are one-to-one (phone or online) and tailored to meet client desires, needs and outcomes. To gain results, I creatively combine a variety of evidence-based coaching techniques I've mastered from accredited courses, reputable professional seminars, webinars and readings.

As a co-author of this book, I feel excited and privileged to contribute to your wellness and self-care. You see, self-care is an important part of your optimal wellness. Self-care enables you to maintain personal health and balance. Self-care allows you to replenish energy and become motivated. And self-care assists your personal growth (Moore et al, 2016).

It is my intention here to show you how you can become your own self-care catalyst for change. With a little guidance, you can discover, learn and maintain any new self-care behaviour you choose. And here are some reputable techniques that can help you:

Ten Self-Care Mastery Strategies

Strategy No. 1

Know and deeply listen to your values so you can focus on what is important to you. By doing so, you'll be able to align the choices, decisions and actions you take and live authentically with reason and purpose. When you create something new and connect it to your values, you 'own' it and this will positively motivate you. (Moore et al, 2016)

How does your self-care align with your values?

To uncover your values, Scott Jeffries has a free values self-discovery process @ https://www.scottjeffries.com.

Strategy No. 2

Identify your strengths so you can positively use them for resilience, achievement and to flourish in life. Remember to be mindful of, focus on and draw from your signature strengths and don't waste time working on weaknesses. (Emerson 2017, Niemiec et al, 2019, Sharp, 2020, Mayerson 2020)

To discover your character strengths, complete the free VIA Character Strengths Survey and your free report will be emailed to you @ https://www.viacharacter.org/survey/account/register .

Strategy No. 3

Believe in who you are, what you stand for, your creativity and what you can achieve. Most behaviour is oriented towards your beliefs. Once you start to believe in self-care you will gather supportive information to affirm your belief and filter out information that doesn't. (Smith, 2019)

Authentically write down your top five self-care beliefs and reflect on them daily.

Strategy No. 4

Appreciate your uniqueness and how you show up in life. Understand your value and acknowledge your self-worth.

To understand your individuality, ask some people who know you well what you are really good at. Then ask what annoys them about you. (Emerson, 2017, Nawalkha, 2019)

Next, proceed to identify the big thing in the world that matters to you most. Maybe it's a religious or political cause or something you're deeply passionate about. Combine the good, the bad and what matters to you most and discover your own unique character map. This is what sets you apart from others. (Nawalkha, 2019)

Strategy No. 5

Define your self-care 'why' so you can feel connected to what you create and stay on track. To do so, answer the following questions:

Why is self-care important to me?

What benefits will self-care bring into my life?

How does self-care align with my values and identity?

Write down, place pictures or take photos about your 'why' and place it somewhere prominent where it will inspire you to prioritise and take action. (Moore et al, 2016)

Strategy No. 6

Dream about and design your self-care future. This will enhance your wellbeing and increase your hope. (King, 2001 cited Moore et al, 2016). Aligning your vision with your values and underpinning it with your 'why' provides you with importance, motivation and many reasons you will want to act. (Moore et al, 2016)

Imagine your self-care life in three- or six-months' time:

- What does your self-care life look like?
- Where are you and what are you doing?
- Who are you with and what are you wearing?
- How do you feel and what strengths are you using?
- Are your self-care activities social and fun?
- Do your self-care activities express your uniqueness?
- Are your self-care activities challenging, achievable and rewarding?

Write down your self-care vision in detail using present tense. Or create your vision on a board by printing, cutting and pasting pictures, graphics or drawings. Place it in a significant place where you will read it or see it daily. (Moore et al, 2016)

Strategy No. 7

Create your action plan for success by creating behaviour goals that make your vision real (Moore et al, 2016). Having clear goals is correlated with happiness and life satisfaction (Healy 2008 cited in Moore et al, 2016). Goals direct, energise, affect persistence and help you access task relevant knowledge and strategies (Lathan 1990, cited in Moore et al 2016). A goal gives you permission to experiment. Once you start your first goal, it will lead you to the next.

You can increase your interest and motivation by creating a goal that's not too easy and a little out of reach, yet achievable. Attending to your goal in this way creates maximum engagement – a state of flow. (Moore et al, 2016)

Goals are best written as three-monthly goals and then broken down into smaller weekly steps. (Moore et al, 2016)

Start with a goal that is related to a self-care activity that's important to you. One that you are confident you can achieve and are ready to do now.

Once you've selected your activity, write your three-month goal and follow with your 'next step' weekly goal.

A proven goal writing formula is to use the SMART acronym (below). Write your goals so they are:

S – Specific
M – Measurable
A – Achievable (not too easy and not too hard)
R – Realistic
T – Time Bound (Moore et al, 2016)

Place your written goal somewhere prominent and schedule a reminder to complete it. This seems like a formal approach; however, by attending your goal in this way, you are more likely to achieve it. (Moore et al, 2016)

Strategy No. 8

Identify and overcome obstacles. Review your goal(s) and identify any actual or potential obstacles that could stand in your way. Stay positive, appreciate your strengths, brainstorm alternatives and mobilise your resources. If you're dealing with internal resistance, seek the assistance of a coach who can help you become unstuck by using motivational interviewing techniques. (Moore et al, 2016)

Strategy No. 9

Understand and handle your excuses. Everyone makes excuses, though it's a choice whether you take any notice of them or not. Dr Tim Sharp (Dr Happy) describes fourteen of the most common excuses and offers helpful insights, tips and advice in his *Habits for Action*. (Sharp, 2020)

Strategy No. 10

Create lasting change: If you're serious about creating new sustainable self-care behaviour, I recommend you read/listen to *Atomic Habits* by James Clear. He advocates keeping activities top of mind, attractive, easy and satisfying while remembering to schedule and repeat new behaviours to maintain them. (Clear, 2018)

Another great author who can help you to form good habits is Gretchen Ruben. In her book *Better Than Before*, Gretchen shows habits to be the key to not only successful change but also to strength, happiness and productivity. She has researched core principles and provides a practical framework to help you understand habits and to guide you in creating lasting change. (Ruben, 2015)

Creating and prioritising new sustainable self-care behaviour requires intention, attention, time, skill and effort. At any moment you can give yourself permission to become, be and have all the self-care you deserve.

You can be just as 'well' while facing challenges, injury, during sickness, recovery and stress as you can in optimal health. So always remember, you are the centre of your universe from which all good things flow. You are your number one. You are the best person, friend and companion you will ever know. You are not vain, inconsiderate or selfish to invest time in caring for yourself. Self-care is an essential requirement for optimal wellness, alignment and living a life you love.

3 Key Self-Care Learnings

Learning No. 1 – Intimately know and understand who you are: your values, strengths and beliefs, your 'why', your uniqueness.

Learning No. 2 – Create and prioritise your self-care dreams: your vision and SMART self-care goals.

Learning No. 3 – Master lasting change: overcome resistance/barriers/excuses and regularly practise self-care behaviours.

Please don't stress. You don't need to change everything at once. Lasting change starts with just one small step. If you'd like to discover your next important, confident and ready-to-do self-care step, request your free Lifenesse Wellness Wheel and Lifenesse Mastery Wheel for self-care @ www.lifenesse.com.au.

I wish you all the joy, peace, happiness, health and wellness that life can offer. Connect with me @ www.lifenesse.com.au/enquire-here if you need some professional insight, guidance, facilitation and/or support for your own self-care journey.

Take care … All the best and God bless!

References

James Clear, *Atomic Habits: An Easy and Proven Way to Build Good Habits and Break Bad Ones*, Penguin Random House LLC, 2018, Audible, Chapter 3

Claire Emerson, *Five Illuminating Ways to Discover Your Unique Advantage*, 15 May 2017: https://further.net/life-advantage

Gretchen Ruben, *Better Than Before, Mastering the Habits of Our Everyday Lives*, 2015, available on Audible

Neal H. Mayerson, 'The Character Strengths Response: An Urgent Call to Action', *Frontiers in Psychology,* 21 August 2020: https://doi.org/10.3389/fpsyg.2020.02106

Margaret Moore, Bob Tschannen-Moran, Erika Jackson, *Coaching Psychology Manual*, China: Wolters Kluwer, 2016

Ajit Nawalkha, 'How to Highlight Your Uniqueness as a Coach', Evercoach by Mindvalley, 2019, Facebook video

Ryan M. Niemiec, Robert E. McGrath, The Power of Character Strengths: Appreciate and ignite your positive personality, 2021, Audible

Tim Sharp, *Habits for Action: How to stop the excuses and do what you know you should*, Sound Kitchen, Sydney, 2020, Audible Original

Scott E. Smith, 'How Do Our Beliefs Affect Our Behavior?', *Capital Gazette,* November 2019: https://www.capitalgazette.com/lifestyles/ac-cn-column-smith-20191105-w5tf6han4raq3afvzwup3m-toie-story.html;

Bio

Ruth Morgan is a health, wellness and 'life in flow' coach and founder of Lifenesse, Sydney, Australia. With forty plus years of specialised nursing and more than thirteen years of patient support experience, as well as professional coaching skills, Ruth delivers an individually tailored service.

'I've mastered a unique combination of reputable coaching methods. My inner core values are truth, empowerment, wellness, expression and love. And my signature strengths are honesty, love, appreciation of beauty and excellence, self-regulation and kindness. Put together, these deliver a unique and positive coaching experience.'

Ruth helps career driven professionals master behaviour change to achieve their number one health and wellness priority. She navigates clients towards new visions of health, wellness and life. Ruth facilitates alignment of choice with values, balance creation, positive thoughts and emotions, overcoming barriers/resistance and assisting in planning achievable actions that bring lasting change.

'By gaining deep insights from my professional and personal experience, I believe that many people don't live the healthy, well, aligned, balanced and meaningful life that they deserve. So many people are busy and don't think to prioritise their self-care. I help clients identify "unworkability", make necessary changes and improve their quality of life. My deepest passion and mission are to enhance "global wellness!"

'I wish you well with your self-care journey.'

Qualifications:

- Professional Health and Wellness Coaching Certificate
- Registered Nurse
- Graduate Certificate Intensive Care Nursing
- Graduate Certificate in Diabetes Education and Management

Work with Ruth:

Self-care is central to wellness! To help you begin, Ruth offers a free Lifenesse Wellness Wheel and Lifenesse Mastery Wheel for self-care by request @ www.lifenesse.com.au.

Start your journey by connecting with me at www.lifenesse.com.au, via email to coach@lifenesse.com.au or message Ruth (Thornton) Morgan via LinkedIn.

Connect with Ruth:

Linkedin: https://www.linkedin.com/in/jruthmorgan/

Website: www.lifenesse.com.au

Email: coach@lifenesse.com.au

EATING CHOCOLATE IN THE BATHTUB AND OTHER SELF-LOVE RITUALS

Angelika Klotz

Love yourself first and everything else falls into line. You really have to love yourself to get anything done in this world.

– Lucille Ball

My hands were slicing through the crystal-clear water. My legs were making waves in the Olympic-sized pool. Even with the excruciating back-pain I had been suffering from for months, I was swimming. Swimming at the crack of dawn was my self-care routine during the summer while I was visiting my parents in Germany. Being in the water was the only time of day when I didn't feel my pain. Pain-free, surrounded by fluid freshness and being carried by water during a time of despair was a huge relief to me.

Lap after lap, I prayed for a miracle that I would exit the pool without pain. The miracle was not granted. Instead, after yet another physiotherapy session, one protruded spinal disc finally ruptured, leaving me without any control of my legs.

Taking care of myself in a time when I had lost control over my body felt like a massive accomplishment. Practising self-love by swimming was the only thing I was able to give myself physically, emotionally, mentally and even spiritually. For the rest of the day, I wasn't really able to drive, and I could hardly walk or even sit normally on a chair. The constant pain had eroded my thought processes, and the only thing I could think of was how I could escape from this pain.

In the end I found myself in surgery, where the particles of the ruptured disc were scraped out of my spinal canal. At last, my pain was gone. A long four weeks of convalescent stillness followed, where I wasn't allowed to do much. But the moment my wounds had healed and I was able to move again, I was back in the pool doing laps.

Many years later, I experienced one of the biggest 'aha' moments in my life. While reading Gary Chapman's *The Five Love Languages*, I finally understood how I could satisfy my heart's desire and comfort the longing of my soul. Gary Chapman's message was that you only feel truly loved when your personal top two of the five love languages are regularly expressed to you by your partner: physical touch, quality time, words of affirmation, acts of service and gifts.

I have found that the same is true for your acts of self-care. I am a big fan of regular acts of self- love. Some don't need extra time or extra money because we are easily able to fit these acts of self-care into our usual routine.

My personal top love language is physical touch. Women who operate on the same self-care love language may want to schedule regular massages or spa days. The no-extra-cost version for you ladies who love physical touch as well are soft blankets or crisp sheets that are hitting the sweet spot when turning in at night. A lovely skin care routine in the morning would set the right tone for the day. Stretching your arms and back every hour in front of the computer would give the right impetus to power through the day.

My client Susie was at a crossroads in her life. Her marriage was hanging by a thread because she and her partner had given up caring for each other. She was physically exhausted holding down a full-time job and taking care of her two boys in an environment that was not supportive of her. She was emotionally exhausted because of the constant yelling and fighting that was going on at home, and her spiritual connection could hardly exist as her self-confidence was vanishing more and more every day. It seemed that nothing she did mattered.

Susie came to me because she was looking for support. She did not feel acknowledged and listened to. We were able to uncover and release a few childhood traumas that would still trigger her whenever her husband gave his suggestions on how to approach things. After seeing me for a few sessions she was slowly getting better at setting boundaries for herself.

One day she came to see me raving about a hot yoga class that she had found. At first, she would go only once a week; soon it became an almost daily activity. For her, holding poses in a heated room while she felt her sweat dripping down onto a towel under her feet was the epitome of self-care. It relaxed her, it gave her strength and it made her feel confident. She would go through great lengths to get her self-care. Driving to the class would take her half an hour. The class itself would take ninety minutes. She'd prepare dinner for her boys and husband before she left and she would come home exhausted yet ecstatic, despite having to face piles of laundry and other chores. But nothing would keep her from going to hot yoga because the class would give her the right amount of physical activity that is part of physical touch. More than that, hot yoga gave Susie confidence in her own strength, the physical detoxification she needed to clear her emotional turmoil and the connection to other women in the class that provided support for her as she no longer felt alone in her struggles with everyday challenges.

Susie found the right self-care routine to take care of her so many needs. Once you've uncovered what it is your body and mind really need, you'll have no difficulties in making it happen – neither spreadsheets nor complicated scheduling are needed. Your self-love self-care will be un-folding organically and you'll keep on doing it because it will feel sooo good.

Little mindful additions to your daily routines show yourself that you care. This might be deep abdominal breathing while slicing the potatoes for dinner, singing loudly with rhythmical moves while vacuuming, doodling with colourful art chalk while having a conversation with your mum on the phone, lighting a candle while eating your food, listening to daily affirmations while driving to work, holding a yoga pose while watching TV, meditating while you're having your nails done or getting a blow-wave, or it might be eating chocolate while having a bath.

Sometimes it's just about changing your mindset and reframing an activity or task into the language of caring self-love. Recently, I had to read to my little two-year-old grandson before putting him to bed. It was tiring. My mind was preoccupied with endless lists of emails I had to answer, webinars to listen to and phone calls to make. Reading to him was just the means to get him to sleep so I could continue with whatever was on my schedule. Every time he wanted yet another repeat of the same digger story, I would get increasingly annoyed – until I had an epiphany: I thought about self-care and how reading to this cute little guy, who I love to bits, was satisfying my need for meditation and physical touch. We curled up under the cosy blanket, and the soft flow of words was like a breathing meditation. Now I cherish these nightly routines because I feel cared for while caring for him.

This mindful quiet time with my grandson was a meditative activity that satisfied my second most important self-love language: spending quality time with myself. Like I did with this nightly reading ritual, incorporating self-care into your life should be easy. It shouldn't be a hassle nor a duty; it should be a stressless personal priority.

My client Melissa was always on the go. She earned good money and had no problems spending it. She invited family members for coffees and dinners. She went on luxurious weekend trips with her girlfriends. She would speed date in order to find the man who she wanted to share her life with. She talked endlessly on the phone while driving to and from work. She jumped into her daily exercise class and would go to a painting or cooking class, gardening group or book club right after. Melinda was hardly ever alone, she was never sitting still and she was not sleeping.

We worked with her brainwaves to support healthy night rhythms, but really an adjustment to her lifestyle was needed. While talking to her, it became clear that her love language was quality time, but she was spreading herself too thin to make time really matter. She wanted to make sure everybody in her circle would get quality time with her; that was her way of showing she cared. What she forgot about was giving quality time to herself. I encouraged her to drop a few afternoon and evening classes and learn meditation instead. She fell in love with transcendental meditation and, soon after, with a man.

Melissa is a changed woman today. Spending quality time alone doing things she really loves and cares about brought back her congruent and aligned self, a joyful and gratified life, and rejuvenating and regenerating sleep.

If you thrive on words of affirmation, giving yourself permission to change limiting self-talk into positive affirmations, incantations, mantras and encouraging belief statements can be a life-changer. Journaling your thoughts can be a great way to stop the endless mind chatter of self-doubt. There is something supportive and encouraging about putting your sentiments on paper. The physical release runs through the arm and hand while the pen glides over the paper putting your reflections into written form. You might never look at what you've written again, and there's really no need to do so because, once unveiled, whatever hits the paper is no longer bugging your system.

Jacqueline found a great way to take care of herself with words of affirmation. She would draw an oracle or angel card every morning to set a positive vibe with a kind and supportive theme for the day. Because she feels supported by this self-love routine, she has an entire shelf filled with boxes of wonderful cards. Finding the perfect one every morning and drawing a card has become second nature to Jacqueline, like brushing her teeth.

Kathleen, who was seeing me for various health concerns, was on the lookout for a self-care routine until she found the perfect job. She landed a job in hospitality as the restaurant manager for a high-end dining experience. This job suits her self-love language of acts of service so well that her job has become her major self-care. She loves writing schedules for staff and waiters, she enjoys delegating, and seeing the restaurant run smoothly and patrons being served well gives her great satisfaction.

If you operate on the same self-love language of acts of service, you might want to try having a beautiful daily planner, where acts of kindness, therapy sessions and meetings can be organised and arranged. Or hang a big calendar on your fridge, where every member of the family finds their activity timetable. Make a beautiful photo calendar, where holiday times and upcoming exotic travel destinations are clearly marked. Try having a soft-coloured calendar in your bedroom, to show scheduled date nights. These are all ways to give constant messages of self-care to your subconscious mind. These messages keep us happier and more joyful – emotions that lower stress levels significantly.

You may also love arranging things in life. This could be putting beautiful flowers on the table, cleaning and sorting the mess in your garage or clearing out your wardrobe. Having a therapy session might be just the act of service that your heart has been longing for for far too long. Offering your self-less service by volunteering at your favourite charity will make you feel sooo good.

Enjoying little indulgences like handmade chocolates or an artisan crafted smooth wine could be just the right gifts to yourself if your love language is receiving gifts. There are endless possibilities to make you happy: adventure trips, city tours or weekend discoveries; supply shopping for your hobbies or crafts, gardening, painting or music; boutique hopping to find some nice new outfits or accessories; stocking up on beautiful candles, fragrant aromatic oils or stationery.

My student, Mandy, loves the gift of investing in herself. She loved learning in school but hated that she wasn't allowed to follow what she desired. Now, the World Wide Web is her oyster filled with affordable lessons – from learning how to play the piano, to Thai cooking; from increasing her memory to hairstyling; from writers workshops to feng shui expertise. If your self-love language is receiving gifts, the possibilities are endless. Learn a new craft or an instrument. Try an adventurous sport like kite-surfing or heli-skiing. Join a self-development course to heal something within yourself. If you are not in the position to spend a lot of money for your indulgences, get creative. The small little flower picked on a walk through a park could be the gift to yourself that adorns the table. The essential oil spreading its aroma from the burner could be the gift to yourself that sets the mood in your living space. The rainbow-coloured vegetables you prepare for your dinner can be the gift to your digestive health. The very deep breath you take in the morning when the sun just rises over the horizon can be the life-sustaining gift of air that carries you through your day. The gift of gratitude you show for the little joys in life will be just the gift to yourself that keeps on giving.

Have you figured out your self-love language yet? If you're having trouble in pinpointing what the best approach is to take care of yourself, hop on over to bliss-balance.com and take a quick test in order to serve yourself best.

Get your favourite tool as well.

See you over there, Angelika
@ Angelika Klotz 2021

Bio

Angelika Klotz is certified in the practice and teaching of aromatherapy, aromatic kinesiology, esogetic colourpuncture, energy emission analysis and reiki. She is also certified as an advanced BodyTalker and PaRama practitioner, and she holds a diploma for traditional Chinese medicine.

Growing up in Germany, Angelika was always interested in health care and in learning ways to assist others. She trained in allopathic medicine and worked as a laboratory technician and paediatric nurse. Being over-stretched as a young mother resulted in back surgery, which sparked her interest in complementary healing and seeking support of other women.

While living in Asia for fifteen years, Angelika turned to studying many alternative healing modalities influenced by Eastern philosophies. She has created a very unique blend of these therapies in her practice supporting women who are stressed by modern day life, cracking under the pressure that is put on them by society and who are at a crossroads in their lives. Education, self-care tips and rituals play a big role in encouraging women on their path to becoming healthy and whole again.

In 2005, Angelika made Auckland, New Zealand her home. She resides there with her husband of forty years, her daughter, four grandkids and 102 essential oils.

Besides teaching other practitioners and running her private practice, Angelika is currently creating further online trainings and retreats to support the global community of women on a healing journey.

If you are on the path and would like to get to know your unique self-care type head to bliss-balance.com and take the quiz.

Connect with Angelika:

Facebook: facebook/bliss.balance101

Email: hello@bliss-balance.com

Website: bliss-balance.com

ORGANISED SIMPLICITY: AN ORGANISED HOME LEADS TO AN ORGANISED LIFE

Jordy Fabian

The question of what you want to own is actually the question of how you want to live your life.

– Marie Kondo

Ever since I can remember, I've always wanted a career that is meaningful and through which I can help people. I worked in marketing for over fifteen years, and I've started but, for various reasons, not finished, degrees in both policing and nursing. As fun and challenging as working in marketing can be, it doesn't quite bring me the satisfaction I get from organising someone's home, knowing I have helped improve their quality of life, or that I've made them genuinely happy by helping them accomplish a task they never thought they could.

Organised Simplicity was born when I realised that my love for organisation and styling could be more than just a hobby. If you asked me if I'd rather get a facial and a massage or go to Kmart, Kmart would win every time. In my own home, I'm forever decluttering, reorganising, moving things, creating new systems and updating the look of each room. One day I thought: How could I turn this into something more? How could people benefit from my passion for organisation? Would this be something that could really help people and make a difference to their lives?

So, I put a post on a local mums group, asking if anyone would be interested in this service. The rest, as they say, is history. Fast forward to the present day, and I now have a small team who have helped me declutter and organise hundreds of people's homes. What fulfils me the most is the look of joy on a client's face when the job is done. When their mouth drops open because they can actually see the floor of a once cluttered, unliveable room. Or they cry because their linen cupboard is no longer a cascading pile of linen and miscellaneous household objects that causes stress and overwhelm every time they open the door. It's helping the elderly, ill and disabled. The time poor, exhausted parents, the people whose homes are overrun by clutter and they have no idea where to start or how to fix it. By implementing systems into their homes that help to increase their confidence and independence, that's what I love about what I do.

SELF-CARE TOOLS

CLUTTER AND YOUR HEALTH

It has been scientifically proven that clutter can make us feel stressed, anxious and depressed. Research from the United States found raised levels of the stress hormone cortisol in mothers whose home environment was cluttered, leading to depression. (www.racgp.org.au)

It has also been found that clutter can lead to you living in a constant state of fight or flight, which is a huge stress on your body. This can in turn affect your physical health, making you more susceptible to illness. (www.racgp.org.au)

When you live in a space that is clean, organised and full of things that make you happy, many wonderful things happen. Your mood lifts, you are instantly more productive, you are less overwhelmed and you are able to think clearly. You are able to focus on the task at hand rather than stressing out about the mess that surrounds and, often times, consumes you.

There are many positives to gain from organising your home, so remember this when you start out and feel overwhelmed by the task ahead. Take a deep breath and focus on one small area at a time. It doesn't matter how long it takes you, as long as you start and keep the momentum going. I promise you, the reward is definitely going to be worth your time and effort.

HOW TO DECLUTTER

If you're still reading I gather it's because you're interested in decluttering or organising your own home, so let's get started! When you have the time, set aside an hour or two, whatever you can dedicate to the task without being interrupted. Grab some garbage bags and head to an area of your home that you know needs attention. Every time you pick up an item ask yourself these questions:

1. Do you love it? (Or, as Marie Kondo™ would say, does it spark joy?)
2. When was the last time you wore or used it?
3. Are you going to wear or use it again?

Next, allocate it:

- If it's in good condition, but it no longer serves a purpose in your home or life, put it in a bag to donate or sell.
- If it's worn out or broken, put it in a bag to throw.
- If you still wear it, use it or it brings you joy, then put it in a pile to keep.

Once you've done this a few times it'll become obvious with each item you pick up which bag it needs to go into. Continue this until you're satisfied the area has been completely decluttered. This could take a few hours, a few days or a few weeks. It doesn't matter, as long as you don't give up!

When you've finished, remove all rubbish, post items for sale online straight away and put all items that don't belong in this space where they should go. You should only be left with items that belong in the current room or area you are in.

CATEGORISE

Now that you've donated, sold or thrown out anything you don't use, you should only be left with what you want to keep, so it's time to categorise. This is where you group like items together. For example, if you are organising your linen cupboard, you may group like items together as follows:

- linen (by bed size – this includes quilt covers, sheets and pillowcases so you can grab everything you need for a bed change in one go)
- bath towels
- hand towels
- bath mats
- beach towels
- spare toiletries (toilet paper, bath/shower products)

- blankets
- quilts
- pillows
- mattress/pillow protectors

ORGANISE

Now comes the fun part. It's time to shop and organise! If you're not sure what products you should purchase, I tell my clients to have a look on my Instagram or to search Pinterest for inspiration. On Pinterest, if you are organising your linen cupboard, search 'linen cupboard organisation' and hundreds of photos will appear. This is a great way to figure out what look you love, therefore what type of containers, boxes or baskets you'll need.

Once you've purchased all your products, you'll need to create zones. Creating dedicated zones for items to live in makes it easier to maintain them as you know exactly where things need to go. Once these zones start to overflow and become unmanageable, you know that you're starting to accumulate more stuff and another declutter may be required.

Say we have a single door linen cupboard; this is an example of the way I would set up the zones:

- Spare quilts and blankets, pillows, larger items
- Bath & beach towels, hand towels, bath mats
- Quilt covers, sheets and pillowcases (group as sets by size)
- Mattress/pillow protectors, miscellaneous
- Spare toiletries, toilet paper, cleaning products

Baskets are a great way to organise items in your linen cupboard, and they look great. Make sure you add a label for easy identification of what's in each one.

KEEP IT GOING

Congratulations! You've successfully decluttered and organised an area of your home. You should be so proud of what you have accomplished.

If you've only just started out on your journey, the important thing is to keep the momentum going. This is done by setting yourself small, achievable goals. Don't tell yourself that you'll declutter and organise your entire home in a weekend, because it won't happen. Decluttering is an exhausting process, both mentally and physically. We become attached to our belongings as many of them represent a time, place or person that we once held dear. It can be incredibly painful to make the decision to part with something of such relevance. It can also be quite cathartic.

MAINTAIN IT

The goal of organising your home is to only be left with items that you love, serve a purpose and have a place to be stored. Personally, I love décor, so I have lots of décor around my house. A rule I've set for myself is when I buy something new, I must sell or donate an item that I no longer use or love. A great rule for you to live by is 'for every one thing you bring in – something needs to go out'. This ensures you are not bringing new items into your home without purging old ones. Remember, the systems and zones that you set up during the organising phase accommodated for everything you had at the time. These need to be managed to ensure they don't overflow. Personally, I do a mini declutter every few months to avoid items accumulating. I recommend setting yourself a one-, two- or three-monthly reminder (depending on how much you like to shop!) to do a mini declutter to help you stay on top of everything.

TOP FIVE

The most popular areas that I am brought in to organise are the kitchen and pantry, wardrobe, office, kid's bedroom and toy room. Below I've given you a cheat sheet so you can organise these rooms yourself.

KITCHEN

The kitchen is the most utilised area of the house and often one of the most disorganised too. There are many reasons why kitchens can be disorganised and dysfunctional, including:

- lack of storage space
- excess cookware, Tupperware, crockery and appliances
- bulk or excess quantities of food

The best way to approach organising your kitchen is to first do a big declutter. This includes every single cupboard and drawer in your kitchen. Go through absolutely everything and get rid of anything that is broken, expired or hasn't been used in the last six to twelve months.

Items to purge

- expired food/spices
- broken appliances, Tupperware, cookware and crockery
- anything you have not used in the last six months (excluding those used on specific occasions such as Christmas)
- unwanted gifts such as crockery (yep, that includes the Royal Doulton set you were given at your wedding ten years ago and haven't used once)
- duplicate dinner, cutlery and glassware sets – you only need one to two depending on the size of your family.

Set up your drawers and cupboards

Every drawer and cupboard should be set up as a specific zone and ideally house no more than one to two item categories. Below are some loose categories for you to follow:

Drawers

- cutlery
- utensils
- alfoil, cling wrap, sandwich bags, garbage bags
- tea towels, dish drying mats

Drawers/Cupboards

- pots and pans
- Tupperware
- baking accessories
- cooking accessories/small appliances
- plates and bowls
- cups and mugs
- lunch boxes, cooler bags and water bottles
- medication/vitamins/wellness

Pantry

- oils/vinegars/sauces/condiments
- spreads
- spices
- cans
- meal kits/dinners
- pasta, grains and rice
- dried fruit, nuts and seeds
- long life milk/drinks

- snacks/school snacks
- sweets
- baking
- cereals
- backstock (this area houses duplicates of items you already have in dedicated zones)

Fridge

- dairy
- yoghurt
- cheese
- deli meats
- dinners/meal kits
- drinks
- fruit
- vegetables
- spreads/condiments
- cooking (minced garlic, ginger, curry pastes)
- lunches
- use me first (items about to expire)

Wardrobe

- Rotate your clothes depending on the season. If you have the room, store seasonal clothes in storage bags and only have current season clothes hanging up and in your drawers. Swap everything over at the change of season. Use this opportunity to do a mini declutter of items you haven't worn!
- Use shelf and drawer organisers or baskets if you have the room.
- Hang: shirts, dresses, skirts, pants, tops, jumpers, jackets.
- Fold: underwear, shorts and swimwear.
- Store shoes on shoe racks.

- Store smaller bags inside larger ones.
- Purchase storage solutions for makeup, jewellery and accessories such as trays, boxes or baskets.

PRO TIP: Hang all items with the hangers facing towards you. When you use something, put it back so the hanger is facing away from you. At the end of the season anything that has not been turned around (worn) can be donated or sold.

Home Office

- Use desk organisers such as pen holders, trays, folders and magazine holders to sort and store paperwork and stationery.
- Use small drawer organisers to organise smaller stationery items.
- If you have a lot of paperwork, purchase a file storage system that works for you, such as a filing cabinet or folders, trays or even magazine holders. Make sure you group paperwork together, such as manuals and warranties, receipts, bills and important documents.
- Cube units and bookshelves are a great way to store books, folders, paper trays, boxes with stationery items and printer paper and can also be used to display photos and décor.

Kid's Bedroom

- Follow the same rules for their clothes as outlined in the wardrobe section.
- Use a cube unit with inserts or a bookshelf to store toys and books.

- Label each insert with a word or picture label so you know what is stored in each one.
- If you have other areas to store toys, such as a toy room, move as much as you can in there to avoid overcrowding the bedroom.
- If your child is in school, set up a desk space for them to sit at to do their homework.

Toy Room

1. Categorise, categorise, categorise. Some example categories include:
    - Lego
    - Barbies/dolls
    - dress ups
    - trucks/cars
    - puzzles
    - books
    - arts and crafts
    - games
    - remote control toys
2. Store like items together in tubs, baskets or boxes. Cube units with inserts and the TROFAST range from IKEA are ideal for organising toy rooms.
3. Label every cube, box or basket. Use image labels if you have young kids. You're always going to have toys that don't necessarily fall into a category and that's okay so make a 'miscellaneous' or 'assorted' tub for these to live in.
4. Set up dedicated zones, for example a reading nook, arts and crafts table, play kitchen or Lego table. If possible, store the relevant toys close to these areas.
5. If there isn't enough room for all the toys that you have, utilise

baskets or boxes in a wardrobe or cupboard (if available and you have the space) and rotate toys on a monthly or bi-monthly basis. If you're still having trouble with finding a home for everything, you may need to go through and choose items to donate or sell with your child. Involve them in the process – kids love to help!

6. Donate excess toys and books to your child's day care, pre-school or school (check that they're open to donations first) or to your local Vinnies, Salvation Army or charity bin. The key to decluttering and organising a toy room is to get rid of toys and books that are no longer age appropriate, that have parts or pieces missing or that your child simply isn't interested in anymore.

WORK WITH ME

I offer several services that range from virtual organisation packages, personalised home organisation guides, in-home decluttering and organisation, product recommendations, interior design, moodboards and more. If you are interested in any of these, please feel free to email me at organisedsimplicity@hotmail.com or send me a message via my website www.organised-simplicity.com.au or Instagram www.instagram.com/organisedsimplicity. I'd love to help you achieve your goals!

Bio

Jordy Fabian is the owner of a boutique home organisation and styling company, Organised Simplicity.

Born in Sydney, Australia, Jordy began her career working in digital marketing for high profile clients such as Toyota, Coca-Cola, Diageo, Unilever and Nestlé before taking on a more traditional communications and media role within the public service and settling down in Brisbane.

In 2019, after almost fifteen years of working in marketing and advertising, Jordy decided to change career paths and commenced studying a Bachelor of Nursing. Although she enjoyed studying, she was still longing for a creative outlet. In 2020, Jordy decided to turn her passion for organisation and styling into a business, and Organised Simplicity was born. Soon after launching, the demand for her services became so high that she deferred from her degree to focus on building up her business.

Jordy has organised and styled countless homes, but her speciality lies with creating 'Instagram worthy' pantries. As the demand for her trademark style continues to grow, Jordy has been lucky enough to travel all over her home state of Queensland, as well as NSW and the ACT to help her clients achieve their dreams of living in an organised, functional home.

What sets her apart from others is her eye for detail and her perfectionist approach when it comes to styling, whether it be a pantry, cupboard or an entire house.

Jordy currently resides in Brisbane with her family and enjoys helping people regain control of their lives by ridding their homes of unwanted clutter and implementing systems that are easy to maintain.

Qualifications:

- PRINCE2® qualified Project Manager

Work with Jordy:

Free fifteen-minute consultation including recommendations for products to organise any one room or area in your home.

Connect with Jordy:
Facebook: www.facebook.com/organisedsimplicity
Instagram: www.instagram.com/organisedsimplicity
Website: www.organised-simplicity.com.au

SCHEDULING TIME FOR YOU

Marissa Rehder

Your life is always speaking to you. The fundamental spiritual question is: Will you listen?

– Oprah Winfrey

How are you feeling? If you're anything like many women, the answer is 'depleted'. You're working hard to take care of others – your family, your friends and your career – but often neglecting yourself. It's a vicious cycle. You don't have time for self-care because you feel guilty about taking it. And then, when you finally do find some time for yourself, guilt sets in again as soon as you start thinking about what else needs to be done.

This is a problem. These cycles can't go on forever, and they'll only get worse if you don't make some changes to your mindset. You deserve to take care of yourself as much as anyone else in your life needs you.

Acknowledge that this guilt isn't helpful. It's just another way that people are trying to control the way you live your life. It doesn't have any bearing on how good or bad a person you are. If something matters enough for someone else, then they should be able to do it themselves. And now we're back at square one with self-care again. It feels like an impossible task when it seems like there are so many things pulling us away from taking time.

I can attest to this firsthand. It wasn't many years ago that I too was waking up each day to just go through the motions, hoping that things would magically get better. There is not much worse than living a life filled with stress, overwhelm and brain fog that keeps you from fully being present and enjoying life. I would wake up, go to work, come home to my husband and three girls exhausted, only to do it over and over, day after day. My girls were constantly getting 'left over mom' which is what I referred to myself after giving my all to my students in the classroom all day. I was constantly living in either the past, dwelling on my mistakes, or the future, thinking that if I could just get a job I truly loved, build a house, take a vacation or any number of other things, I could finally be truly happy. I was at a place where I couldn't even understand the idea that some people were truly happy in life.

My negative self-talk manifested into physical struggles that, once again, kept me from fully enjoying my life and my family. I had even gone as far as convincing myself that I didn't need to do the things I used to love because I chose to be a mom and a teacher so by making those choices, I was choosing to give up myself.

I'm here to tell you that there are so many flaws in how I was living my life during the early years of my marriage. And the biggest one was not allowing myself the time and space to rejuvenate myself through self-care. This isn't something that is just going to happen, it has to actually become a lifestyle – one that you choose day after day. It takes intention and consistency to rewire your ability to put yourself on your to-do list.

Society often tells us that self-care isn't selfish, that it's a must-do activity. Society has also led us to believe that self-care is a form of pampering, including facials, massages, long bubble baths, sipping wine while watching your favourite TV show. While these things can be considered self-care, they are not the only options. I think we need to start by defining what self-care really is. It's any activity that allows you to feel renewed, less stressed and less overwhelmed. Self-care is also not to be confused with self-indulgence, which might make you appear to be happy in the short term but can have the reverse effect in the long term. I'm sure you've heard the saying 'you can't pour from an empty cup'. But this raises a question for me: Why are we expected to pour from our cup at all? What if I told you that the true secret to practising self-care is to fill your cup so full that it overflows into the cups around you. *Cue excuses* – 'I'm too busy to take time for myself', 'It's just another task on my to-do list', 'blah, blah, blah ...'

The truth is, you're not too busy. You just don't value yourself enough to invest in your own wellbeing. And it's a self-perpetuating cycle. The more stressed and overwhelmed you feel, the less likely you are to take care of yourself. The less time there is for taking care of yourself, the more you're feeling stressed, making you even worse at caring for your needs.

Knowing what I know now, it's honestly hard to believe that so many people make self-care a chore because they feel like they don't have time. With the right planning and motivation, you can find ways to take care of yourself without feeling like it takes too much time out of your day. Here are some tips for scheduling self-care into your life:

- Figure out what your priorities are. Is it yoga, running, reading, or journaling? Maybe you need an afternoon nap, rather than time at the office, or you need to create solid morning and nightly routines.
- Figure out which activities make you feel rejuvenated and prepared for your day. After that, schedule them in!
- Think about when during the day will work best for each activity with some consideration to how long that would take. For example, if I want to do thirty minutes of yoga without

interruption, this could easily happen right after I finish eating breakfast before getting ready for school/day care. On weekend mornings, because there aren't other demands on our time, I might try doing forty-five minutes of yoga.

In order to help you get better organised, here are my top three tips for scheduling your self-care:

Create routines that work best for you; this might mean going to bed early, journaling or reading during your morning or nightly routine, doing yoga with friends every Saturday morning or waking up ten minutes early to meditate in the quiet before your family wakes up.

1. Write down what helps make sense of your life and get organised. Practical self-care includes things like decluttering your spaces, creating and sticking to a budget, cleaning, keeping a planner, and so much more.
2. Build solid habits. Use strategies like habit stacking (adding your new habit to an existing one), using visual cues (setting timers, posting notes around your house or anything else that will remind you of your habit), and tracking your new habits (mark down each time you perform your new habit on a calendar or habit tracking page). These are all going to help you build a self-care centred lifestyle. Remember – self-care isn't selfish, so squash the guilt and negative self-talk that creeps in when you think of building this new lifestyle.

Now what? Using a planner, calendar or journal is going to be imperative to scheduling your self-care. Figure out what works best for you and get in the habit of checking it regularly. Check your self-care items off as they are completed or make sure not to book too many at once so that each one is given adequate time.

Self-care can be anything from a walk outside, writing in a journal, reading an inspiring blog post or taking some much needed me-time by going to the spa! Whatever fits your needs will work just fine. Just make sure it rejuvenates your soul. Take five minutes right now to close your eyes and do something nice for yourself, like meditating or listening to music with headphones while no one bothers you (don't forget about breathing!).

Once you have determined where you're going to physically schedule your self-care, it's time to create an action plan to help guarantee your success. Start small, create a mantra, give up your excuses and show up for yourself ... Because you're worth it!

When you embark on this new journey to develop and schedule your self-care routines and habits, it's important to start small. It can be overwhelming and frustrating to set huge goals and not achieve them because you took on too much. Start with one goal that you know you can achieve. It might be as simple as reading ten pages in a new book before bed each night. Once you've created a solid habit from that, move on to the next habit you want to create. Creating a mantra allows you to rewire your subconscious brain into believing you're the type of person who is going to build these new habits. Start by writing out all of the objections you have to your new habit and write them down. Write the opposite of these negative beliefs, using words and phrases that evoke meaning and emotion. Use these statements to create a mantra. When I first started using this strategy, I was determined to become a morning person. My mantra was: 'I love waking up to a new day; my goals and I are worth getting up for.' I had spent so many years believing I wasn't a morning person, I needed to rewire my thoughts that surrounded waking up early. This will help you ensure your success.

The last piece of creating this new lifestyle is to give up your excuses. Life happens to everyone, and it's up to you to quit giving into your excuses and start taking charge of your own destiny. You need to make the decision right now that you are no longer the type of person who makes excuses. Wake up each day fully believing you're the type of person who lives a happy and self-care filled lifestyle.

The time has come to make a change with your self-care routine. You can start by scheduling some easy self-care activities into your daily schedule and getting rid of excuses that hold you back from doing so. Soon, you'll find yourself with solid habits and routines that will leave your cup overflowing into those around you. Remember, if it's important enough for you to do, then find a way!

Quotes

Your life is always speaking to you. The fundamental spiritual question is: Will you listen? – Oprah Winfrey

You are one decision away from a completely different life. – Mel Robbins

In the long run, we shape our lives and we shape ourselves. The process never ends until we die. And the choices we make are ultimately our own responsibility. – Eleanor Roosevelt

If you get clear on the what, the how will be taken care of. – Jack Canfield

A goal without a plan is just a dream. – Dave Ramsey

Mantra: *I am worthy of making changes for. My life is happy and I am present.*

Bio

I'm **Marissa Rehder,** a life coach who focuses on helping overwhelmed women develop self-worth and true happiness in order to design and live their best life.

A former teacher, I found a love for supporting other teachers through my own process of self-discovery. On the verge of burnout and being ready to leave the profession, I decided there had to be a way to overcome the intense feelings the stress of being a teacher, wife and mom was creating. Throughout the next two years, I was determined to create a 'happy life framework' that would benefit more women than just me.

It was throughout this journey that The Nourishment Haven was developed, which is an online community where women can come for support and personal development. I have also started coaching women on how to create the life they have always dreamed of through the process of discovering the best version of themselves.

Qualifications:

- Certified Life Coach
- Certified Life's Purpose Coach
- Certified in Journal Therapy

Work with Marissa:

I work with people in one-to-one coaching sessions, masterminds and through an online membership program. If you would like to work with me, you can find me at https://marissarehder.com/work-with-me

You can check out our monthly membership by going to: www.thenourishmenthaven.com/membership

Connect with Marisssa:
Instagram: https://www.instagram.com/marissa.rehder/
Facebook: https://www.facebook.com/marissarehder
LinkedIn: https://www.linkedin.com/in/marissa-rehder-405587168/
Website: https://marissarehder.com/work-with-me

MASTERING THE ART AND SCIENCE OF THE MORNING ROUTINE

James Yates

Awareness is key to transformational Change

– James Yates

Set up for morning success.
Success doesn't happen by chance; it happens by choice.

Hustle. That's what we all believe we need to do in order to succeed. The thriving entrepreneur of today must be defined by the hustle – the fourteen-hour workdays and seven-day work week – otherwise they're not on the road to success. Holidays are for slackers. And self-care … Who has time for that?

The 'hustle' is glorified. After all, an entrepreneur with dreams doesn't need to sleep, one hungry for success doesn't need to eat, and one so occupied with living out their purpose doesn't need to take time off to recharge. That's how the hustle is packaged, and that's the mindset I bought into years ago when I began my own entrepreneurial journey. It was then that I discovered the dark side of the hustle and the reality behind true sustainable success – both in business and in every other dimension of our lives.

You see, for more than a decade, I 'hustled' to win. I travelled the world as an entrepreneur and worked my backside off day in and day out. And every moment I wasn't in front of people or developing my business, I was at the gym pumping it up. It took a while before I realised that despite my 'success' and growing demand, I was seriously unhappy. I was working as hard as I could, pushing myself with sheer willpower most days, but my relationship, my health and my overall wellbeing were in decline. The truth was, the cracks were starting to show and I was overcome with burnout – emotionally and mentally broke. In an attempt to remedy that, doctors prescribed all sorts of medication and therapies. But as you can imagine, as my lifestyle of hustle continued, those interventions were all in vain. Life had become nothing but a dark whirlpool, and I was spiralling downwards.

All that changed when my wife and I were told we would never be able to have any children of our own. That one line, delivered by a medical expert, shook us and our relationship to the core. It was then that we were presented with a choice – to create impactful change or to stand and stagnate. It became clear that the 'modern' way of life with its hustle and bustle was not working for us. Since then, we have come to realise it isn't working for many others either!

From that moment forward, I realised everything in life needed a drastic shake up, and it would take enormous internal and external shifts to make that happen. Over the course of three years, I called on all of my personal resources, mentors and experiences to dive much deeper into my personal growth journey with one goal in mind – to upgrade all facets of my life. This journey, coupled with the wisdom of our ancestors and advancements in modern science, allowed me to reach the heights of my energy and potential. A newfound sense of fulfilment was flowing into my life. And for the first time in years, I was genuinely happy.

A few years later, our son was born. The first phase of the journey I had set out to accomplish was complete and my eyes opened to the realm of infinite possibilities. Since then, I've shared my story, and my secrets to success, with thousands of people suffering from burnout, fatigue, and overwhelm. And today, I'm sharing it with you.

The thing is, modern society has conditioned us to live very unbalanced, unhealthy and fast-paced lives with no pause for internalisation, introspection and simply being present in the moment. However, by turning our backs on the small joys of life and by neglecting the self-care piece of the puzzle, we risk losing everything we're trying to build from the ground up. After all, we are the foundations of our success, and only when we nail that piece do we have a real shot at experiencing fulfilment, joy and abundance in our lives. And that piece is what I call Mastering Your Morning.

Mastering Your Morning

Starting our day right conditions us to step into the right headspace and helps set the right tone for the day. In fact, when we make our morning routine non-negotiable, we take control of the autopilot habits that are draining our morning glory.

Consider the seemingly harmless habit of reaching for the phone as soon as you wake up. Did you know that around seventy-nine per cent of people – or four out of five smartphone users – do that within the first fifteen minutes of waking up? Worse still, sixty-two per cent of those people are doing so immediately upon waking. This means they've reached for their phone before even greeting their partner. They scroll through social media, check their emails, catch up on private messages or read the news. As a result, their brain is bombarded with external information, urgency and negativity before it's even had the chance to rev up. Instead, they switch gears into the fight-or-flight response, flooding their system with stress hormones that shut down the part of the brain responsible for logic, decision-making and reasoning. Their emotions are wired, their muscles tense and their day is riddled with reactivity. In this state, peak performance is almost impossible.

Now imagine starting your day in a way that enhances your wellbeing, triggers the release of feel-good hormones that spill over into the rest of your day and reduce stress. Visualise yourself being pumped up on dopamine (the pleasure and reward hormone that boosts productivity and focus), serotonin (the happy hormone that enhances memory and learning), endorphins (the pain-relieving and calming hormones that magnify strength and confidence) and oxytocin (the love hormone that deepens bonding and trust). This chemical combination is a powerhouse of productivity, energy and happiness that can be induced through the three primary habits and three secondary habits that constitute the morning manifesto: MBI-GEC.

Move

Breathe

Intentions

Gratitude

Earthing

Connection

Starting your day with these six habits is sure to magnify your health and wellbeing, priming you for a lifetime of sustainable, well-rounded success. So, let's get right into it.

Move (minimum of twenty minutes)

Physical activity is essential to a healthy and happy life. There's a ton of evidence that suggests exercise contributes to treating various chronic diseases, increasing longevity and enhancing our mental health. A good exercise routine is not simply a nice-to-have. It's a fundamental habit that kickstarts the release of serotonin and endorphins, thereby improving our mood and boosting our energy.

In fact, moving is the first thing I do in the morning, and it could be extremely beneficial for you too! After all, our bodies are an intelligent machine that operates on a precise internal biological clock. By moving in the morning, we effectively jumpstart our metabolism and decrease the levels of cortisol (the stress hormone) which played a role in waking us up. It allows more oxygen to reach the brain, thereby enhancing our mental processing power throughout our day. And believe me when I say that you need to be feeling at your best in order to respond to the day-to-day stresses of entrepreneurship.

To incorporate MOVE into your morning routine, consider the following:

MOVE for at least twenty minutes as soon as you get up for maximum results. You don't need to spend hours at the gym every day to benefit from moving your body. Start simple – going out for a walk or practising yoga. It doesn't have to be an intensive workout, and you don't need to run like you're training for a marathon. Aim for a light sweat. Whether you are a first-time mover or a regular exercise junkie, ensure you go at your own intensity. Refer to a healthcare professional when you wish to make changes to your physical activity and, above all, stay safe.

Breathe (minimum of ten minutes)

We've left breathing to nature. Most of the time, this involuntary function of the body is paid little attention to, if not completely taken for granted. But what if I were to ask you to bring your attention to your breath and become aware of your breathing style and pattern? Do you breathe through your nose or mouth? Is your breathing deep, or is it shallow?

You may have not heard this in school, but there's a wrong way to breathe and a right way. The wrong way is through the mouth, which results in shallow and short breaths. It's estimated that up to thirty per cent or even as much as fifty per cent of modern adults breathe through their mouth. This leads to trauma of the soft tissues of airways, enlarged tonsils, dental decay, bad breath, a greater chance of snoring … and the list goes on! It's not that we've consciously made a decision to breathe like this. Rather, we often change our mode of breathing as a way to deal with the stresses of the modern world. I've observed regularly that a majority of my clients go one step further, holding their breath for long periods of time without even realising it. With that said, awareness is the key to transformational change.

The right way to breathe is through the nose – deeply, slowly and gently. Nasal breathing helps prevent respiratory diseases and increases the efficiency of your lungs by ten per cent to twenty per cent. It also helps reduce the heart rate, improves cognitive performance and strengthens the immune system. By breathing an average of ten to twelve breaths a minute, we regulate the amount of oxygen that enters our brain, thereby breathing our way to better health.

Here's how you can incorporate BREATHE into your morning routine:

Observe the way you breathe generally, and identify whether you breathe more often through your nose or mouth. If you are a mouth breather, consider speaking to a healthcare professional about ways to make nose breathing permanent in your case. BREATHE for at least ten minutes every morning. Do that by consciously observing your breaths. Inhale slowly and softly through your nose then exhale slowly and softly through your nose. Remember to keep your attention on your breath for the duration of the practice.

Look into different breathing techniques that can help spice up your morning BREATHE routine and improve your health, focus and energy. Such techniques include belly breathing, alternate-nostril breathing, the Wim Hof breathing method, and many more.

Consult a healthcare professional when you are trying out any new breathing technique or if you are taking medication.

Intentions (minimum of ten minutes)

Intentions are the energy behind goal setting and achievement in life. You can think of intentions as the gateways to action. They hold the key to transformative actions and change. Like a compass, intentions guide our actions and add a sense of purpose to that which we aim to achieve.

Setting intentions increases the neuroplasticity of your brain, which is the ability of the brain to form connections between neurons that enhance cognitive functioning. The higher the brain neuroplasticity, the lower the risk of dementia, trauma and mental health challenges.

I've found that setting intentions first thing in the morning increases energy, performance, and productivity throughout the day. When we set intentions, we tune into the present moment and use positive thinking to channel energy into what we desire to achieve. It enhances our feelings of wellbeing, allowing us to feel like we've already achieved our goals. Moreover, it empowers us with resilience to take on our day and work around the obstacles that inevitably pop up.

Here's how you can incorporate INTENTIONS into your morning routine:

Spend around ten minutes every morning setting your intentions for the day. By doing so, you will be clear on what you are looking to accomplish, and you'll find it easier to remain focused on your goals.

Record your intentions from the perspective of you at the end of the day. So instead of writing 'I will make five business-related calls today', write 'It's 3:00 pm, and I feel wonderful after making five business-related calls today'.

As you are setting your intentions, tap into how it would feel to go through with them. Acting upon your intentions is always a rewarding feeling. Visualise how happy, satisfied, proud of yourself, confident and inspired you would feel.

You can take it a step further and turbocharge your energy by practising these three secondary habits to turn every morning into the beginning of greatness:

Gratitude: I love to spend at least five to ten minutes every morning journaling what I am grateful for and sharing it out loud with my family. We hold space for each other to share, and this creates smiles and happiness all round. Gratitude can impact your health, relationships and success. It reminds you of all the wonderful things that are going for you and opens you up to all the amazing things that are yet to come.

Earthing: Also known as grounding, this practice of directly connecting with nature through physical contact with the earth helps your body come back into alignment. In as little as thirty minutes, earthing has been shown to activate healing, reverse inflammation, and magnify feelings of wellbeing. To that end, often I will exercise or walk barefoot so that I can earth whilst still accomplishing other areas of my morning routine.

Connection: Research has shown that when we enjoy powerful

connections, we have a fifty per cent increased chance of longevity. I make a conscious effort to connect with those I love every morning. Whether that be physically with my immediately family, or reaching out to my greater tribe for a meaningful interaction over the phone. You see, connecting with those we love is invaluable – enhancing our self-esteem, offering emotional support and alleviating loneliness. Social connections give life added meaning, so be sure to nurture them consistently. And remember that nothing boosts our love hormone, oxytocin, more than a good old hug.

The MBI-GEC morning routine is one of the most impactful tools in my arsenal. It underpins everything I teach and it's the first thing I prescribe to those I mentor, coach and guide. It's the foundation of my success, and it is sure to become the foundation of yours.

Stop focusing on other people's glory and get focused on building your story.
Success comes from creation rather than consumption.
You'll attract what you want when you're grateful for what you have.
The art is to dream big and the science is to remain present. Embrace the now and start experiencing what is possible.
Awareness is key to transformational change.

Call to Action

Are you looking to embark on a powerful self-care journey? As the founder of Reignite Enterprises, I would like to personally invite you to The Reignite Retreat.

The Reignite Retreat is a transformative four-day self-care retreat that provides you with a place and a space where you can elevate your energy, wellbeing, and happiness. You will be guided and supported by world-class experts that will hold a space for you to renew your energy, nourish your wellbeing, rewire your mind and optimise your habits and behaviours so that you can leave with practical tools that can enhance your life moving forwards.

Hosted in what can only be described as a haven – where you are surrounded by nature, wildlife and are a stone's throw from the ocean – The Reignite Retreat takes you on the ultimate adventure. Here, life-long connections are made and the discovery of our deep connection with our Self is had.

Renew. Nourish. Rewire. Optimise.

To learn more about The Reignite Retreat, simply visit: www.reigniteretreat.com

Bio

James Yates is a high performance coach, speaker and entrepreneur. He is the co-founder of Reignite, a life enhancement company that creates unique programs, products and experiences that bring people

together for causes that support the evolution of consciousness and the expansion of human potential.

James specialises in both human optimisation and conscious entrepreneurship. He has worked extensively with a wide range of individuals and corporations to improve and amplify their personal and professional performance.

Calling on a wide range of practical tools, techniques and biohacks that he has developed and utilised with great effect over a twenty plus year career, James' high impact events and programs are all built on real life experiences he ensures are personally tried and tested.

James has spoken at hundreds of events across the world and co-founded the internationally renowned experience, The Reignite Retreat, which attracts hundreds of people each year who are looking to perform better in all areas of life. He has also received praise for a variety of professional accomplishments, including being recognised as one of the world's top three home business trainers and being celebrated as the number one sales recruiter in two large multinational companies, where he developed, supported and coached various high performers and their teams.

James is extremely passionate about helping as many people as possible live their calling and do what they love. He has countless testimonials from people whose lives have been transformed by the strategies and techniques he has helped them to master.

Work with James:

To find out more about James' offerings, visit jamesyates.me.

Connect with James:

Facebook: https://www.facebook.com/JamesYatesCoach

LinkedIn: https://www.linkedin.com/in/jamesyatescoach/

Website: jamesyates.me

SECTION 10:
PROFESSIONAL SELF-CARE

INTRODUCTION

Tracey Jewel

No matter what you do for a living, it can create stress. From managing deadlines to managing teams, professional self-care is a must for carving that career path to success. Workplace stress won't simply disappear on its own. There will always be something that dials up the heat and puts the pressure on.

A healthy work life is important, even if that workplace is toxic. You may not be able to change where you currently work at this time, and even if you do, there's no guarantee the next place you go will be any less stressful. That's why it's up to you to put things in perspective and manage your own stress so that you can be calm when navigating the stormy seas ahead.

Do you take breaks at work and get up to stretch your legs? Do you forgo your earned vacation days instead of using them as you deserve? How often do you take work home? If you're not getting back what you put into work, it's time to look at career self-care and give yourself what you need to feel supported at your job.

Simple acts like leaving your desk to eat your lunch, taking a brisk walk through the corridors on your break and learning when to say 'no' to things and set boundaries, will all help you manage your work-life balance and boost your professional self-care. On the following pages, you'll learn how to make your own successes, achieve your goals for your career and leave that work-related stress behind you – even in the face of deadlines.

PROFESSIONAL SELF-CARE: HAPPINESS AND BALANCE AT WORK

Erin Devlin

You before business.

We give so much of ourselves at work – more than a third of our waking life. What if we could get up every workday, achieve great results and leave feeling energised, satisfied and proud?

As a working mum of twin toddlers, running two businesses and volunteering, I understand how busy life can be. I've travelled the world, danced as a professional ballerina, pursued a nearly fifteen-year career in recruitment and have recently published my first book, *Get the Job You Really Want*. Throughout all of this time, I have always kept family and friends front and centre. It's not been easy balancing everything, but it's certainly been enjoyable, rewarding and incredibly fulfilling.

Over the journey, I've developed and applied strategies that have helped me to balance workloads, family, commitments, goals, health and values. I believe that everyone deserves to feel happy, fulfilled and engaged at work. Achieving balance in work and life can be difficult, but it is easier when our goals, values, time investment and energy are all in alignment.

Self-care at work starts with you. It means you always come first – before business. There is no business without you, your health and your happiness. It's that simple.

Here are ten key principles that I follow in my professional working life, which I hope can help you to manage the demands and challenges that every day brings and look after your health and wellbeing at work:

1. Align your values and career goals with the right job, career and employer.

Wish you could leap out of bed excited for the challenges and the opportunities of the day? Finding this feeling starts with aligning your values and career goals with the right job, career and employer.

First, develop a career vision that you would like to work towards. Perhaps it is one that gives you balance and flexibility in your job, or maybe it takes you towards a particular level of earnings or gives you meaningful work opportunities. Decide what is important to you and set a career vision to work towards. Next, assess yourself in the following areas to help set your career direction:

Interests – What do you love doing? How do you spend your spare time?

- Motivating factors – What would make you excited to go to work every day?
- Strengths – What are you good at? What are your natural abilities?
- Values – What are your core values? What principles do you hold dear?
- Achievements – What have you achieved in your life and career to date?

Next, set some career goals, using a formula like George T Doran's S.M.A.R.T goal acronym.

S.M.A.R.T. stands for specific, measurable, assignable, realistic and time-based. For example, you might say 'I'd like to be a market leading expert in UX Design within the next five years'. You can set one major goal, plus several micro goals that help you to achieve particular skills or objectives.

Build your assessment of interests, motivating factors, strengths, values and achievements, plus your career goals, into a career plan. You can also work with a career practitioner to explore your options further.

If you would like to access a free career plan template, visit people-2people.com.au.

Lastly, assess your current employer or potential employers for their alignment with your goals and what's important to you. Look at values alignment, culture, benefits, career progression, training and development, flexibility and work-life balance, location, environment and performance. You may also look at how much emphasis each employer puts on creating meaningful work opportunities. Do they offer challenge, opportunity to help others, give back, support your community or improve environmental sustainability? Will you feel fulfilled, supported and enriched by working there? Self-employment might be on the list of options to consider, so if you are thinking of going out on your own or with others, run your self-employment opportunity through the same lens.

If your career goals and values are aligned with your employer's, then you are much more likely to enjoy your work, feel balanced, be happy and thrive. Greater alignment means better outcomes for both you and your employer and better opportunities for you to progress in your career.

2. Set goals in your job

Once you feel that you are in the right job, with the right values alignment, you can set specific goals that help you develop and progress within your career. Ask yourself:

What would I like to achieve in this position in the next twelve months? Or the next five years?

- What action do I need to take to make that happen?
- What support, training or resources do I need from my manager, organisation or externally to get there?

To help achieve your career goals you can seek out mentors, engage in networking, undertake further training and education and work with a career practitioner. It's also a great idea to communicate your goals with your manager so that they can assist you in developing and achieving them sooner.

3. Set boundaries and manage expectations

As someone who loves to be a team player and help others, it's tempting to always say yes to work, opportunities and requests. But what if the word 'yes' is making your life unbearable? It's time to rationalise, prioritise and politely draw a line.

Perhaps you would like to commit to having dinner with your kids every night or join a six-week fitness program? Maybe you need more 'me time' or availability to see your friends? Think about what's important to you and what you'd like to spend more time doing. Then carve out time for those activities in your calendar. Set time boundaries and prioritise your work to finish on time. Easier said than done, but with discipline in prioritising yourself, you can enjoy better work-life balance.

Managing expectations of key stakeholders is an important part of achieving balance at work. By communicating when you believe you can get a piece of work done, or by giving more context about your current workload, you can help others to understand what they can expect from you and when. Skilled expectations management can reduce the pressure on you, free up your time, and release you to go and do the things that you love doing.

4. Big rocks, little rocks

Feeling a sense of satisfaction at the end of the day is one of the most important ways to tell your body and mind to switch off. If your workload feels incomplete, it can plague you into the evening and into your personal time. Rather than carrying this burden home, set some micro-goals that you can achieve within the day. To do this well, I recommend focusing on no more than three 'big rocks' each day. Choose three objectives you'd like to meet and make these your focus. Your meetings, emails, internal communications and phone calls can then fit around these. By prioritising your own objectives first, you can feel a sense of accomplishment each day, switch off at the end of it and make your personal time truly yours.

5. Done is better than perfect

Want more time back in your day? There are some tasks that need to be done to perfection – a client proposal, an email to a stakeholder, a publicly available advertisement or a conference presentation. But there are many tasks that can simply be done much faster by using Pareto's principle – the 80-20 rule. Pareto's principle states that eighty per cent of the results come from twenty per cent of the action. Clear away the 'noise' on your desk by focusing on what really matters and what gets results. Focus on the goals, projects and tasks that contribute to your personal or organisational objectives. Move swiftly through tasks and duties by using perfection at the most appropriate times, and at other times remembering the mantra coined by Sheryl Sandberg, 'Done is better than perfect'.

6. Do, delegate, delay, delete

With every task that comes your way, you can either do it quickly, delegate it to someone else, acknowledge it but delay it, or delete it. These steps can help to reduce clutter and noise in your workday and can also improve your wellbeing. Don't delay quick things, get them done and move on.

Don't do things you can delegate – teach someone to do them well if you have the resources and move on. You can delay large projects, but block out time to complete them and manage expectations of others of when they will be done. Delete or remove tasks, projects and activities that take you away from what you would really like to be doing. For me the equation is easy: do I spend this time working with a client that isn't really the right client, or do I spend this time with my family? Decide what is important to you. There is an opportunity cost for every choice, so treat your own time with respect.

7. Systemise and automate

Systemise and automate repetitive tasks in your professional and personal life. For example, rather than writing a response from scratch every time for an email you receive regularly, create a template for it. Rather than receiving a notification every time something happens in your work customer relationship system, create a dashboard, and check it daily or weekly. Learn shortcuts, and put systems, processes and instructions in place, and you will gain more time back in your day.

8. Time versus objective blocks

A strategy I love to use at work and teach to my team, is to organise each day into time versus objective blocks. This is particularly helpful for managing competing priorities. I set myself a period of time, usually forty-five minutes, and an objective that I would like to complete in that time. For example, I might say that I'd like to write a 700-word article in forty-five minutes. If I reach the 700 words before the forty-five minutes is up, then I move onto the next task. If I reach the forty-five minutes and have tried my best, but I didn't quite meet the objective, I move on. This is great if you sometimes find yourself stuck on one task. It can help you to spread your time across multiple opportunities and ensure you invest time in key priorities.

9. Close the gap to happiness

Happiness is often the gap between expectations and reality. If you have a realistic expectation of yourself, you can set yourself up for success. Be clear about what can actually be achieved in one day and make a plan. When you get close to the end of your day – about an hour out from when you finish – this is a great time to take a step back, assess your priorities, and put your plan in place for the day ahead. By doing this with an hour's notice, you give yourself ample time to complete any preparation, reading or tasks required. You can then leave feeling confident, clear and ready for the next day, and you can genuinely switch off in between.

10. YOU before business

No business, job or project is more important than you and your health. Sure, there will be days that you have to put in long hours, and there will be days when something important comes up and must be done. But this can't be the norm, or you and your mental health will burn out. You are the person who comes first – along with your health and wellbeing. If you are fit, healthy and happy you will not only feel better, but you will also be more productive, effective and enjoyable for others to work with.

Always put yourself before business, and you can enjoy a long and rewarding career. Whether it's aligning your life and career plans, setting goals, giving yourself realistic expectations or setting boundaries, there are many ways you can put your own wellbeing first and thrive both at work and at home.

References

G T Doran, (1981) 'There's a S.M.A.R.T. Way to Write Management's Goals and Objectives', *Management Review*, 70, 35-36

A W Flux, Vilfredo Pareto (1896) Cours d'Économie Politique, Tome Premier, *The Economic Journal,* Volume 6, Issue 22, 1 June, Pages 249–253

https://www.businessinsider.com.au/sheryl-sandberg-lean-in-2013-2?r=US&IR=T

Bio

Erin Devlin GAICD MRCSA is an experienced business leader, author, board director, engaging speaker and recruitment industry leader. In 2021 she published her first book *Get the Job You Really Want*. She was the RCSA SEEK Professional Recruiter of the Year 2017 and a finalist for the 2021 RCSA Industry Leader Award. Erin is the managing director of people2people Recruitment Victoria and leads a team of professional recruitment consultants. As CEO of Infront Sports Consulting, she has also worked with over 500 professional athletes and coaches on career transition and planning. With nearly fifteen years' experience in recruitment, she is a board director for the Recruitment, Consulting and Staffing Association (RCSA) and a graduate of the Australian Institute of Company Directors. Erin is a regular guest speaker with ABC, Seven Network, Nine Network, Foxtel, 2UE, Fairfax and Shortlist on careers and employment. An established author, Erin's first book, *Get the Job You Really Want* helps job seekers, career changers and professionals to secure engaging, meaningful and satisfying jobs and promotions. Published in 2021, it is available from: people2people.com.au/resources.

Follow Erin on social media for career advice and tips.

Connect with Erin:

Instagram: @erin_devlin_

LinkedIn: https://www.linkedin.com/in/erindevlin/

Twitter: @erin_devlin

Website: https://www.people2people.com.au/consultants/erin-devlin

PAY CHEQUE PERIL: WHY YOU MUST ENJOY MEANINGFUL WORK

Brian Klindworth

May your internal voice drown
out the external chorus.

– Author unknown, and not
bold enough to call my own.

That's it I'm done. I don't need any more amazing stories to impress others. As tantalising as the anticipation of holding the attention of loved ones whilst telling my story had been, I was done. That wasn't fun, and I didn't enjoy completing a marathon. For decades I had been climbing mountains, jumping out of aeroplanes, travelling around the world, chasing trophies on the sporting field and in the office: grander titles, more money, international postings, million-dollar deals. All for what? Pursuing other people's notion of success so I could be loved and accepted.

It was time for me to work out what I wanted and do it for myself. To love and accept myself.

Do you want to be happy, or do you want to appear happy? Never mind what the world tells you to do to be happy. Be truthful to yourself and discover what you really want. – Haemin Sunim

What role does work play in your life?

Eighty-five per cent of people in full time jobs globally are unhappy in their jobs. – Gallup

Has it become your number one priority? By that I mean, do you plan your life around work? Setting your alarm clock to get up so you can be at work on time. Stopping work at the end of the day only when your job is complete. Coming home and switching off because you have nothing left to give. Perhaps living it up on the weekends or stopping completely so you can survive the next week at work.

I refer to this as working to pay the bills. I did this across five careers, in three countries, and experienced three redundancies and divorce during that time. Success sounded something like: get a good education, get and keep a well-paying job, get married, buy a house, start a family, then hang on for dear life until you can retire and then start living life as you really want to.

The role of work in my life has had two significant reincarnations. One as the vehicle to support the life I want to live, and two as a vehicle of contribution. Exploring and answering the question of what this work thing is all about, inspired me to write down the life I wanted to live. Not in that moment, more what I was building to, what I considered the most rewarding and exciting time of my ideal life. I pictured myself as a husband and father of four kids living in and owning my own home fifteen kilometres from the Melbourne CBD. That was just the start of the image and details. This process of imagining my ideal life has guided a continual evolution of my relationship with work.

Work became no longer the highest priority in my life as described above. I was no longer just working to pay the bills. My work was being shaped to not only provide the financial resources required, but to provide the time to participate in and not just bankroll the life I wanted to live.

Tony Robbins' model of the six core human needs awakened me to the importance of connection and contribution for happy humans. That is, humans need to be connected to and making a contribution to others. His model provides insight based on the idea that all our actions are motivated by a desire to meet our needs. Those behaviours may be unconscious or conscious, and even graceful or disgraceful, with the same purpose of meeting a need. Given the time we spend at work, that makes it the vehicle for our greatest contribution to whatever cause or population we choose to serve.

Your mission is within waiting to be expressed without.
Your heart is the gateway of its inspired expression.
– Dr John Demartini

Now I live and talk about enjoying meaningful work. At one level a job is a group of tasks. Most jobs are filled with tasks that people are good at and can get paid to do. What is often lacking, or non-existent, are tasks that an individual loves completing and or finds meaningful.

What is a task that an individual loves completing? Take a moment to reflect on a giddy childhood moment. You know, the moment that inspires a smile that takes over your face, warms your heart and has you expressing yourself without a care in the world. Yeah, that moment. It's a feeling I want you to capture. How often do you experience that level of energy in your work?

What is a meaningful task? Have you considered whether your job makes a difference? What about who or what is impacted and how? I encourage you now to take moment to reflect on a time in your life when you righted a wrong or saved the day. I am picturing you standing tall, chest up, with just the edges of your mouth turned up in a satisfied grin. Well done you, you made a difference. When was the last time you embodied that energy, having completed a task you felt was important in your day job?

While our days are filled solely with tasks that we are good at and can get paid to do, we are externally motivated. You know, the experience of turning up because you are paid to do so or because your boss tells you how wonderful you are. Or maybe you hang around because the job is just flexible enough to leave behind while you connect with the people and activities most important to you.

Jobs that contain tasks that you love and find meaningful allow you to access internal inspiration. Inspired individuals don't need to be told when to start or to keep going. They are more organised and structured. They see challenges as opportunities to grow and do indeed become masters of their craft. This allows them to take on more complex challenges, which sees them valued more highly by themselves and others.

Top two regrets of the dying: 1. I wish I'd had the courage to live a life true to myself, not the life others expected of me. 2. I wish I didn't work so hard. – Bronnie Ware.

Those who enjoy meaningful work no longer have their job on a pedestal and build a life around it. They have integrated their work and life so they facilitate and support one another. Each day is no more important than another and can be lived fully.

So how do you create a relationship with work that helps you take care of you and live your ideal life? Try some or all of the following:

Life Design

Take some time for you and write down what you want to create for your life – from today right through to whatever age you believe you will live to. Give thought to who you want to share it with and how you might pay for it. What level of health and wellbeing would be needed to support it, and who would you need to be to make it happen?

Ideal average day

Write it down, everything. When does it start? Where does it start? What do you do? Who do you share it with? Now you are started, keep going.

Ideal job

This is more than what you put into a Seek or Indeed job search engine. Keep going until you have twenty features that will have you doing what you want in a way that you will have to succeed.

Task Audit

Reflect on your last week and all the tasks you completed, yes, even the one's not worth mentioning. Then put them in one of the following four categories:

The most valuable contribution you can make
Those that energise you
Energy suckers that leave you flat
What could be delegated?
What changes could you make?

Values alignment

Do you complete a to-do list? If no, start. If yes, align your tasks to your values. It is amazing how much more important those 'meaningless' tasks seem when aligned to your values.

Gratitude

At the end of the day, join the dots to see how your work supported you in living your ideal job that supports your ideal average day while building the life you have consciously designed.

Health and Wellbeing

Define what it means to be healthy and well for you. No, don't get distracted by what it is not; focus on what it is. For a gold star include physical, mental, emotional and spiritual wellbeing. A mantra or statement might do the trick.

To focus solely on what you have to do is a missed opportunity, for we must be before we can do. So, who do you need to be to take one or many of the actions above? Kind? Courageous? Playful? That's up to you. I have read that our values are inspired by our voids. What is or has been missing in your life? I have also read that aspirational values are a choice and might be whatever emotion we wish to experience. I am a fan of observation and lived wisdom. Choose up to three, and perhaps start with just one. Filter your decisions through this value and take actions in alignment with it. Then be still and reflect on what impact it had on you. Then trust that feedback, trust you, and be the person you want to be.

So, what are the perils of a pay cheque?

sixty-seven per cent of adult Australians are overweight or obese.1

forty-five per cent of Australian adults will be affected by mental illness at some time in their life.2

forty-four per cent of marriages globally end in divorce.3

The working poor is over ten per cent in some countries in Europe.4

fifty-one per cent of Australians experience loneliness every week.5

To say one's work is solely responsible for the statistic above is overly simplistic. Ignoring the role of work in populations that these statistics have come from might be a decision to live in fantasy.

Enjoying meaningful work will improve your health, relationships, wealth and the legacy you leave. Be intentional. Be conscious. Be wise in choosing what role work plays in your life so you can benefit from enjoying meaningful work.

References

Australian Institute of Health and Welfare:
https://www.aihw.gov.au/reports/australias-health/overweight-and-obesity

Better Health Channel:
https://www.betterhealth.vic.gov.au/health/ServicesAndSupport/mental-illness-statistics

Unified Lawyers
https://www.unifiedlawyers.com.au/blog/global-divorce-rates-statistics/

Tutor2U:
https://www.tutor2u.net/economics/reference/working-poverty
Australian Loneliness Report 2018:
https://www.psychweek.org.au/wp/wp-content/uploads/2018/11/Psychology-Week-2018-Australian-Loneliness-Report.pdf

Bio

Brian Klindworth is a career coach supporting humble explorers to discover and or reconnect with living and working their ideal lives.

Brian's first impression of working was that it was a bad thing, something to minimise as an individual worked to live.

He began his career chasing other people's definition of success working as a recruitment consultant with firms like Michael Page and Link Recruitment. He spent the next ten years working out what he wanted to be when he grew up. This included working in six different careers across three countries and experiencing redundancy three times. During this time he helped hospitals raise funds, individuals improve their fitness, companies relocate executives around the globe and companies develop and recruit individuals utilising psychometric assessments. This breadth of experience helped him understand what it truly meant to live and work his ideal life – to live his definition of success.

Thirteen years dedicated to personal development and consciously living his definition of success allows Brian to share his hard-won wisdom to accelerate others on their journey to living and working their ideal lives.

Qualifications:

- Bachelor of Commerce
- Life Coach, The Coaching Institute

Work with Brian:

Design your ideal life and a way of working to support it with me. Quote this book for a 40% discount on your first month's work to living and working your ideal life.

Connect with Brian:
Website:www.brianklindworth.com
LinkedIn: https://www.linkedin.com/in/brian-klindworth-career-coach/

FROM CAREER TO CALLING

Taina Maarya Jara

The greatest gift you can give the world is to become who you really are.

– Taina Maarya Jara

What tends to happen when we think that we have our life sorted? Life knocks us off course, so that we can get on the right course – we wake up from our illusions and start becoming who we really are, so that we can start doing what we are here to really do.

This happened to me for the first time in 2007 when I realised I was in a 'golden cage'. I had worked hard to build a career that matched the societal expectations of 'success', and I had obtained a permanent position with the Austrian Federal Government specialising in international relations. This had been an 'impossible' dream for a Finnish country girl and university graduate who was 'crazy' enough to believe she could do it.

Indeed, the first years in that role were amazing. I was a member of a team responsible for preparing and running the Austrian presidency of the Council of the European Union in 2006. That time was filled with exciting projects, interesting people and international travel.

After the presidency was over, we entered a quiet period at work, and I fell into a deep hole. I had a lot of time to think. I started to feel there was something else for me, but I had no idea what it was. It felt terrible to think that I was wasting my life sitting in that office.

I then saw a series of images of a yellow flower in my mind's eye. In the first image it was blooming brightly, but then it gradually went down until it died in the last image due to lack of nourishment. This is how I was feeling – that I was dying inside.

I was trapped in a golden cage. I had so many benefits that kept me loyal to a career I no longer aligned with. I lived in one of the most beautiful cities in the world, Vienna, had a 'reputable' job for life and a nice superannuation waiting for me. My mind kept telling me that I would be mad to give it up.

But the hard truth was, I was no longer happy. My inner voice was so loud and clear that I couldn't ignore it, as uncomfortable as it was. I had no idea what was going on with me or what I could do about it. All I could do was to start asking and searching.

I also started to question the foundations upon which I had built my career, namely environmental and sustainability policies. The political narrative no longer made sense to me, and I started to see through all the hot air, smoke and mirrors. I was waking up to the matrix. It was as if my whole world was turned upside down and the rug pulled out from under my feet. Everything I had lived for turned out to be an illusion. It was shocking and scary at first, but connecting with my inner truth was much more important and felt very liberating.

And if that wasn't enough for 2007, the adventurer in me became active and demanding. I had visited my sister in Australia and got an idea of applying for permanent residency over there. That seemed like an exciting adventure and another 'impossible' dream as I had heard how difficult it was to obtain, especially with my background in social sciences. I decided to demonstrate that I could get it and went to work. Fifteen months later I held a permanent visa grant letter from Australia in my hand.

The transition from Europe to Australia was a powerful catalyst for shedding off the 'old me' and discovering the 'real me' and my purpose. It was a difficult and lengthy process, but it happened in the divine timing. I had to face and overcome many fears and challenges, including life crises. Sometimes the ride was smoother, sometimes tougher.

Each time my eyes opened more, as the Spirit was leading me closer to my purpose. The last drop came in August 2017 when I had a multidimensional experience at work (I had settled into an Australian version of the 'golden cage'). I received a message from the Spirit saying: 'This is not going to make you happy.' After the initial emotional shock, I started to see clearly and decided to change my life. I decided to build a life that I loved and help others do the same. I had no idea how I'd do it, but the decision was firmly made. In the coming months, one thing led to another, and in January 2018, I launched my coaching business.

I was so excited about the new chapter of freedom and fulfilment in my life, yet the reality turned out very different. I became a lonely solopreneur, which wasn't aligned with my personality, vision or values.

Once again, I had no idea what to do. But I also knew that I hadn't come this far to settle. I turned to God and asked for guidance. 'There must be a joyful way of building a business. Please help me crack the code!'

Two months later, I received a hunch from the Spirit and acted on it without knowing what to expect. I was divinely guided to the entrepreneurial community and collaborative business model I had been asking for without even knowing if it existed.

Sometime later I remembered the image of the wilting flower I saw while in Austria, and realised that the nourishment I had been lacking to follow my calling and collaborate with other like-minded people.

The highest form of self-love and self-care is to commit to your life's mission.

Then everything else falls into place.
– Taina Maarya Jara

In my experience, the highest form of self-care is to commit to our true purpose in life. Our purpose is written in our soul, and the Spirit is always calling us towards it. We don't need to do anything 'special' or go anywhere 'special' to hear the call. All we need to do is to be honest with ourselves, and listen without preconditioned expectations. The Spirit speaks to us all the time, and if we pay attention, we'll receive the messages.

The calling of the Spirit might seem very subtle, but it is extremely powerful. It is connected to our reason for being in the world and is so powerful that it doesn't go away, even if we try hard to ignore or suppress it. The Spirit keeps sending us signals until we listen, and the more we refuse to listen, the stronger the signals must become.

If we refuse to listen on the mental and emotional levels, the signals might become physical. This has happened to me several times when I 'needed' an injury, illness, relationship breakdown, unemployment or another shock to stop me in my tracks because I was insisting on continuing in the wrong direction. These signals are important wake-up calls, and they make us stronger and wiser if we learn and readjust accordingly. We should never have regrets about the past though, because all those experiences prepared us for what is meant for us.

There are many different ways in which we can express our purpose in life, both personally (such as raising children) and professionally (such as running a business). At this point I'd like to make an important note about goals, intentions and strategies that we use to express our purpose. It is very important that 1) the goals and intentions we set are truly ours, and 2) the strategy we follow is designed to get us there, while we also enjoy the journey. It's so important that we get this right! Otherwise, we end up in an endless rat race of chasing goals that only fulfil us temporarily, if at all. Or we sacrifice our quality of life in the here and now in the hope that things will be better 'when we get there'. These approaches only lead to frustration, exhaustion and burn-out – I've experienced this myself.

When we set our goals and intentions in alignment with the calling we receive, and use our intellect wisely by choosing a strategy that supports those goals and intentions, then not only do we feel fulfilled on all levels, but the entire process of 'getting there' becomes deeply rewarding. We are on purpose every day, and not only in some rare highlight moments when we have a big win or breakthrough.

When we do this, we won't need many of those self-care practices to get some relief from the stressful daily life – instead we may choose to do them because we enjoy them. This is the difference between being 'on course' instead of 'off course', and very important for purpose-driven entrepreneurs who are here to transform the world for the better, while keeping their own cup full along the way.

What You Can Do Right Now

I would like to help you start applying to your own life what I have just shared – no matter where you are at. You may be at the very beginning of this journey, or you may have followed this path for many years and are now ready for the next level.

The first and most important thing is to give yourself permission to be fully honest with yourself. Allow your heart to speak to you, while you listen with an open mind. Often, we run from one coach or healer to another, hoping to get clarity about our life's purpose and the next right steps. At the same time, we haven't given ourselves permission to do what we're called to do. In this way, we block ourselves and are unable to hear and follow the guidance that's trying to reach us.

Secondly, take a moment in your day to connect with yourself. Shut out all distractions and go into your own space. Close your eyes and take a couple of deep breaths. Then imagine that you're lying in your death bed and looking back on your life. Now ask yourself with all honesty: 'Is there anything I regret for not having done, even if I really wanted to, just because I was afraid?' Pay attention to the answers you receive, and take note of them. Know that these are your heart's desires and a part of your purpose. Then return to the present moment and reflect: 'Have I committed to these desires? If not, what is holding me back? Am I willing to commit to them now?'

Thirdly, I'd like to make an important note about self-care. When people talk about self-care, they normally refer to soothing, calming and relaxing practices (such as meditating, taking a bath or a massage or taking a day off social media). This is the feminine-energy side of self-care, of winding down and withdrawing. But sometimes we need the exact opposite to show love and care for ourselves. Often, we feel agitated and stressed because we are holding ourselves back and not expressing what we want to express. This is the masculine-energy side of self-care, of action and expression. It is very important to know the difference between these two, and understand which we need at any time to be aligned and in balance.

A good exercise related to this last point is to make an inventory of how you habitually spend your time. The exercise goes like this:

1. Choose a typical day in your week – a Tuesday or Thursday, for example.
2. Write down all the activities you habitually do from the moment you wake up in the morning to the moment you go back to sleep at night.
3. Go through the list and mark with green those activities that you feel are directly related to your life's purpose (and inspire

and uplift you), and with red those that are not directly related to your purpose (and drain you).

4. Take note of how much green versus red you have in your day and what you can do to make it greener.

This exercise helps you become aware of how you're spending your time, and to make the necessary adjustments to align more with your purpose. Please remember: Small changes lead to significant improvements!

I'd love to close this section with an affirmation that has helped me tremendously, each time I felt guilty for prioritising myself and my purpose: 'The best thing I can do for others is to love and respect myself.' I hope it will help you in your journey!

Living your purpose requires a strategy.

It can be daunting enough to try to figure out what your life's purpose is. But, after that, another question arises: How do you express it in a way that nourishes your soul, supports your health and brings you abundance?

This was my experience in my early journey too. I kept asking what my purpose was, but each time I ended up in confusion and lack of clarity and direction, because I was interested in so many things!

In the subsequent years, I learnt two important lessons:

1. We don't find our purpose; our purpose finds us (if we're willing to listen and follow).
2. To express our purpose, passion is not enough. We also need a strategy that is designed to bring our vision, values and aspirations to life.

Most people only focus on their passions and expect it to bring them everything they need. This can be a very frustrating and disappointing experience, especially if you're seeking to build a healthy and thriving business that allows you to live your purpose – both personally and professionally. An inappropriate strategy can extinguish your passion, while an appropriate strategy ignites your passion. This is why choosing the right strategy from the get-go is pivotal.

If you are like me, you are probably not interested in figuring out business strategies on your own. The great news is that you don't have to because you don't need to create a strategy to use it. You can tap into existing strategies and systems that do a lot of the heavy lifting for you so that you can focus on your purpose and achieve more in less time.

Bio

Taina Maarya Jara is a freedom business mentor and advocate for healthy and purpose-driven businesses. She partners with ambitious and spiritual women and men worldwide to build and grow healthy, thriving businesses online. She does this by helping them align their purpose with a supportive business model and entrepreneurial community.

In addition to her beautiful home country Finland, Taina has lived in Austria, Australia, Belgium, Germany and Spain. She is a global citizen, passionate about connecting with like-minded people worldwide, and is fluent in English, Finnish, German and Spanish.

Taina started her career in international relations specialising in the environment and sustainability. She was a high achiever and drove herself into a burnout and health crisis in 2002. This led to her spiritual awakening and a profound journey of self-discovery, which she pursued in parallel with her career in the government, university and not-for-profit sectors.

After an impactful personal experience in 2017, Taina started to transition from her career to her calling. She launched a coaching business, just to realise that the traditional solopreneur business model was not aligned with her vision of a joyful business that allowed her to fulfil her purpose and create freedom.

She continued searching and found an aligned business model and community, which she now shares with other high achievers who want to build and run purpose-driven businesses in a healthy, joyful way.

Qualifications:

- Master's degree in Social Sciences (Research)
- Diplomas in Mindset Training and Coaching, Counselling and Bioneuroemoción®
- Certificates in Adult Training and Aromatherapy (medically audited).

Work with Taina:

If you'd like to explore how my purpose business strategy and community could benefit you, please contact me via the link: https://www.tainamaaryajara.com/contact. I look forward to guiding you to your next right steps!

Connect with Taina:

Facebook: facebook.com/tainamaaryaj11

Instagram: instagram.com/tainamaaryaj

LinkedIn: linkedin.com/in/tainamaaryaj

Website: tainamaaryajara.com

RECLAIM YOUR ENERGY: BEYOND BURNOUT

Wendy Nash

Burnout is commonly described as a state of emotional, physical and mental exhaustion caused by excessive and prolonged stress that occurs when an individual feels overwhelmed, emotionally drained and unable to meet constant demands.

(Ref. helpguide.org Authors: Melinda Smith, M.A., Jeanne Segal, Ph.D., and Lawrence Robinson)

Times are changing, and we need to change the point of view that if you want to get somewhere you need to overextend yourself and put in the hours. When you keep taking on extra projects, working late or taking work home, sooner or later the signs will appear – insomnia, more caffeine or alcohol, digestive problems and energy slumps in the day. Everything starts to feel harder, even overwhelming, and continuing this stress cycle long term just doesn't work for you, your family, or the company. You reach a point where you're functioning on overdrive all the time and running on adrenal energy, while the voice inside whispers: 'I wish I could just stop, just for a while'.

While burnout has long been associated with job-related stress and heavy demands in the workplace, I believe burnout is just as prevalent, if not more influential, in this new digital world, where more of us continue to work from home. Burnout has become easier to hide behind our screens and digital communications.

I found burnout to be more a soul-tired kind of exhaustion from prolonged stress, inadequate support and lack of work-life balance and self-care. Basically, it's when you're contributing to others more than yourself.

How does burnout manifest?

Burnout can manifest in many ways. It may be an increasing feeling of overwhelm – 'I can't keep going' – and is often the result of prolonged stress, an excessive work overload, unrealistic expectations, lack of adequate support, poor work-life balance and insufficient or a total lack of self-care!

Who does it affect?

More commonly businesswomen and entrepreneurs in their thirties, forties or early fifties experience work related burnout, as they're trying to juggle the demands of corporate life or small business with relationship and in some cases children. Other critical stages can be at times of divorce, or later when being carer as the health of elderly parents declines.

Why is burnout important?

Burnout is your soul's way of getting you to pay attention and to listen to your body. It's a chance to recognise when something's off, to take a step back and look at what might need to change in your life. Is it your job, environment, relationships? What is draining you or not serving you? Do you need to up your self-care? What would you change to bring you more joy? What would bring greater possibilities?

Wendy's story

Growing up in Melbourne, I had two passions: dance and horse riding. I learnt dance from the age of four and had my own pony at age seven. These passions quickly became an integral part of my world. From age twelve, riding grew to play an even greater role in my life, when I began spending my weekends riding in the country and boarding nearby. When I gave up dance at fourteen, my passion for horse riding only grew, leading me to find immense joy and a sense of accomplishment in both leisurely and competitive riding for many years to follow.

It was much later in life, when I had spent years climbing the corporate ladder, at that time living in Sydney, that I was struck with burnout and chronic fatigue. I was stopped in my tracks, and it took me down a transformational path to physical, emotional and spiritual wellbeing. It was a pivotal time that led me to see the incongruence between how I was showing up in my outer world and my true nature. My life was lacking balance, and I was running on the adrenal energy triggered by long term stress. I was missing that heart connection, the mind-body connection, those golden nuggets previously instilled in me from my early passions for dance and horse riding.

For over twenty-five years now, I have devoted my knowledge and professional skills to mentoring others to greater self-empowerment. I have been a facilitator for Access Consciousness® classes, mindfulness-based stillness meditation, Wu Tao dance teacher training and performed on the main stage at Mind Body Spirit Festivals. I facilitated my own Wu Tao and art therapy retreats and meditation classes at The Yarra Valley Living Centre and was guest dance therapist on occasion for Dr Ruth Gawler's retreats. I have also assisted Dr Ian Gawler and Dr Ruth Gawler at their Seven-Day Therapeutic Meditation Retreat.

Currently I offer a range of online programs to help business-women and entrepreneurs to reclaim their energy and beat burnout, using mindfulness-based stillness meditation, the Passion Mapping™ technique and spiritual mentoring-energy healing. I also co-host international Passion Cafés in collaboration with Passion Maps™ International.

My personal experience with burnout came as a wakeup call that I was on the wrong path. I was a high achiever working for a fast-growing publishing company in Sydney, with a growing staff to manage. In the thrill of such a role, my determination to go above and beyond took on a life of its own, and it wasn't long before I was unknowingly running on the fumes of what adrenaline I had left.

Life was fast and fun. I loved the challenge but was subconsciously aware that I no longer had anything that was feeding me at a soul level to give me balance. My years of dance were behind me, and I had given up horse riding in my early twenties. The demands of corporate life quickly infiltrated any time I had once devoted to myself and my two great passions. There was the office environment, long hours, more demanding projects, business lunches and, after late finishes, meeting for dinner with work colleagues, before going home to get up and repeat it the next day. It was exciting, though not sustainable for my body and soul long term.

It was at this point that I first experienced burnout and chronic fatigue. I developed pleurisy and, as an individual who never got sick, naïvely thought it was just like a bad cold. Take a bit of time off and get back to the office, I thought.

When the pleurisy symptoms went, I was left feeling physically and mentally depleted and totally burnt out. I couldn't function normally. I struggled to get out of bed, often lying there wondering if I could make it to the kitchen or the bathroom. I remember lying in bed, my arm against my side feeling like dead weight. I'd wonder how I could move it or roll over in bed. I was uninterested in quick fixes thrown at me by western medicine, like antidepressants, and there really weren't any other treatment options available.

I had totally missed the signs. Many weekends I would retreat to my studio apartment and emerge only to return to the office on Monday morning. My boss couldn't understand how I would spend all weekend locked away without interacting with another human. The thing was, I was accountable for so much during the week – making sure the office was running smoothly, on the phone continually – that I needed some 'space', to not have to talk to or be with another human. I just wanted it all to 'stop' for a while.

Another sign perhaps – though I loved the jobs I'd had across various industries, moving every couple of years to take on a more challenging role, my private time was spent reading psychology and motivational books. I was intrigued by what makes people behave and react the way they do, myself included. There was an obvious gap between how I'd been spending my work hours and what I was passionate about.

I had a sense this was happening for a reason. And I had an inner knowing I was to make changes and look for answers elsewhere if I was to reclaim my energy and wellbeing. The thought of going back to an office was 'ughhh' – it felt so heavy. I never wanted to set foot in an office again! This raised questions around identity. What else could I do? Who am I without the suit/corporate clothes? The title/position I held? What was I meant to learn from this?

I had a strong inner knowing I needed to leave the business world and trust my intuition, as I explored various natural therapies for my own recovery. I was at a crossroads, and a path led me to studying new modalities. By following those, I had success with gaining skills as an energy therapist and slowly reinventing my life.

Burnout was a pivotal time in my life. I was unable to work at all for a couple of years and tried many different modalities and read up on various practices searching for ways to get well. The way back meant I had to make different choices, be open to new therapies, change my eating habits and, in time, take a new career path. It required me to pay attention, listen to my body and really make conscious choices that were right for me.

As I looked for ways to restore my energy, I discovered and came to understand at a deep level that we create our own reality. Also, that we are more than a physical body, we are energetic beings surrounded by energy in all living (and non-living) things. All our thoughts, feelings, emotions and language carry energy, and illness shows up in our energy field long before it manifests in our physical body!

Gradually, through detoxing my body (by changing to mainly a plant-based diet), meditation, energy healing, yoga, Chinese medicine and time in nature, I reclaimed my energy, resilience and wellbeing. I supported this by making time for things I was passionate about, the things that brought me joy.

Self-Care Tools

Accept what is

Start where you are. Know you can choose how you react to things. What can you learn from this experience? Learn patience with yourself and others.

Simplify your life

Get clear on who and what is important to you. Release what no longer serves you.

Clear your energy

At the start and end of the day, or any time you're feeling off or scattered, take three deep breaths and clear your energy bubble (the energy field surrounding you) of any thoughts, feelings, emotions, judgements and projections.

Passions and Joy

Do the things that bring you joy; express yourself creatively; choose books or movies that motivate, uplift you and feed your soul.

Integrity

Choose what is right for you! Being true to yourself restores your energy, inner strength and true nature.

Support

Work with a mentor or energy healer, reach out to family or friends if you need help.

Food as medicine

You need clean healthy eating to nourish the body. Eating plenty of fruit and vegetables and eliminating sugar, dairy and red meat is a good start.

Stress

Let go of what or who is causing stress in your life, and change the way you react to stressful situations.

Pick a ritual and begin

Morning pages – First thing on waking, write at least three pages of whatever comes – just let your thoughts empty onto the pages in totally free form writing.

Meditation – Ideally listen to a relaxing body scan or Yoga Nidra meditation.

Mindful movement – Perform yoga, qi gong, Wu Tao dance or tai chi.

Walking in nature – Walk by the beach, in the countryside, barefoot on the grass.

The thirty-six breaths – Begin by counting your exhalations (one, exhale, inhale … two, exhale, inhale … three, exhale, inhale, and so on). Count until you have completed thirty-six breaths. If you lose count, you can start again. This can be done at one time or throughout the day, counting in four groups of nine. Allow your breathing to unfold naturally. In time, your breathing will automatically become deeper and more rhythmic.

(Ref: The Touch of Healing - Alice Burmeister with Tom Monte)

Bio

Wendy Nash is a change maker, spiritual mentor and energy healer, Passion Maps™ facilitator and mindfulness meditation teacher.

Born in Melbourne, Victoria, her deep knowledge and professional skills initially came from her own challenging journey, from success on the corporate ladder to severe chronic fatigue. It led her on a transformational path to physical, emotional and spiritual wellbeing.

For over twenty-five years, she has focused her deep knowledge, talents and professional skills into mentoring others towards greater self-empowerment.

She has been a facilitator for Access Consciousness® classes, a Wu Tao dance teacher trainer and has performed on the main stage at Mind Body Spirit Festivals.

She has presented her own movement and art therapy retreats and meditation classes at The Yarra Valley Living Centre and was guest dance therapist on occasion for Dr Ruth Gawler's retreats.

Wendy is currently facilitating her own online courses helping businesswomen and entrepreneurs beat burnout and facilitating online Passion Mapping™ courses and spiritual mentoring-energy healing. She also co-hosts international online Passion Cafés in collaboration with Passion Maps™.

Qualifications:

- Diploma Passion Maps™ Coach
- Personal and Relationships Mapping,
- Access Consciousness® Bars and Body Facilitator
- Mindfulness-Based Stillness Meditation Teacher
- Qi Gong Level 2
- Diploma in Small Business Management
- Diploma in Forensic Healing
- Diploma Wu Tao Dance Teacher and Teacher Trainer
- Transpersonal Art Therapy and Transpersonal Counselling
- Kinesiology
- Reiki
- Chinese Acupressure
- Australian Flower Essences and Aromatherapy.

Work with Wendy:

Book a strategy session:
https://calendly.com/wendynash-mentoronline/30mins
or access the freebies: https://wendynash.com.au/freebies/

Connect with Wendy:

Facebook: www.facebook.com/wendynashmentoronline
Instagram: @wendynash_mentoronline
LinkedIn: www.linkedin.com/in/wendynash1/
Website: www.wendynash.com.au

THE FUTURE MINDSET

Alex Ma

The human mind is a beautiful learning engine. And if our work and contribution to our community has a finite timespan then what we learn is as important as how much.

What if there was a way to target the most desirable skills required over our lifetime and learn how to make the most of a rewarding professional career? Having your skills desirable isn't about doing what others want. It's about creating the cornerstone moments that uncover pathways of opportunity in your life and career. The more moments you create, the more future opportunities will also present themselves. This is called having a **future mindset**. This mindset is built by immersing yourself in wholesome mind food that will inspire your career.

My name is Alex, and I'm the head coach of Future Mindset. I've got the professional development recipe to help you find success and a rewarding career, one which is perfect for the time in which we live. In our rapidly changing world, technology and engineering is changing many aspects of our lives. The pace of change now is astonishing. There has never been a more important time to give our careers and lives the space to invest in skills and knowledge that are evergreen and highly valuable. I want to help others in their pursuit of a rewarding career because it enriches the quality of our lives. I believe we should help each other become the best version of ourselves, and my framework puts this concept into practice. Those I have coached have found that gaining these desirable skills sometimes outweighs the satisfaction of landing a promotion, because the skills can be taken with them wherever they go and remain useful time after time. Constantly learning new skills is the foundation of a mindset that will bring your career perpetual accomplishment. I personally never stopped learning. From my background of engineering, I learnt about project management, which helped me lead teams; I learnt about finance, which helped me at work but also in my investment decisions; I learnt about business partnering, which has led me to become a better leader; and the list goes on.

In this chapter, I will show you some examples of the most desirable and evergreen skills that have emerged, and put a framework around forming opportunities and career cornerstones. Whether you're between jobs, pursuing a side project or working part-time or full-time, adopting this future mindset grows your opportunities by investing in knowledge and personal growth.

Distilling down to a framework

When I think about distilling down to the components that create someone's career, I think about a collection of cornerstones. Picture someone, from any profession, reflecting upon their successful career and passing on their story. What moments would they mention? Of course, having the right relationships and being in the right place at the right time will often come up. But when you peel back what you can't control, you'll find there were very actionable steps that led to the cornerstones. What would be your actionable steps? If creating cornerstones makes sense in hindsight, it would make sense that we explore how we can create these moments into the future and how to make them count.

For my journey, some of these cornerstones included the opportunity to create something impactful, being able to collaborate with fantastic minds and be given the opportunity to make mistakes and fail forward. I truly believe that many of these cornerstones were a result of something I learnt, and the knowledge and skills I acquire continue to grow and continue to serve me for the rest of my journey. It is on this notion that this framework was built, and many have now benefited from this life-long learning approach.

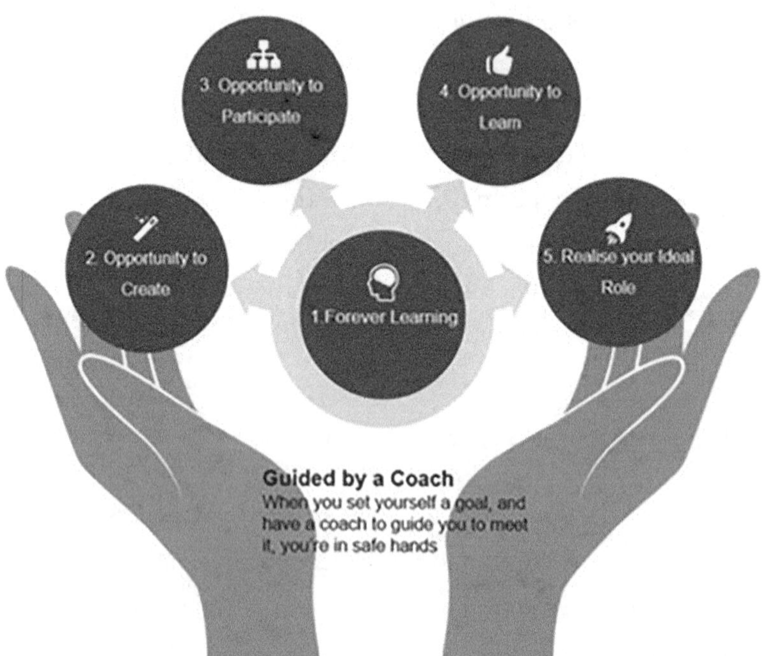

Here's the secret to the framework. Half of your effort will go towards a life-long approach to learning, which I'll cover under the title of Forever Learning and STEM, forming the foundation. The remaining effort is put into the tools, concepts and techniques that create the four types of opportunities that are the components that move your career. I'm going to firstly go through some examples of why this life-long learning approach has been so worthwhile for me and those that I've mentored. Secondly, I'll share some of the techniques to be purposeful with our human interactions, explain why those moments matter and how to make them matter. Lastly, we will cover why the role of a coach is instrumental.

Forever Learning and STEM

The centre is the concept of forever learning with the future in mind. Think about those times when you stumbled across an article that made you wonder how you could apply it to your work, or how a business would thrive with the idea. This goes to activating a growth mindset, which keeps away limiting beliefs, self-doubt and fear of failing. To take that next step to grow your career, you'll need to stay open-minded, have a sense of digital curiosity and embrace STEM (STEM stands for Science, Technology, Engineering and Mathematics and is often referred to in education and industry as a knowledge area with significant demand). In this future world, where collaboration, creativity, inclusion and diversity are going to take centre stage, it's never been more important to master the human connection as well as valuable STEM skills.

Why do I know this? After dedicating a large part of my life studying and working in STEM, I can say there's a growing gap between the number of workers that have these desirable skills and the number of workers needed to create a rapidly digitalised and purposeful future. Digitally fluent workers are able to extract more value from all the data our businesses collect than someone who cannot. One particular study has shown that sixty-eight per cent of data collected by companies don't ever get worked on. Because we live in a time when the data we collect is expanding at an exponential rate, there's a strong case for roles that utilise this data to make good decisions to exist. We can see this in all types of businesses from the mum and dad small business all the way up to large corporations, where skills in data science, coding, digital marketing and robotics are in extra high demand. You don't have to look far for examples: fitness tracker and sports analytics are making data easy to consume, off-the-shelf digital marketing funnels are tracking performance and search engine optimisation (SEO) is boosting traffic. There's now a huge difference between traditional businesses and a business which has strong data maturity. This is why STEM skills and the growing digital space are going to be highly desirable for decades. It's a good thing that coding, data science and digital marketing are examples of skills that are really easy to learn, and anyone can pick them up.

What I help others with, is after understanding what career and industry is ideal for them, I can show you the complementing evergreen and highly desirable skills and how to learn them.

Call to action: Prioritise regular exposure to learning.
Every Week: Prioritise reading about new technologies and developments and learning the relevant skills for growing trends.
Every Month: Prioritise time to learn a new skill no-matter how small.

Opportunity to Create

Your contributions to your current job matter to you and your team. Perhaps in your quest for a more rewarding career, you are looking to have a bigger impact to your company or industry, or perhaps you're looking to create some career cornerstones that can lead to your next promotion. By having a set of subskills, you're more likely to be assigned special initiatives and side projects if you work in a team environment, and these are often the best opportunities to leave your mark. You will never know when one of these side projects you've completed for your team or your company end up becoming a career cornerstone for you.

An example of an area I'm passionate in is my STEM volunteering work has led me to work with great organisations such as Qantas, CSIRO, BHP Foundation, University of Queensland, QUT and Channel Ten's Coding@Home series, where others have recognised my passion and impact and they have thus attracted more opportunities. It all started just from my supervisor seeing my passion in STEM. Sometimes you may not have a relationship with your current boss that gives you space to take on special initiatives. What I help others with here is also to create good support systems and interpersonal skills that give space for opportunity.

Call to action: Plan and seek out opportunities to use your new skills to create memorable impact. These are often a result of following your passions and areas of curiosity.

Opportunity to Participate

There's a common feeling out there that if you spend many years in an industry, the years of experience speak for themselves. The downside of this, for those who want to accelerate their career, is that you get shut out of jobs with 'minimum years of experience'. Compounding this, most, but not all, STEM professions are male-dominated and, until recently, have very small talent pipelines of females and people from diverse backgrounds. My job as a coach, is to help you beat this natural progression line and break the myth of this 'years of experience' yardstick – and it is to do with creating opportunities to participate. Companies worldwide have proven that inclusion and diversity is better for employees and also for the bottom line. Everyone has the right to thrive, and if you're a minority in the industry, your right to thrive has never been stronger! So get amongst it, and get to know more people than ever before!

Despite how much I believe digital skills are highly desirable in the future, we must also embrace empathy and the human connection. What I helped others with here is to build their confidence and to help them seize their right to thrive. That's when you really get noticed. Many of my clients find it hard, as their industry is dominated by middle-aged Caucasian men, which I've also had to overcome as the only Asian in the room for most my career. You just don't know which person you meet can potentially be a cornerstone to your career, such as when a hiring manager remembers your work, remembers having worked with you, or felt a genuine connection with you.

Call to action: Get involved. Make yourself available to explore ways to collaborate with your colleagues. Take on tasks at work that give more visibility to your work. Ever wondered how you actually know you're getting value from your networking? I have a step-by-step process for how to make networking work for you.

Opportunity to Learn

I have very vivid memories of my mistakes and, from the early days of my career, fear of failure and fear of exposing my weaknesses. In the world of project management, where managing change is bread and butter, I made my first significant mistake pretty early on – two years into my career – when I stretched myself to take on a large responsibility. This engineering mistake cost the project a precious week and $200,000. For the next two years I would regard change management as one of my weaknesses. In my sixth year, in preparing for an interview for a high-profile commercial role, I realised that the follow-through to fix my own mistake and the lessons learnt was a great example of my character. When my moment of sharing and vulnerability was over in the interview, the hiring manager chose to focus on my authenticity and ability to change the plan when needed, and he gave me the job. I had learnt the valuable lesson of *failing forward*. I went on to implement an unpopular organisational change that saved the company over a million dollars.

Looking back, I have learnt the value of mistakes, and that success and failure are both part of the same building blocks that make you stronger. Had I not shared this failure through a moment of vulnerability, I wouldn't have discovered and put into use one of my great strengths.

This story and many others came to define my strengths as an individual and as a leader, and added depth to my personal story. What I help others do is to discover their current strengths and then prepare a game plan to explore many of their other strengths. And by quickly learning about their target industry, I can draw on a global network of industry professionals to give them access to learn about those industries.

Call to action: Know yourself well. Keep building up your strengths. Be open-minded; you have strengths you don't know yet, and exposing yourself to new skills and challenges is the best way to uncover them. Once you find them, build them into your story.

Opportunity to land your ideal role

These cornerstones to some are their ultimate goal, but reaching your goal is just the beginning, you've still got all of the previously mentioned cornerstones to establish in this new role. These are also the most vital of the cornerstones, because you've worked on your game plan and converted your opportunity.

What I help you do here is teach you how to close your gaps with an advertised job, convert a strong resume, cover letter and recommendation into an interview, and lay out tips to increase your chance to be the final candidate no-matter what type of interview format – online, telephone, in-person, presentation, panel or assessment centre. And whether you've landed a new role or you're looking at the year ahead in your current role, know your value in the market and be able to negotiate your pay.

Call to action: Be ready for game day. Know your brand, your CV and cover letter, your digital reach, and know your worth on the market. Keep an eye out for opportunities, and don't be afraid to apply for a job that will be great for you.

What a coach can do for you

As your coach, I will work with you to form a strategy around your job readiness, your pathways to your ideal role and discovery of your future strengths. Together we will build a personalised plan to maximise your opportunities, alongside actionable personal development against your ideal role. The core of our Future Mindset program also covers interview training and CV and cover letter editing to help you look your best. We constantly hunt for quality training material for highly desirable and evergreen skillsets that prepare you for the future. Our masterclasses with targeted readings, key learnings workbook and pathways will be great mind food to complement your journey. The future mindset is yours to keep.

I work with people just like you to build purpose into their career pursuit. The difference between the 'future you' that has already landed their ideal job and the 'you' that has played it safe is just the commitment to do something about it, and the hardest step is to just start. A mentor will often give you good advice but a coach will work with your goals and target timeframe to get you to your ideal role. A coach will be there every step of the way to help you reach your goal.

Bio

Alex Ma is a future-minded people leader and a long-time advocate for inclusion, diversity and STEM (Science, Technology, Engineering and Mathematics). He has coached like-minded professionals to uplevel with a future mindset and skills that stay desirable and evergreen, so they can create rewarding careers and be part of projects of the future.

Alex has studied at prestigious universities around Australia and the world, including the University of Melbourne, Queensland University of Technology, EDHEC Business School and Vienna University of Economics and Business. As an advocate of these desirable STEM skills, he has partnered with or been featured by like-minded organisations, including Qantas, CSIRO, BHP Foundation, University of Queensland, Queensland University of Technology and Channel Ten's Coding@Home series.

Qualifications:

- Master of Business (Applied Finance)
- Bachelor of Engineering (Mechatronics)
- Bachelor of Computer Science

Work with Alex:

Alex will work with you to form a game plan and create pathways to your ideal role. You'll be growing highly desirable skills that you can take with you for a lifetime. Alex excels in the virtual one-on-one coaching format, making it easy for anyone to connect world-wide.

Special Offer – Mention this book for an extra 30% discount on your first two sessions in the Future Mindset program.

Connect with Alex:

Facebook: https://www.facebook.com/MTCfuturemindset

LinkedIn: https://www.linkedin.com/company/MTCfuturemindset

Email: future.mindset.pc@gmail.com

FROM REJECTION TO RESILIENCE

Natalie Tran

Every time I thought I was being rejected from something good, I was actually being re-directed to something better.

– Dr Steve Maraboli.

It was early 2001, and I remember the excitement of being headhunted for a role which came with a relocation to another country. The year was then filled with discussions and meetings with human resources managers and divisional leaders via phone and in person, sometimes at the airport if our work travel schedules lined up. I even had a final interview onsite overseas to finalise details and to have an office tour. The transition and relocation plans were definitely set in motion. The months leading up to the departure day were filled with packing things for storage in Melbourne or to be shipped overseas. We gave things away that we didn't need anymore, sold our apartment and car. My husband resigned from his role in Melbourne to come along with me for the new journey. We had farewell parties with family and friends. I was so excited and, as with all transitions, a little anxious, nervous and sad to leave family and friends and the life we had in Melbourne.

To add to these feelings, like the rest of the world we witnessed the unforgettable explosive scenes with buildings on fire and chaos. First, like most who had just seen the footage, we didn't understand what was happening. We soon learnt of the extent of the September 11 attacks in New York, leaving us completely shocked, saddened and devastated. We went to bed every night thinking we would receive some news from the company about our flight and what to expect given what had happened. However, we did not get any updates and proceeded to drive to the airport on our day of departure.

Just a couple of hours from boarding the plane, I received a phone call. Without saying much, the company had decided to rescind the contract they had offered and I did not need to board the plane anymore. It was a very brief call, and I was not given much time to respond to what was relayed to me. There was also no follow up comment to say they would call back another time to debrief or discuss further on the matter. It was pretty much 'Sorry, we need to rescind your contract in light of the current situation. You do not need to board your flight anymore.' There was no 'Are you okay? Can we do anything for you? Let's have a chat later to see if we can still accommodate you working for us or is there anything we can do to support you to settle back into Melbourne?' Instead, I was left reeling, feeling the biggest shock, disappointment, hurt and rejection I had ever felt. It was unlike anything I had experienced before, a punch in the gut, and as the hours passed, I got more disappointed and frustrated. And then the feelings of failure and pain set in. I called back wanting to have further talks, but the company did not want to entertain any discussion. That thirty second call I received was final.

As the days progressed, I felt worse, and that feeling of failure really got me. I felt I couldn't talk to anyone as it was just so painful, and I didn't know how I could share it without putting on a façade that I was okay. After all, I am that friend and family member who always had everything together, who could do anything she set her mind to and who overcame challenges easily.

This time it felt very different and my invincibility dwindled down to nothing. I didn't have any closure as to why the company who had been chasing me for almost a year stopped all communication and dealt with their decision in such a blunt and uncaring way. It was as if nothing had happened and all the planning for the year and all that my husband and I had given up didn't matter. The only thing that kept me sane was hearing we were able to extend the time on handing over our apartment to the new buyers.

What had been the biggest opportunity had turned into a nightmare: the worst day of my life at the time. We were both out of a job and sleeping on the floor of an empty apartment. All the clarity I had, disappeared, and if I had to rate my confidence in resuming life in Melbourne, it was two out of ten at best. I did not know how to bounce back, something which normally came easily to me did not this time. It affected my whole body – poor posture, lack of appetite and a lack of energy. I could not work out why I couldn't cope with this event, which came with immense feelings of hurt, anger, anxiety and failure. Doubt crept in from all levels. I couldn't help but wonder if I'd done something wrong or I wasn't good enough for the company and September 11 was just the excuse they needed to reject me.

That began my journey in learning how to deal with rejection and rebounding on a level I have not experienced before. It made me think about what resilience means to me – the way I responded to the rejection, how I worked with the emotions associated with it and how I came out on the other side with increased self-awareness, another perspective and growth. I want to share with you my thoughts on rejection and resilience and three important strategies which helped me to improve my resilience.

Defining Resilience

As a career coach I cherish the times I receive news of successful transitions from my candidates and clients, but I also feel the frustration and disappointment when they face rejections. In fact, rejections and obstacles will be met by all of us when we embark on and navigate through any transitional journey, whether it's in finding another role, creating a new start up or taking a business opportunity. Each time we receive a rejection, it can feel like a punch in the gut. In fact, scientific research has shown there is correlation between emotional rejection and physical pain.

Not only is it then crucial for us to recover, but to also come back stronger than before. How can we do this, and how do we practise self-care and look after ourselves when we face rejections as we transition in our careers?

There are many definitions of resilience, and they are along the lines of the ability or capacity to bounce back or to recover from tough times. My experience of resilience involves:

- embracing and processing pain effectively and to use it as fuel
- continuously learning and growing even in difficult times; and
- having compassion for ourselves and others, where helping someone else to become more resilient is part of growing our own resilience.

Strategies to Build Resilience

Here are three strategies to help you respond to and build resilience when you face rejection and career setbacks:

1. reflecting on and facing your emotions
2. reframing how you see rejection
3. building certainty into your day through self-care.

Reflection

Reflection is one of the biggest and most powerful skills in building resilience. Ray Dalio coined the equation 'pain + reflection = progress'. The pain of feeling rejected should be expected as part of any transition journey, and we often do one or more of three things when we feel this pain: avoid it, try and distract ourselves from it or numb ourselves to it. As the equation goes, we should acknowledge and reflect on it.

When I was in pain, it was hard to reflect. However, we need to reflect because only then can we see the value in the pain and turn it into progress. Reflection is not the same as overthinking or procrastinating on taking action. If we choose to reflect, we can grow and also help others around us do the same. Reflection will lead us to gratitude, perspective and building resilience. It is a skill and muscle which is under-utilised and can be strengthened. It is about self-awareness and asking questions, such as what is it that we value in our life, learning about what we are trying to achieve, simplifying what is going on and stepping away from the situation to gain perspective. It is easy to think that resilience is just about getting up, wiping the dust off and getting on the horse again. And although that may be the end goal, part of the journey to improved resilience is to consciously observe how we feel and spending time to explore our emotions and feelings with curiosity and compassion. This self-awareness will help us next time we feel challenged or feel distressed.

I have also experienced false resilience, where we are able to carry on because we have suppressed our emotions. According to Dr Deborah MacNamara, this false sense of resilience does not allow us to be flexible and may cause further pain in the long run. 'True resilience is about being hardy …' It is thus important for us not to quash the feelings but to embrace them. Yasmin Mogahed said, 'Resilience is very different than being numb. Resilience means you experience, you feel, you fail, you hurt. You fall. But, you keep going.'

Mindset and reframing

When we reframe the setbacks in our paths, we open the door to opportunities we might not have seen otherwise. In fact, rejection is redirection. I had a choice to get angry and upset or to see it as an opportunity to be redirected. Do not take the rejection personally. It's your application that has been rejected not you. Do not take the no response or vague generic feedback and make it specific about you and let self-doubt or negative thoughts creep in. What we should do is view the rejection with curiosity. Observe the process and see where we can learn from it and refocus. If we let rejection or someone else dictate our failure, we also let them dictate our success as well.

Resilience walks hand in hand with confidence. Failure does affect us and we can hurt, but do not let it define us. It is how we frame the failure that matters. Failure is only the end or final if it makes us quit. I had to say to myself, 'I am in the middle of something, that's all.'

We also need to hone our energy; we cannot fight every battle. It is not only exhausting, it is also not always helpful. We can lose sight of what is important, and it can lead to an unhelpful mindset. It is better to focus on those battles that have meaning to us or have long term implications. Don't waste your energy and resources on things that do not matter. This was certainly an area I had to work on with what I was going through.

Building certainty into our day through self-care

The inspired actions we can implement to build resilience when we experience any form of rejection in our journey is based around building some kind of certainty into our day. I share ten strategies I have used to help build some certainty into my own day. It may be hard to start them all at the same time, so pick one to two to focus on each week. These activities remind us that we have some control over our environment and that we should take new action, even small steps forward.

Practise mindfulness and meditation including breathwork.

1. Practise gratitude – writing down what you are grateful for.
2. Prioritise sleep.
3. Engage in regular exercise or movement.
4. Share your problems and connect with others.
5. Examine your strengths, and seek out resources to help you understand more about your strengths.
6. Clarify your values by asking questions such as 'what is one thing that is missing from my life right now?'
7. Seek guidance in the stories of others who have gone through difficult times, and study how they built their resilience (Nelson Mandela, for example, or mentors in our circle or community who are a few years ahead of us).
8. Create morning and night-time rituals and routines, whether it's reading, setting intentions for the day, journaling or repeating affirmations.
9. Keep the job search activities going. If we compare it to gardening, a fruitful harvest requires us to tend to our garden consistently. The amount of effort we put in is likely to be proportionate to the amount of product we get. Likewise, the more we put into our career transition process, the better chance we have of finding the next best career path.

Examples of these daily activities to build resilience:

- To bolster your resilience, think of all the times you have been resilient before. Think of those moments and write them down. Were there lessons you have learnt, or unexpected benefits? What kind of success did they lead to? Where did they redirect you to? Reflecting on these moments puts you in a better headspace. Affirmation: 'If I lived through that, I can do anything.'

- Journaling – Practise expressive writing for five, ten or twenty minutes a day about an issue. It is not about perfecting the writing, but about releasing your thoughts and feelings to paper each day and making it a daily routine to confront issues head on, giving them a structure and gaining a new perspective on them. It may help to release your thoughts and worries each day. You can also practise gratitude in your journaling by writing down one to three things you are thankful for each day.
- Practise the ancient Japanese technique of centering yourself, which can help turn panic, stress and feelings of anxiety into positivity. It is about deep diaphragmatic breathing to relax all your muscles by clenching then releasing them. Then, in your mind, gather all your worries and fears into a balloon and release it. Watch it float away above your head. Once you have done this use your out breaths to focus on visualising your goals.

Unless we try to do something beyond what we have already mastered, we will not learn and grow. What I have certainly learnt sitting in an empty apartment in those challenging weeks, is that these difficult situations and setbacks teach us useful lessons. But we have to be tuned in to get the most out of them, and to choose growth even in tough times. We then need to focus all of our energy, not on fighting the old but building the new.

Bio

Natalie Tran is an executive and business coach and a career management consultant, specialising in the delivery and facilitation of career, wellbeing and leadership development programs for individuals and purpose-driven businesses and start-ups.

Her holistic and practical perspective is firmly grounded in over twenty-five years of experience gained across a number of diverse industries including banking, finance, funds management and professional services. Natalie holds a Bachelor of Commerce degree from the University of Melbourne and has completed the chartered accountants program. She is accredited in the use of Management Drives and Birkman® tools, Fire-Up Coaching Mindset Coaching Program, Certificate IV in Training and Assessment and is a qualified Pilates instructor and AntiGravity Yoga teacher.

Having navigated several career transitions herself, Natalie enjoys coaching and supporting clients to connect to their sense of purpose and to gain clarity to pivot to a more meaningful career that better aligns to their unique skills, interests, experience, goals and values.

Natalie is passionate about supporting her clients holistically through her current consulting and coaching work, with core focus areas around self-awareness, resilience, wellbeing (physical and mental), energy management, self-care and having a positive and growth mindset.

Work with Natalie:

Natalie is offering 30% discount on your first two coaching sessions. Just quote the book *The Art of Self-Care* to receive the offer. See http://www.transitionwithpurpose.com.au/ for more information and to book a session.

You can also access free resources on her website: http://www.transitionwithpurpose.com.au/free-inspo.

Connect with Natalie:

LinkedIn: https://www.linkedin.com/in/nattran/

Website: http://www.transitionwithpurpose.com.au/

Instagram: @transitionwithpurpose

Workfolio: http://www.natalie-tran.com/

FINAL WORD

Tracey Jewel

So many elements make up intentional self-care. It's important to give each of these areas your full attention so you can fully care for your own needs. You might excel in taking time to nurture your physical self-care, but perhaps you're neglecting that spiritual focus. Balance is the key to achieving your own personal growth in the direction that you want to go.

How should you use what you've learnt from this book? Reading each section and engaging in the exercises will move you forward. However, having a greater understanding of them is the first step. Some areas of intentional self-care may come easier for you than others. Know that this is completely normal, and that self-care evolves and opens up differently for each of us.

When your lifestyle is balanced, you achieve positive wellbeing no matter what obstacles present themselves. It's the key to better all-around health too. These areas of focus will help you live life on your terms and be present in the moment rather than dwelling on things that drag you down.

And how do you get that balance? Tuning into all these areas of self-care is the start of a beautiful transition for you. You'll find your own harmony in a way that makes sense for you. Take care of your health in mind and body with nourishing foods and activities that move you. Keep your mind sharp by learning more and banishing negative thoughts. Feel like you have time for yourself when you balance work and life. Engage with social connections and spend time with friends that fill your heart with love.

You'll need to look at what areas of your life require the most attention. For some, work may be the most stressful part of life. For others, it may be family life at home. By using this book to zero-in on what is out of balance, you can create what you need to find your true happiness.

You truly deserve that happiness and that fulfilled feeling, you really do. But the only way you will get it is by taking time to intentionally and deliberately focus on your own self-care.

Love yourself. Forgive yourself. And open yourself up to the new possibilities that await you. Your future is waiting for you. All you need to do is live in this moment with what you've learnt from this book and the doors will open, leading you to where you envision.

Bio

Tracey Jewel has been coaching wellness professionals all over the world for the past twelve years. She created the self-care lifestyle program to empower women.

Tracey is the author of three female personal development books (*Goddess Within,* 2011, *Don't Mess with the Goddess,* 2016, *This*

Goddess Means Business, 2018), a professional speaker and a wellness entrepreneur.

She appeared on one of TVs most viewed programs *Married at First Sight* in 2018, the *Married at First Sight Grand Reunion* specials in 2021 and *Sunday Night,* where she shared her deeply personal anxiety story.

Tracey was a guest on *The Oprah Winfrey Show* in May 2011 and has loved sharing her journey through the many interviews over the years on radio, online, YouTube, newspapers, magazines and TV as well as with her 165,000 Instagram followers and 70,000 blog subscribers.

She spends her time between coaching wellness professionals with marketing strategies and collaborating with wellness experts all over the world to bring new self-care practices, products and wellness modalities to you!

For more: traceyjewel.com